School Vouchers and Privatization

A Reference Handbook

CONTEMPORARY EDUCATION ISSUES

School Vouchers and Privatization

●◆ A REFERENCE HANDBOOK

Danny Weil

A B C ● C L I O

Santa Barbara, California • Denver, Colorado • Oxford, England

Library of Congress Cataloging-in-Publication Data
Weil, Danny K., 1953–
  School vouchers and privatization : a reference handbook / Danny Weil.
    p. cm. — (Contemporary education issues)
Includes bibliographical references (p.) and index.
    ISBN 1-57607-346-7 (hardcover : alk. paper); ISBN 1-57607-753-5 (e-book)
    1. Educational vouchers—United States. 2. Privatization in
education—United States. 3. School choice—United States. I. Title.
II. Series.
LB2828.8 .W45 2002
379.1'11—dc21

                                                                    2002153378

06 05 04 03 02   10 9 8 7 6 5 4 3 2 1

This book is also available on the World Wide Web as an e-book.
Visit www.abc-clio.com for details.

ABC-CLIO, Inc.
130 Cremona Drive, P.O. Box 1911
Santa Barbara, California 93116-1911
This book is printed on acid-free paper.

Manufactured in the United States of America

Contents

Chapter Five: Vouchers and the Law:
Drawing Conclusions from Research   127

Chapter Six: Private Scholarships and
Faith-Based Charitable Contributions   179

❧ Series Editor's Preface

The Contemporary Education Issues series is dedicated to providing readers with an up-to-date exploration of the central issues in education today. Books in the series will examine such controversial topics as home schooling, charter schools, privatization of public schools, Native American education, African American education, literacy, curriculum development, and many others. The series is national in scope and is intended to encourage research by anyone interested in the field.

Because education is undergoing radical if not revolutionary change, the series is particularly concerned with how contemporary controversies in education affect both the organization of schools and the content and delivery of curriculum. Authors will endeavor to provide a balanced understanding of the issues and their effects on teachers, students, parents, administrators, and policymakers. The aim of the Contemporary Education Issues series is to publish excellent research on today's educational concerns by some of the finest scholar/practitioners in the field while pointing to new directions. The series promises to offer important analyses of some of the most controversial issues facing society today.

—*Danny Weil*
Series Editor

◦◦ Preface

This book will begin by looking closely at the privatization of education as an ideological construct—teasing out what it actually implies about learning and examining the impact of myriad privatization efforts on our nation's public schools. We will look at what privatization efforts signify for education and public policy and how they continue to evolve. Privatization efforts are complex and controversial, and in these pages we will examine multiple points of view about this unquestionably new direction in public policy and the educational strategies that privatization implies—from the commercialism of school curriculum to private voucher programs. We will explore the changing nature of public education and private partnerships on a state, national, and international scale as well as the economic theories underlying our nation's change in educational polices and examine the underlying historical basis for these changes.

In exploring and assessing carefully the concept of privatized education, this book will focus on the debate over private choice and school vouchers. The ideology of private school vouchers will be critically analyzed from numerous points of view, with information on vouchers and the laws that govern them in various cities and states. The book will also include a historical overview of the private voucher movement and other market-based reform efforts in education in an attempt to help explain claims made regarding privatization by a diverse range of educational policy investigators and pundits.

The call for private choice through school vouchers is not the only attempt to privatize schools and refigure the current educational community. Because the issue of privatization extends beyond private choice and school vouchers, this book will also examine how privatization has appeared in little-known market-based educational reform measures such as the for-profit management of public schools, commercialism in the classroom, philanthropic tuition-sponsorships, faith-based charities, educational tax credits, the development of corporate curriculum, exclusive executive agreements between companies and schools, and advertising in school core curriculum.

This book will also look carefully at the development of private curriculums and educational materials by corporations and the impact of these materials on the teaching profession. Through an extensive discussion of privatization efforts that goes beyond the issue of private school vouchers, readers will be better able to assess and evaluate the privatization endeavors that today's public schools are facing. As a result, readers will be in a better position to act as critical citizens and education consumers in an era of continuous and enormous political, personal, and social change.

In addition to examining private choice and vouchers, the book will also analyze various scholarship funding organizations that directly affect vouchers and private choice by subsidizing the costs of private education. The book will examine relationships between partisan think tanks and privatized scholarship funds, both of which allegedly seek to erode civic support for public education by subsidizing students' exit from public schools so that they might enter into the private school of their choice.

The book will also examine the controversial issues and agendas of faith-based charitable organizations. Many groups now support the provision of public funds to faith-based organizations and charities that provide social services. Currently, these services are limited in scope, but in the future these activities might be construed to include the privatization of schools through federal public subsidization. Finally, the book will examine maturing market-based reform measures such as the outsourcing of essential and vital public school services to private corporations and the for-profit management of schools.

The book includes a directory of organizations and public policy institutions, lists of print and nonprint resources, and contact information for corporations and organizations that are involved in the privatization of schools and organizations that are resistant to privatization efforts.

❦ Acknowledgments and Dedication

I would like to thank Alex Molnar, Rethinking Schools, People for the American Way, and Monthly Review Press. I also wish to thank Holly Anderson, my wife, lover, friend, and teacher, who has always believed in my ideas. Thank you, Holly, for your time and copious editing skills that allowed this book to become a reality and for being there when I needed you, as always. Thanks also to Turwanire Mandla for his insights and help with chapter 1 of this book. Finally, I would like to extend my heartfelt love and appreciation to my friend Lenny Sandroff. Although he is not here physically to support me in my efforts, Lenny showed me again and again what it means to live a public life of love, empathy, courage, and intellectual accomplishment. To you I dedicate this book, Lenny, for we once again carved our names on the tree of life. Bless you, my brother; know that you are in my thoughts each and every day.

Chapter One
⚬⟶ Introduction

PRIVATIZATION AND EDUCATION

Most of us have heard the term *globalization,* which has come to refer to the economic, social, and cultural forces that "unify" the world, creating the so-called global village. Discussion of globalization is often confined to its *economic manifestations*—the benefits or burdens that result when private corporations compete in a worldwide market. The expansion of the global market has brought a movement toward less government involvement and greater privatization, a movement that has sparked a fundamental debate about the management of public educational institutions. The debate concerns whether the best education for today's students can be provided by democratically elected governments or by corporations. During the past ten years many students, politicians, teachers, parents, political radicals, businesspeople, and religious leaders have expressed dissatisfaction with U.S. public schools. Educational and social conflicts among various constituencies over diversity, religion, race, gender, social class, teacher power, unionization, and the nature of U.S. culture have all found expression in the turbulent controversies over the future of public education. These controversies are complex and contentious, and they have critical and far-reaching implications for the future of U.S. public policy in general and education in particular. Those who propose that public education be dismantled in favor of the privatization of public schools and public school services are questioning the very notion of a truly public education.

The privatization of education is not a simple matter of shifting funds from public schools to private schools. Privatization is part of a broad economic movement, a national and an international model of social management, a paradigm that suggests that market-driven forces are the panacea for all of society's ills, not just those affecting schools.

WHAT IS PRIVATIZATION?

Any real understanding of the discussions of privatization must recognize both its current and its historical context. The definition of *privati-*

zation stems from the economic theories of Adam Smith in *An Inquiry into the Nature and Causes of the Wealth of Nations,* first published in 1776. Smith's economic theories are known collectively as economic liberalism, or laissez-faire capitalism, and today's successors of Smith's ideas are called neoliberal economics. Adam Smith's theories of economic liberalism are the basis for today's neoliberalism, and one of neoliberalism's central tenets is privatization. Thus, any discussion of educational reform through privatization must take place within a larger understanding of neoliberalism, of the original theory of economic liberalism, and of the actual application of privatization to society.

Neoliberal economic theory makes the following basic assumptions about human behavior:

- Men and women operate out of self-interest, with the central expression of this self-interest being the search for financial gain. People are motivated by what's good for them as individuals, and what's good for the individual and, by extension, for incorporated individuals is good for everyone.[1]
- Cooperative behavior is not as rational as competitive behavior. In the economic sphere this natural predominance of competitive behavior is expressed as healthy marketplace competition.[2]

Human progress is measured by sustained economic growth as indicated by the gross national product (GNP), an indicator of national consumption rates. A corollary of this is that the more one consumes, the greater one's contribution to the social good.[3]

- Humans are, by nature, unequal and do not possess equal attributes. Some individuals have more potential than others.
- Only the free, unregulated market can ensure optimum efficiency and rational allocation of limited resources.

The debate over privatization is a debate over which sector is more effective in reforming education (and other arenas)—the free market, as touted by neoliberalism, or the public sphere. Traditionally, transnational corporations have been the principal players in the free markets, while government and civic society have been the principal players in the public spheres. Privatization involves a shift of this balance, with corporations taking a greater role in the public sphere.

But just what is the distinction between the public and private spheres? Paul Starr, noted author and contributor to the *Yale Law and*

Policy Review, has devoted a great deal of time examining this question, and for him the distinction is quite clearly that between the more open common interest of the public sphere and the more closed self-interest of the private sphere. Starr argues that with privatization, there is a general retreat from the traditional public sphere—a radical shift of individual involvement from the whole to the part—that is, from public action to private concerns. The public sphere, with its myriad institutions, may be conceived of as the open, accessible, and visible—for example, one might think of public theaters, the public marketplace, public institutions, and public sociability—and the privatizing of public institutions thus results in a shift away from this kind of communally motivated behavior to behavior that is more focused on private interests.[4]

The argument over privatization in education, that is, the shift of education from the domain of government and civic society to that of the corporate free market, departs in a fundamental way from traditionally conceived notions about funding education. The debate centers on how the education market should be or should not be regulated, and what elements of education, if any, should be a commodity in the market. The notion of education as a commodity is intricately linked with the notion of private property, the underlying principal of privatization. In a private property–based society such as the United States, land, consumer goods, production equipment, and more recently, even ideas have been classified as private property. The realm of private property is now being extended to services that are essential to a civilized existence, such as health care, social security, and education. But some are questioning this extension of private property: Is education a simple commodity that can or should be viewed as private property—the methods, costs, and mode of its delivery wholly determined by the rules of the free marketplace? Or is it a public right available to all children regardless of race, ethnicity, culture, and socioeconomic class?

Today the privatization movement is emerging as a movement opposing the growth of government and especially opposing the New Deal government policies associated with Franklin Delano Roosevelt. The privatization movement is not limited to education—reforms involving privatization are being recommended throughout the U.S. public sector. Nor is the current debate over privatization only about returning education and other public services to the traditional private sector, shifting them from civic public interests to private, market-oriented, corporate interests. The debate is also about the competence and desirability of public provisions and institutions, and as a result it is about how we want to live our lives, build our communities, construct our institutions, and define our identity and culture. Proponents of privatization assume that government is by its nature inefficient and ineffective. Government is often condemned for a myriad of our social ills, whereas privatization is advocated as a panacea for problems involving the production, distribution, and consumption of society's resources. In the beginning of the new millennium, U.S. society has shifted slightly, from believing government can do nothing to the belief that the marketplace can do everything. Privatization calls us to reexamine the need for collective or public social action; it questions the role of individual citizens as the primary decision makers in society. Privatization calls into question the continued dominance of government as the expression of the people's sovereignty. It calls us to reexamine how we will define our social, individual, and national identity.

There is little doubt that when the categories of the public sector and the private sector are actually put into play, distinctions between them can become blurred. The state is influenced by private interests, and private corporations are in turn regulated by the state and depend on the state for financial support (e.g., research grants, subsidies). Through tax credits, institutional partiality, zoning preferences, direct aid, and state guarantees, the government plays an active role in helping the private sector, in effect socializing the costs of doing business while privatizing the profits. Government also establishes regulations and arbitrates adherence to the law and to some degree of normative business ethics.

So, for example, the Securities and Exchange Commission regulates the private affairs of the stock market and its participants. Airport authorities regulate air traffic in the interest of private airlines and consumers. And, of course, the utilities form a special public-private partnership—themselves the object of deregulation and privatization.

The question facing Americans in all areas in which privatization is proposed as a solution to today's problems is relatively simple: Do we as citizens having a degree of sovereignty wish to retain an element of control over key aspects of our lives currently residing in the realm of openness, visibility, public accountability, democratic scrutiny, and public sunshine laws—the public sector? Or do we wish to trade this sovereignty for the marketplace efficiency in the provision of goods and services promised by the private sector, with its closed board meetings, profit projections, management and marketing cost analyses, self-interests, and invisible decision making? Our decisions on these matters must be informed; we must understand that the trade-off for more sovereignty is some inefficiency, and the trade-off for greater efficiency is some loss of transparency. Which of these options reward a democratic society in the long haul? Will there really be greater overall societal happiness in a market system that seeks to privatize many, if not all institutions, and thus to move the public provisions and institutions we have shared as community resources into the private sector, where the bottom-line, that is, market reasoning, is the determinant and greater efficiency is the possible result? It is in this context and within the framework of these and other questions that this chapter briefly explores the larger socioeconomic concept of privatization and attempts to examine critically the concept from varied frames of reference.

SOME EXAMPLES OF PRIVATIZATION

Public schools are being affected by privatization in many ways. In the last decade, the number of agreements between public schools and corporations has increased steadily. The last decade has seen phenomenal growth in the number of corporate-sponsored public schools, privately run charter schools, private choice measures, and private school voucher proposals. For example, the corporate headquarters of American Bankers Insurance Group in Miami includes a learning center for children from kindergarten through second grade. The school is limited to the children of company employees, but Dade County Public School District pays the school's expenses with taxpayers' money. Honeywell operates a similar school under a similar agreement with the local school district in Clearwater, Florida. In public schools in New York City, American Express sponsors "Academies of Travel and Tourism," where students study geography and culture to prepare for work in travel and tourism. The city of Celebration, Florida, founded and owned by the Walt Disney Company, has a school for the children of residents that is run jointly by the Disney Company, Stetson University, and the Osceola County School District.

For-profit management of schools is becoming big business. For example, the Edison Project, headed by Chris Whittle of Channel One, runs twenty-five schools in eight states and enjoys revenues of about $70 million. Advantage Schools, Inc., operates eight charter schools in seven states.[5] And this is just the beginning. Referring to the rise of the health maintenance organization, the *Wall Street Journal* has called these for-profit educational companies "educational maintenance organizations."

The movement toward privatization in education is not without its critics. After signing an exclusive contract with the Coca Cola company, a school board in Madison, Wisconsin, ended that contract after protest from parents, students, and activists concerned about the effect of junk food on children's health. The protesters argued that marketing by Coke and other snack food companies was only exacerbating the higher levels of obesity and Type 2 diabetes in school-age children. Despite such protests, many schools remain strapped for cash, and Coke and other companies find no lack of business partners in education. For its part, Coke intends to continue forming business agreements with schools. Partly in response to the protests, Coke has made what it calls an "education-based decision" to offer more "nutritious" drinks, and it now encourages nonexclusive contracts with school districts whereby Coca-Cola vending machines will be placed in strategic places on school grounds.[6]

Of course, the privatization movement is not limited to schools. The Cato Institute, a conservative, libertarian think tank, argues for the privatization of Social Security. Michael Tanner, director of the Cato Institute, recommends that Social Security taxes be deposited in individually owned investment accounts.[7] Privatization, the Tanner argues, would thus allow the poor to save more retirement benefits than with the current system. Privatizing Social Security would benefit everyone, working to end poverty among the elderly by creating increased financial security. Privatization of Social Security has also been the object of a presidential task force. The penal system is also undergoing privatization, as the prison "system" becomes the prison "industry." At a California correctional facility outside San Diego, inmates sew T-shirts for U.S. clothing companies, including Seattle Cotton Works and Lee Jeans. The contracting company, CMT Blues, pays minimum wage, half of which goes to the prisoners and the other half toward prison costs. The California Department of Corrections Joint Venture Program and CMT Blues owner Pierre Slieman say they are providing the inmates with jobs and skills that they can use when they are released.[8]

Of the more than 2 million people imprisoned in the United States, over one-quarter are employed in the privatized prison industry, which is dominated by eighteen private prison corporations. One of these corporations, Corrections Corporation of America, also operates private prisons in Puerto Rico, Australia, and the United Kingdom and is planning to open a new, private prison in South Africa.[9]

Another example of privatization can be found in the arena of art and culture, where public funding has been cut in recent years. In response, corporate funding of public art and technology exhibits has risen dramatically; in the late 1990s it was up 47 percent from previous years. In return for corporate sponsorship, museums offer companies what amounts to advertising, with billboards and products right alongside the exhibits. For example, Subaru sponsors the Franklin Institute

Science Museum's Traveling Science Shows, which are transported from site to site in Subaru station wagons. Attendees are given "goody bags" containing, among other things, an invitation to come in for a Subaru test drive. Meanwhile, TWA, another sponsor of the Franklin Institute shows, featured a history of aviation with TWA memorabilia and products for sale.[10]

Medicare and the nation's health care industry has also become the object of privatization efforts. The National Bipartisan Commission on the Future of Medicare has been pushing for privatization reform of Medicare since late 1999. Congress established the commission to come up with possible solutions to the Medicare "crisis." After two years of work, the commission suggested that the current Medicare system, which guarantees medical services, should be replaced with a voucher system. Seniors could use the vouchers to purchase private medical insurance or to stay in the Medicare system with an additional premium. The commission's recommendation assumes that by forcing seniors to pay a portion of their premiums, the voucher system would cause anywhere from half to three-fourths of seniors to leave the Medicare system and enroll with private HMOs.[11]

Local governments are accepting privatization proposals as well. Sacramento, California, for example, inaugurated a project in 1998 called "Capital Spirit," under which the city nominated an official rental car, an official soft drink, an official telecommunications provider—all in return for corporate funding. Now, rather than having to raise taxes, cities can sell their endorsements directly to private corporations. Surf City, California, declared Coke its "official beverage" and gave the Coca-Cola Company the exclusive right to sell nonalcoholic drinks in city parks and beaches; in return the city will receive $300,000 per year and in-kind contributions.[12]

This spectacular growth in corporate involvement in education and other parts of the public sector has not been accomplished without the help of private think tanks, both liberal and conservative, who seek to shape and manage public perception regarding educational policy. There has also been a steady increase in corporate philanthropy, as evidenced by the growth and development of private scholarship funds. The contracting-out of vital and essential school services—ranging from landscaping services to cafeteria services—has also been on a steady rise. These developments, along with the more widespread use of corporate-sponsored educational materials (CSEMs), in-school, private advertising, and exclusive agreements between public schools and private corporations, have been the subject of controversy for more than a decade. The protests of parents and activists against corporate advertising in schools exemplify the concerns of many Americans about privatization in general. The debate over privatization really gets to the fundamental issues regarding the kind of society we wish to see—issues that must become the content of our decision making.

WHY PRIVATIZATION?

Privatization is proposed and implemented under the banner of efficiency, effectiveness, personal liberty, and social freedom. Although privatization proponents differ on many issues, the most zealous privatization advocates believe that the government could and should be virtually put out of business in most affairs other than the defense of national sovereignty. The assertion made by most privatization champions is that the public sector is an incompetent monopoly incapable of providing the quality of goods and services citizens need and want. This failure is due to the fact that government is allegedly sheltered from the competitive characteristics of the economic market and as such is inefficient, qualitatively inferior, and not cost-effective. Private contractors and entrepreneurs, privatization advocates contend, are in a better position to provide the quality goods and services Americans need; because of the constant market pressures they encounter, private companies must provide quality products at competitive prices in order to stay in business.

However, Paul Starr makes the point that privatization is far more complex than this. First of all, he argues, privatization should not be simply equated with a reduction in government and a consequent increase in competition. Public sector services that are privatized can be vulnerable to lack of competition, as with monopolies. For example, private monopolies were created when publicly owned British Telecom and British Gas were privatized under the Thatcher administration. New government regulatory agencies had to be created to monitor the takeover and the new corporate entities. There was no effort to liberalize the economy to encourage more competition; in fact the opposite was true—the share prices of companies that controlled former public institutions were protected from such competition. Conversely, the nationalization of privately owned institutions can involve liberalizing policies, as seen in the French nationalization of the banking system in the early 1980s, which resulted in a liberalization of the financial markets.

Starr also points out that the private sector does not have a corner on competition. Public school systems can implement a competitive system wherein families choose among a variety of public schools, with government funds for education allocated according to student population. Government contracts can be given to private companies in a competitive bidding system.[13]

Nonetheless, the theory and practice of free-market dominance and laissez-faire populism, which would limit the role of government to only what is necessary to protect national security and property rights, has seen a tremendous ideological advance within the last decade. As early as 1991, for example, Stephen Goldsmith was running for the job of mayor of Indianapolis and asserted that he could run the entire city with just four contract managers.[14] His vision of limited government was promoted by the writings of Robert Poole, architect of the Libertarian Reason Foundation and one of the staunchest proponents of privatization in the United States. Poole envisioned a city run entirely on contractual arrangements between a small government and a host of private providers.[15]

Libertarianism is based on the notion of a limited government and a free market; it can best be described as market liberalism. As a political and economic theory, libertarianism promotes no government regulation of any sector of the economy or of any political structure. Libertarians believe that society is best served if all institutions are privatized, which is similar to the neoliberalist view that societies should be organized according to the Adam Smith's economic principles.

Many Americans today are feeling adulation for the market system we know as capitalism and a deep cynicism regarding the public sector's ability to provide vital human services. The reasons for this are varied and complex, resulting in great controversy. This exaltation of privatization has had specific consequences for Americans, including the expansion and increasingly widespread public-policy practice of providing public services and goods through contracts with private entities or through outright privatization.

As Starr points out, several views of a "good society" justify privatization as a public policy strategy. The most obvious is that of liberal and neoliberal economics, which states that if laissez-faire individualism, property rights, and the free market are protected from the interference of government, they will produce the most efficient product and the most individual choice. A second view, also common in recent neoliberal theory, defines privatization as a political strategy for diverting power from government. Alongside these views is a more socially minded justification for privatization that calls for greater reliance on traditional, private institutions for the provision of social services. This view, presented most convincingly by Peter Berger and Richard Neuhaus (conservative religious authors who write and speak extensively about public issues), argues that the service organizations of modern government have undermined the work of private social institutions like churches, voluntary organizations, self-help groups, and the family, thereby interfering with their "value-generating" and "value-maintaining" work and alienating the very individuals who need help. Berger and Neuhaus, among others, propose that the government should instead support these private institutions to take back many of the social tasks currently done by government. Others argue that the state should have no role in this empowerment of traditional institutions. In any case, it is argued that this movement of power from the state to the private institution will ultimately result in the empowerment of local communities.[16]

Clearly, these three views overlap, and they are all used by pro-privatization activists and policy analysts. However, they must all be examined individually, as they each have very different implications and envision a different kind of society.

Another important aspect of the privatization movement is that it is not confined to the Western industrialized countries. In fact, with the development of the World Bank, the World Trade Organization, and the International Monetary Fund, privatization efforts have expanded as these institutions have required Third World governments seeking membership or funding to dismantle social programs in an effort to force privatization through social and economic restructuring. In fact, a great debate about such restructuring has been held throughout the Third World and in the halls of the U.S. Congress, as many believe the effects of privatization have been disastrous. Interestingly enough, it appears that many of those who would support privatization in the United States are critical of such efforts in many Third World countries. They argue correctly that the activities and policies of the World Bank, for example in countries in Africa, have contributed significantly to spiraling economic decline and social conflict, both of which have led to civil violence.

The movement toward privatization must be understood as a unique and global historical trend appearing during a particular stage of political, economic, and social development as we enter the twenty-first century. The many individual efforts to privatize American schools can best be understood in the broader historical context of economic, ideological, and political history. Educational privatization efforts are born of peculiar historical relationships. Couching the debate over privatization of our nation's schools within a historical understanding of privatization theory and practice enhances our understanding of this unique public policy concept.

A BRIEF EXAMINATION OF ECONOMIC THEORY: THE HISTORY BEHIND THE PRESENT DEBATE

The fundamentally simple argument for privatization goes back to the eighteenth-century liberal economic theories of the philosophical father of capitalism, Adam Smith. Smith's theories, expounded in his treatise *An Inquiry into the Nature and Causes of the Wealth of Nations*, were based on the claim that only the profit motive, free economic markets, and competition provide the proper incentives for efficiency and quality in the production of the goods and services a society and its individuals need and want. Smith maintained that market competition, therefore, leads to economic, personal, and political liberty. Smith's theory of economic, social, and human development defined human actions as purely individualistic and human motives as distinctly and innately selfish. Thus his theory was founded on the sanctity of private property rights and private ownership, and he argued for little or no interference with these distinct class arrangements by any governmental bodies or policies.

However, Smith wrote his treatise in 1776, when the United States was fighting for its independence as a nation and U.S. corporate structure was in its infancy. At that time, companies (or the corporate means of production) had far less impact on the daily lives of the vast majority of Americans than they do today. It would not be a stretch to say that most people produced and consumed most of what they needed. Today, in contrast, corporate influence touches almost every aspect of daily life, and some are discussing the possibility that the corporate structure might possibly replace national government. Even in 1776 Smith seemed to anticipate the market's propensity toward collusion and monopoly and pointed out the need for government intervention in matters of national security and international relations.

However, Smith's work advocated the abolition of all government intervention in all matters of economic and social life. Smith endorsed the end of even the few government restrictions on manufacturing that were present at the time. He insisted that there be no barriers to commerce and argued for the removal of government-imposed tariffs. Because he envisioned an absence of state controls on the economic workings of capitalism, Smith's ideas were characterized as "liberal" economic theories.

Understanding Smith's ideas requires an understanding of the social, economic, and political conditions of the times. Smith's ideas arose during a time when the American colonists had suffered severely from government intervention by the oppressive British crown. Writing in colonial America at the end of the eighteenth century, Smith was responding to the economic tyranny of the British Crown and the impediments it placed upon the colonies in their efforts to achieve economic development. The British Crown had severely limited free trade, both within the empire and between the empire and outside forces. American colonists could not trade on the basis of economic advantage but had to adhere to the requirements of British imperial protectionism. We must also understand that self-sufficiency was one of the primary economic characteristics of the times; a large percentage of Americans produced much of what they consumed. The colonial American economy was run by small farmers and businesspeople, not by large multinational corporations. In this regard David C. Korten, formerly a member of the faculty at the Harvard Business School and an operative of the U.S. Agency for International Development and now president of the People-Centered Development Forum in New York, describes the economic environment and theories of Adam Smith's time in the following way: "Adam Smith's ideal was a market comprised solely of small buyers and sellers, each too small to influence the market price of the commodities exchanged. Thus, Smith's concept of a competitive market was one in which there were no large businesses with monopolistic market powers."[17] Of course, in Smith's preferred world of small artisans, farmers, and shopkeepers, ownership and management were almost always in the same hands.[18]

Clearly, the economic terrain has changed considerably since Adam Smith penned his treatise. Today, we speak glibly of the globalization of economic markets through major transnational corporations (TNCs), not through small shopkeepers and artisans. We routinely associate business with the giant corporations that control the consumer items we have become so dependent upon in daily lives. This contrast explains the use of the term *neoliberalism* to indicate the new or further development of Smith's original ideas. The radically changed historical circumstances also set up neoliberalism for strident criticism, as many are seriously questioning whether neoliberalism can so dogmatically claim a direct relationship to Adam's Smith's theories as the legitimate roots of their ideas.

Smith called for "free enterprise" and "free competition," and with his formulation the idea of the economic market as a guiding social and individual force received its first theoretical defense.[19] Although this form of economic liberalism prevailed in the United States throughout the 1800s and early 1900s, in the late nineteenth century economic liberals saw that their theories of unregulated, laissez-faire, capitalistic economic development were becoming vulnerable. Corporate power was beginning to become consolidated throughout the developed countries, especially in the United States. Economic crises became regular and reoccurring features of capitalism, and American society witnessed the development and emergence of socialist movements and evidence of collectivist tendencies among many people. Many Americans were involved in movements seeking limits on the activities of corporations and increases in individual rights and freedoms; factory acts, restrictions on child labor, public health measures, the regulation of working hours, the women's suffrage movement, calls for social insurance, and provisions for free education, as well as a movement to establish free libraries, all emerged during this period.[20]

The demise of classical liberal economic theory was hastened by the extended world economic and political crisis encompassing World War I, the Russian Revolution, the Great Depression, the rise of fascism, and World War II. Claiming that full employment was necessary for the growth of capitalism, the early twentieth-century British economist John Maynard Keynes proposed that governments and central banks should intervene in the economy to increase employment. Keynes's economic theories were an attempt to arrest social and economic crises, especially during the Great Depression of the 1930s. His economic interventionist theories greatly influenced the public policies of Franklin D. Roosevelt and the New Deal social administration adopted before, during, and after the Great Depression, and they presaged and pointed the way toward an era of greater government intervention in the U.S. economic and social fabric of everyday life later in the twentieth century.

By the 1940s, the era of widespread faith in the liberal, self-regulating market originally advanced by Smith seemed to be coming to an end. A new theory of a mixed economy began to surface, one that combined capitalist markets with government planning for private investment, and a new social compact between government and capital corresponded with the emerging power of the United States throughout the world directly after World War II. For the next several decades of the twentieth century, most Americans accepted the assumption that government had a role to play in the economy and that government's role was to advance the public good. The New Deal political philosophies and Keynesian economic theory assumed that only government employees would staff government programs, and during this time Americans saw an exponential growth and expansion of the public sector. The number of government-employed police officers, firefighters, correction officers, schoolteachers, social workers, health care workers, lawyers, accountants, and other public workers experienced a virtual explosion after World War II.[21]

However, within the last quarter of the twentieth century this belief in the role of government has been challenged by a new economic theory that seeks to revive the original, classically liberal, free-market theories of Adam Smith. A more pure and uncompromising theory of liberalism—known in economic and political quarters as neoliberalism, or neoliberal economic theory—has emerged within the last three decades. This neoliberal theory seeks to challenge the social compact between government and business and capital and labor that was so prevalent during the first three-quarters of the twentieth century.

Neoliberalism, a new economic liberalism patterned on the political, social, and ideological positions originally advanced by Smith, is concerned with liberating private enterprise from any and all regulations imposed by government or nations, while promoting the universalization of market relations through public funding. This reexpression of Adam Smith's ideas at the dawn of a new era of globalization calls for the "liberation" of everything from international trade agreements, such as those used to pass NAFTA or GATT, to government institutions and services, with the ending of all price controls.

The argument for neoliberalism builds on a claim essential to capitalism: that unregulated private markets provide the best chance to increase economic growth, political freedom, and individual liberty and sovereignty, and that free, unfettered markets will ultimately benefit everyone. Neoliberal economic relations are founded on a commitment to a self-regulating market and on the notion of private property relations and a "competitive order" within market economies. According to neoliberalism, one element of the government's role is to encourage the rapid accumulation of private capital by using taxpayer funds to subsidize companies' research, risk taking, and eventual profits. Thus it follows that one of the chief aims of neoliberalism is the contracting of essential public services to private, for-profit firms in an effort to encourage this capital growth and to reduce government and massive public (i.e., government) employment.[22]

Yet not all neoliberal advocates agree that the government is responsible for supporting private enterprise through public subsidies. One of the most notable advocates for neoliberal economic policies in the twentieth century was the Austrian economist Friedrich Hayek, a recipient of the Nobel Prize for economics. In his seminal work, *The Political Order of Free People,* published in 1979, Hayek maintained that any governmental agency allowed to use its taxing power to finance public services should be legally required to refund taxes raised for these purposes to all those who prefer to get those services in the private sphere. This applies to all services in which government maintains or aspires to maintain what Hayek referred to as a "legal monopoly." The only exception to Hayek's concept of privatization is that of maintaining and enforcing the public law and maintaining an armed force for the purpose of public defense, including defense against external enemies. However, from Hayek's frame of reference, all public services should be privatized—from education to transportation to communications, including postal services, telegraph, telephone, and broadcasting services, the so-called public utilities, and the various types of social insurance.

Throughout the late 1970s and the 1980s, a small group of like-minded privatization activists began to create international foundations and public policy think tanks in an effort to promote their causes. For the last two decades, pro-privatization fund-raisers have been investing hundreds of millions of dollars into building a huge consortium consisting of newspapers, magazines, Web sites, think tanks, radio stations, television networks, and publishing houses. A foundation-supported neoliberal constituency has been engrossed for the past quarter of a century in the building of a huge media infrastructure. By purchasing the means of public discourse, this neoliberal constituency has joined ranks with many politicians in an attempt to manage citizens' perceptions about the role of private markets and government policies.

In 1979 neoliberal economic and social policies were given a tremendous boost and social legitimization by the election of Margaret Thatcher as prime minister of England. A disciple of Hayek and a firm believer in neoliberal economic theories and political policies, Thatcher began a neoliberal revolution in England. According to Susan George, a notable scholar on privatization matters, Thatcher's neoliberal doctrines signified a paradigmatic shift in both ideology and social organization. First of all, Thatcher's reforms upheld the central tenet of neoliberalism: the best results are achieved through free competition, from the individual level to the international level. According to neoliberal theory, competition identifies the most effective producers and the most efficient methods of production, and therefore it is the best mechanism for distribute all resources in the most effective way.[23]

However, critics of Thatcher's policies have argued that the country has suffered greatly under neoliberal economic policies. Studies show that before 1979, about 10 percent of the population in Great Britain lived in poverty, whereas since the implementation of Thatcher's policies, which have been continued under Tony Blair and John Major, it is now one person in four and one child in three.[24]

With neoliberalism's new language of efficiency and blame of the government emerging in political discourse, it's instructive to turn once again to Paul Starr, who argues that privatization really seeks to accomplish specific functions. Privatization seeks to move activities and functions from the public, or government, sphere to the private sphere. This requires reducing government spending and regulation. This radical shift would change the very fabric of our laws and institutions, creating a new economic and social life.[25]

During the 1980s, the Western industrialized countries experienced the emergence of politically and socially conservative movements and governments, most notably in Great Britain and the United States. Not coincidentally, privatization began to be more frequently discussed as a policy strategy in political and business circles. In the United States, neoliberalism eventually became associated with Ronald Reagan's economic policy, dubbed *Reaganomics,* becoming perhaps the most ambitious conservative attempt to change the course of American economic and social policy since the New Deal of the Roosevelt administration.

WHAT PROPONENTS AND OPPONENTS ARE SAYING ABOUT NEOLIBERALISM AND PRIVATIZATION EFFORTS

The Argument for Neoliberalism

As we have seen, there are many different positions within the neoliberal camp. Some defenders of neoliberalism suggest that privatization is intended to force public entities, such as schools or hospitals, to be governed by the same competitive forces that make private markets work. Other proponents of neoliberal ideas argue that neoliberalism is merely a form of government reform, not a call for government reduction. They contend that the real goal of neoliberal policies is to expand the role of public subsidies, collected and allocated by the state through taxation to finance private industry.

However, other neoliberal organizations argue that their support for privatization is a way to dismantle public institutions that should be private. The neoliberal Cato Institute, argues that its attempts to privatize public schooling through private vouchers is a way of dismantling what they refer to as "government schools." They do not champion private vouchers as a public policy strategy for securing the continuance and enhancement of public education through competition. Rather, their support for educational vouchers is based on their belief in private, not public education. And this, they claim, can only be accomplished through the separation of government and schools. As we shall see when we turn our attention to the arguments for private choice and private school vouchers, this is precisely one of many arguments that proponents of private vouchers make when advocating private choice. Milton Friedman, the Nobel Prize–winning economist, made this same argument as early as 1955, when he first proposed that parents be given universal vouchers so they might send their children to the schools of their choice.[26]

In order to understand the neoliberal public policy position on the issue of educational privatization, we must critically examine the fundamental ideology behind the privatization movement. The standard argument for privatization assumes that people and companies compete with each other on an even playing field, where all have equal footing and enjoy equal opportunities. As David Boaz of the Cato Institute argues in his book *Libertarianism: A Primer,* by participating in competition, each competitor gives his or her express agreement to the process, making competition a cooperative activity. Thus the competitive search for profits, goods, and services benefits everyone socially and personally.[27]

Arguments for neoliberal policy vary from constituency to constituency, but some distinct areas of mutual agreement can be found. First, neoliberal economics assumes that the free market improves things for everyone. Cutting public expenditures for social services like education and health care through privatization is a necessary step in reducing the government's role in society and thereby reducing people's dependence on government "entitlements" and fostering "individual responsibility." Second, deregulation is needed to "get the state off the backs of businesses and corporations and the American people." It thereby creates larger profits that will eventually "trickle down" to average citizens. Third, the sale of state-owned enterprises to private investors is always preferable to continued public sector ownership. Such privatization should include key industries that are currently nationalized in many countries, such as banks, railroads, toll highways, schools, hospitals, gas and electric companies, and even water companies. In the United States, privatization policies would result in decreased regulation and the outright purchase by private interests of public hospitals and other public services, including highways. And finally, privatization in effect redefines the concepts of public good and community good in terms of individual responsibility and private choice. It implies that people should be required to find the security and happiness they need and want within the private sector.

Elliot Sclar of the Century Foundation, a neoliberal think tank, reminds us that not all proponents of private markets are antigovernment. For example, contracting public services to the private sector is based not on animosity toward government per se, but on the idea of re-organizing societal institutions and revenue collection and distribution policies so that public taxpayer funds can be used to subsidize the costs and risks associated with privatization. Sclar and others understand that privatization is most often suggested in the name of shrinking government, but he also astutely understands that contracting public functions and services to private agencies is a vehicle toward subsidizing costs of privatization and providing a convenient ideological link between the provision of private services and the reduction of state ownership.[28]

If we grant the assumption made by proponents of neoliberalism that competition through the private market is always a positive attribute, then we would have to concede that the market should be the universal arbitrator of all social benefits. And if we also concede the claim that people are unequal by nature, the market serves a societal role, reinforcing a type of social Darwinism that, for the most part, grants rewards to and accepts contributions from only those who are well educated and better positioned. If this were true, there would be no better way to ensure the competitive nature of the market than to downsize or remove government regulations in favor of pure, competitive forces. Burdensome government regulation would not work to ensure public safety but would actually smother market mechanisms and individual initiative.

Regarding the need to shrink government in favor of wholesale privatization, David Boaz passionately argues that the twentieth century revealed the failure of big government. Boaz notes that for-profit companies, faith-based organizations, and other private groups are finding many solutions to problems where government has failed. According to Boaz, this shift in the paradigm reveals, for instance, that private investment markets provide a better solution to the financial problems faced by older Americans than Social Security, and that private, community-based government can better respond to the needs of the U.S. citizens than current local government. Not surprisingly, this argument is accompanied by the claim that private schools are better able to provide quality education at lower cost than are public schools, and that for-profit companies will soon bring about a great reform of education. Furthermore, Boaz claims that private faith-based organizations and charities succeed in doing what the welfare programs have failed to do—find a way for people to contribute to society rather than making them dependent on society. This desire to privatize many aspects of daily life and to bypass government completely is justified by the idea that the services people need will be better provided by a mixture of private for-profit companies, nonprofit agencies, volunteer organizations, and faith-based charities.[29]

However, bypassing government is the last thing other neoliberal activists want. They would prefer to view the government as a source of public joint venture capital that could be given to transnational corporations to assist them in developing, maintaining, arranging, and regulating all social institutions in the interest of profit accumulation. This argument claims that all society members would profit from such an arrangement, not only the vested, privileged, private interests. Many proponents of neoliberalism argue that the U.S. government already provides "corporate welfare" to such key industries as defense and pharmaceuticals by substantially underwriting research and development of products, such as military aircraft and AIDS drugs. They argue this should not be the role of government, and they promote a privatized ideology that reduces the role of government in civic, political, moral, and economic life.

The Argument against Neoliberalism

Yet not everybody supports neoliberal privatization efforts. Those who argue against neoliberalism and its public policies of privatization claim first and foremost that unfettered competition is not the what keeps the market as an even playing field—on the contrary, competition causes inequity and, in effect, burns itself out. Individual competition among citizens gives way to an economic concentration of power and wealth in the hands of a few elite. Opponents of privatization are also quick to point out that, contrary to the neoliberal claim, the truly competitive market is not a desirable or sustainable long-term condition for sellers. Sellers, they maintain, try to avoid "slugging it out" with a host of competitors for a slim profit and instead seek to create monopolistic situations in which the concentration of wealth is significantly greater and actual competition is reduced in favor of larger profits. Diminished competition is what sellers really want, and the greater their market share, the greater their control of the market and the greater their profits.[30] The last thing the market wants, opponents of neoliberalism would maintain, is pure laissez-faire competition. They claim that this is why during an era of unmitigated deregulation and privatization, the world is witnessing some of the largest consolidations of corporate power through acquisitions and mergers of corporate and public entities.

Privatization proponents also claim that, contrary to the standard economic model advanced in liberal and neoliberal thought, not everyone begins on equal footing in the marketplace, nor do all citizens have equal opportunities; because of racism, classicism, and gender discrimination, competition becomes highly selective, discriminating by race, gender, and class. These factors and others must be considered when looking at economic development and the distribution of opportunities and resources. According to opponents of neoliberalism, the possibility of sustaining widespread competition and individual freedom through pure market relationships is more myth than reality. In their view, the markets actually create inequity and have created an economy and culture controlled and configured by large, transnational corporations financed by public subsidies.

Furthermore, many proponents of privatization would agree that smaller government is the last thing they want. Many critics claim that neoliberalism is really a unique and modern form of state intervention: an economic arrangement whereby private economic costs and risks are publicly socialized and borne by the general community while the profits and assets generated are privatized by a select few in the name of a "shared community."[31]

Critics of neoliberalism have the following beliefs in common:

> Neoliberal fiscal policies are imposed on Third World countries by powerful financial institutions concerned with maximizing the profits of transnational corporations.
> Neoliberal policies destroy welfare programs, attack labor rights, cut back social programs, and deny protection to children, youth, and women, both abroad and at home.
> The free market envisioned by neoliberal ideas threatens the environment because it leaves trade unregulated, and decisions are driven by the market rather than by their impact on the environment.
> The neoliberal view seeks to roll back the gains made by working people during the last sixty years in the United States.[32]
> According to neoliberals, private markets produce better outcomes for society as a whole, and the role of government should be reduced to merely defending the nation's sovereignty and assuring civil order.

Harry Magdoff, the editor of the economic journal *Monthly Review*, agrees with these contentions and argues that all government actually works to protect the interests of the business class in U.S. society. Magdoff claims that the role of government is hardly being reduced; instead government is being refigured to intervene in support of the private sector, with loans and subsidies for private companies and fewer and less restrictive regulations. The more the economy depends on financial institutions, the more deregulation becomes the norm of the day.[33]

Noam Chomsky, professor of linguistics at MIT and a notable political observer, agrees. Chomsky asks us to critically reanalyze the neoliberal claims of Reaganomics as it emerged in the United States. Chomsky points out that Reaganomics wanted it both ways—smaller government involvement in social affairs and greater government involvement in support of private business interests. The Reagan administration extolled the glories of the market, lectured the poor about their dependence on government, dismantled federal government programs, and ceded more and more power to the states from the federal government. At the same time, the Reagan administration boasted to the national and international business world that the Reagan policies granted more import relief to U.S. industry than the policies of any presidential administration in more than half a century. So which is it? Is neoliberalism for government regulations and subsidies that socialize the costs of doing business while allowing business to privatize the profits, or is neoliberalism adamantly against government involvement, financial or otherwise, in any area of the private marketplace?

For critics like Chomsky, neoliberalism is not a call for smaller government but rather a move toward larger government and more consolidated corporate power beholden to government subsidies and a new form of state protectionism in world trade. Chomsky argues that neoliberalism encourages business to become dependent on government largess—fostering a corporate "entitlement mentality," if you will—through massive state subsidies, deregulation, and economic bailouts, all paid for with public funds.[34] Without such extreme measures of government interference in the market, claim opponents to neoliberalism, it is doubtful that U.S. automotive, steel, machine tool, and semiconductor industries, among others, would have survived against Japanese competition. The $50 million bailout of the Chrysler Corporation with taxpayer funds in the 1980s provides just one example of this kind of state intervention. Another example is current efforts in California to force taxpayers to subsidize the regional utility, the Pacific Gas and Electric Company, through outright purchase at inflated prices.

Chomsky specifically calls attention to the fact that these interventions and bailouts are actually subsidized and paid for by taxpayers through government-funded research and redevelopment paid for by social funds and then simply bequeathed to the private sector. He points to the Internet as a prime example of neoliberal economic poli-

cies in action. Analyzing the development of the information super-
highway, he argues that the Pentagon started the Internet with publicly
funded research money. Yet the Internet was eventually "kidnapped"
from the public who financed it and handed over to private interests.
Now, with the merger of AOL/Time Warner and AT&T, it is largely operated and controlled by a handful of corporations. The same phenomenon has occurred with radio and television stations that were at one
time public property.

Ironically, neoliberal economists like Stephen Moore, a fellow at
the Hoover Institute at Stanford University, would agree with Chomsky's
argument that the state is currently subsidizing private businesses with
entitlements. As a libertarian, Moore is also opposed to the state functioning in this manner. Federal subsidies to corporations take on many
forms—from direct grant payments to insurance sold at below-market
rates; from loan guarantees to free enterprise zones and other sundry
items such as trade protection, monetary policy, and tax loopholes and
benefits. Despite their promises to downsize government, congressional
Republicans have retreated from any serious attempt to reduce business subsidies. According to Moore, the "entitlement" mentality of
which antigovernment forces speak when lambasting public institutions does not apply to government socializing the costs of business
while business privatizes the profits. In fact, federal subsidies to U.S.
business now cost American taxpayers nearly $100 billion a year.[35]

PRIVATIZATION AS AN ECONOMIC AND SOCIAL PHENOMENON

Robert McChesney, another vocal opponent of neoliberal policies and a
professor at the University of Illinois, claims that whether one is critical
of neoliberal economic policies or not, neoliberalism has become the
compelling economic and social force of our time. Through neoliberal
policies and principles, a few transnational corporations are given a
great deal of influence over our social and economic life. To support
these policies and principles, a broad-based, corporate-financed public
relations effort has brought a near-sacred quality to terms and ideas
such as "free market competition," "personal responsibility," and "the
entrepreneurial spirit." Consequently, many people accept without
question these phrases and the claims they represent, only rarely requiring empirical evidence or a reasoned defense. These phrases are invoked to justify a range of economic and fiscal policy ideas—from decreasing high-income and corporate taxes and undoing or blocking

environmental regulations to privatizing public education and social welfare programs. From the perspective encouraged by this public relations effort, not only is neoliberalism accepted as the most efficient and most democratic provider but anything that might hinder corporate freedom of action is suspect.[36]

However dominant neoliberalism may be now, its critics argue that the world into which capitalism was born was not pervaded by market institutions. Human needs and desires were once satisfied, for the most part, without rendering people wholly dependent on markets for their livelihoods and necessities. Further, government intervention has been quite effective in improving the lives of citizens and communities. For example, it is argued that in the twentieth century alone, government has been a driving force for social good. Public sector successes include the provision of many things we now consider necessities, including electricity and other utilities; protection from seasonal flooding; protection and regulation of food, water, and air; interstate highways; weather forecasts and storm warnings; and protection from crime and foreign attack. The public sector has also given us the National Park system, the space program, and research solutions to medical and industrial challenges.

According to Monthly Review Press, however, neoliberalism radically changes the role of government in all this, not simply by making the marketplace the central forum for the satisfaction of basic human needs and wants, but by shifting the culture so that all members of society are dependent on market forces and competition for their cultural, recreational, emotional, intellectual, and spiritual development and needs. Neoliberal policies maintain that every human capacity, every public policy, must and should be guided to meet the needs of large multinational corporations to accumulate greater and greater profits.[37]

Although the advance of liberal economics was offset briefly in the 1930s with the implementation of the Roosevelt New Deal programs and Keynesian economics, even these government activities were seen at the time as devastating for true liberal believers, and neoliberals are still intent on reversing the New Deal policies. Unfettered capitalism is now the norm of the day, and the privatization movement is simply an effort to do away with public sector social programs while redefining and employing government as a "collection agency"—one whose role is essentially to collect public funds not for social government programs but to subsidize private companies that promise to provide social services more effectively and efficiently than the government can.

However, opponents of this phenomenon contend that the economic consequences of neoliberal programs in the last twenty years have been devastating—both nationally and internationally. Alan Nasser, writing for *Monthly Review,* maintains that neoliberalism has become the new political and economic orthodoxy, which allows the outright erasure of existing business regulations. An example is the March 2001 repeal of ergonomics regulations by the George W. Bush administration. As privatization attempts to take over publicly owned enterprises, it also mandates that the social wage, the aggregate earned income of workers be reduced and income supplements eliminated. As a result, claims Nasser, national income has been moved from labor to capital.[38] Neoliberalism's critics argue that since the Thatcher and Reagan governments, which first embraced neoliberal policies and programs as national and international realities, the world has witnessed a massive increase in social and economic inequality and an explosion in world poverty.

John Gray, noted critic of libertarianism and neoliberal economic policies, suggests that liberal institutions and practices are endangered by what he calls "the market fundamentalism" of the new right.[39] Gray, a former Libertarian himself, now argues that neoliberalism is a recipe for social breakdown and political instability. He maintains that antigovernment, pro-market forces have substituted the belief that government can do little or nothing with a new market populism that claims that markets can do everything. Arguing that the market actually creates cultural instability, Gray claims that the celebration of consumer choice and private demands has undermined communities and devalued stability in personal relationships.[40] For critics like Gray, neoliberalism and market processes erode distinctive cultures, devastate communities, and decimate personal liberty.

In his book, *The Politics of the Rich and Poor,* Kevin Phillips, a Republican economic analyst and former aid to President Nixon, agrees with Gray's conclusions. He argues that in the late 1970s and 1980s, income disparities in the United States rose dramatically as a result of neoliberal policies. Hardly politically liberal, Phillips argues that during the Reagan administrations, American families in the top 10 percent of the income pyramid saw their average income increase by 16 percent; those in the top 5 percent enjoyed a 23 percent increase; and those in the top 1 percent saw a 50 percent increase, from an average of $270,000 to $405,000. Among families at the bottom of the income pyramid, 80 percent experienced a decrease in income during the same period. The poorest 10 percent of Americans, according to Phillips, lost 15 percent of their income, from an already low $4,113 annually to $3,504. In 1977, Phillip contends, the top 1 percent of American families had average incomes 65 times greater than those of the bottom 10 percent. A decade later, the top 1 percent was 115 times better off than the bottom.[41]

Some economic critics of neoliberal social policy, such as former U.S. Secretary of Labor Robert Reich, have argued that the abandonment of Keynesian economic policy in the late 1970s resulted in an atrocious approach to economic management based on the so-called free market. Reich and others claim that the quiet renunciation of Keynesianism resulted in severe austerity measures here in the United States, such as the loss of basic entitlements like health and pension benefits coupled with shrinking wages, along with economic "restructuring" in the Third World that further punished the poor and left countries more dependent on industrialized economies. Critics would argue that neoliberal policies are being forcibly implemented throughout the world. These policies, according to their opponents, have birthed a disastrous global environment, an unstable global economy, and a wider chasm between rich and poor, signaling an unprecedented bonanza for the wealthy and deplorable conditions for the poor.[42]

SUMMARY

Whether one believes that neoliberal privatization policies are necessary for freedom and democracy or lead to monopolization, loss of personal and social liberty, and divestiture of the economic wealth of working people, it is undisputed that these policies are increasingly operative in all corners of the globe. Neoliberalism, unfettered globalization, and unbridled privatization practices and public policies have become some of the most controversial issues facing citizens throughout the developed and developing world. Equipped with a basic theoretical understanding of the concept of neoliberalism, the following chapters focus on how these policies specifically affect and define current issues regarding school choice, private vouchers, and other, less well-known, market-based educational reforms.

NOTES

1. Smith, Adam. (1997). *The Wealth of Nations* (Modern Library Series). New York: Random House.

2. Ibid.

3. Boaz. D. (2000). *Libertarianism: A Primer.* New York: Free Press.

4. Starr, P. (1988). "The Meaning of Privatization." *Yale Law and Policy Review* 6: 6-41. This article also appears in Alfred Kahn and Sheila Kamerman, eds., *Privatization and the Welfare State*. Princeton: Princeton University Press, 1989.

5. Corporate Watch. (1997). The Education Industry Fact Sheet, prepared by the Applied Research Center. Available at: http://www.corpwatch.org.

6. Manning, S. (2001). "The Littlest Coke Addicts." *The Nation.* http://www.thenation.com.; Nichols, J. (2001). "Is Coke in Schools Move the Real Thing?" *The Nation.* http://www.thenation.com.

7. Tanner, Michael. (2002). *No Second Best: The Unappetizing Alternatives to Social Security Privatization*. The Cato Project on Social Security Privatization. http://www.socialsecurity.org. (Accessed July 6, 2002)

8. Light, J. (1999, October 28). "Prison Industry: Capitalist Punishment." CorpWatch Web site. Available at: http://www.corpwatch.org. (Accessed May 23, 2002)

9. Ibid.

10. "Traveling Science Shows." *The Franklin Institute Online.* Available at: http://sln.fi.edu. (Accessed May 23, 2002)

11. Sullivan, K. (1999, July/August). "The Medicare Privatization Campaign: An Inauspicious Beginning." *Z Magazine* 12, no. 7/8, p. 68.

12. Mokhiber, R., and R. Weissman. "Sacramento Corporate Sponsorship Program Takes Commercialism to the Extreme." http://www.flipside.org. (Accessed July 6, 2002)

13. Starr, P. "The Meaning of Privatization."

14. Fantauzzo, S. (1991). *Competitive Government: A Labor Perspective of the Indianapolis Model*. American Federation of State, County, and Municipal Employees, Council 62.

15. Poole, R. W. (1980). *Cutting Back City Hall*. New York: Universe Books.

16. Berger, P., and R. Neuhaus. (1996). *To Empower People: The Role of Mediating Structures in Public Policy*. Washington, D.C.: American Enterprise Institute, p. 33.

17. Korten, D. C. (2001). "The Mythic Victory of Capitalism." In: *The Case against the Global Economy*, edited by Jerry Mander. San Francisco: Sierra Club Books, pp. 186–187.

18. Ibid.

19. Smith, Adam. *The Wealth of Nations.*

20. Spencer, H. (1884/1981). *The Man versus the State*. Indianapolis: Liberty Classics.

21. Sclar, E. (2000). *You Don't Always Get What You Pay For: The Economics of Privatization*. London: Cornell University Press.

22. Polanyi, K. (1944). *The Great Transformation*. Boston: Beacon Press, pp. 135–150.

23. George, S. (1999, March 24–26). "A Short History of Neo-Liberalism: Twenty Years of Elite Economics and the Emerging Opportunities for Structural Social Change." Speech delivered at the Conference on Economic Sovereignty in a Globalizing World. Bangkok, Thailand. *Z Magazine* Web site. Available at: http://www.zmag.org.

24. Ibid.

25. Starr, P. "The Meaning of Privatization," p. 5.

26. Friedman, M. (1955). "The Role of Government in Education." In: *Economics and the Public Interest,* edited by Robert A. Solow. New Brunswick: Rutgers University Press.

27. Boaz, D. *Libertarianism: A Primer,* p. 42.

28. Sclar, E. *You Don't Always Get What You Pay For,* p. 94.

29. Boaz, D. *Libertarianism: A Primer,* p. 124.

30. Sclar, E. *You Don't Always Get What You Pay For,* p. 10.

31. O'Connor, J. (1973). *The Fiscal Crisis of the State.* New York: St. Martin's Press.

32. Martinez, E., Garcia, A. (1996, July 27–August 3). "What Is Neo-liberalism?" Speech published by the British Columbia Teachers' Federation for the Tri-National Coalition in Defense of Public Education. Given at the Intercontinental Encounter for Humanity and against Neo-liberalism in La Realidad, Chiapas, Mexico. Available at: http://www.islandnet.com.

33. Magdoff, H. (1998, January). "The Same Old State." *Monthly Review* 49, no. 8: 9.

34. Chomsky, N. (1997). "The Passion for Free Markets." *Z Magazine.* Available at: http://zena.secureforum.com.

35. Moore, S. (1999). "Welfare for the Well-Off: How Business Subsidies Fleece Taxpayers." Hoover Essay in Public Policy. The Hoover Institution Web site. Available at: http://www-hoover.stanford.edu.

36. McChesney, R. (1999, April). "Noam Chomsky and the Struggle Against Neo-liberalism." *Monthly Review* 50, no. 11: 40–41.

37. See Monthly Review Press. http://www.monthlyreview.org/mrpress.

38. Nasser, A. (2000, December). "Saving Social Security: A Neoliberal Recapitulation of Primitive Accumulation." *Monthly Review Press* 52, no. 7: 42.

39. Gray, J. (1993). *Beyond the New Right: Markets, Government, and the Common Environment.* London: Routledge, p. vii.

40. Gray, J. (1995). *Enlightenment's Wake: Politics and Culture at the Close of the Modern Age.* London: Routledge, p. 99.

41. Phillips, K. (1990). *The Politics of the Rich and Poor: Wealth and the American Electorate in the Reagan Aftermath.* New York: Random House.

42. Ibid., p. 41.

Chapter Two

✦ Chronology

The following is a brief chronology of the development of public policy efforts to privatize education. Whether one considers judicial decisions during the 1900s or public policy debates, the efforts to privatize schools has a long history. This chapter will familiarize the reader with both the judicial history and the public policy behind the movement to privatize education.

1892 An important example of judicial preference for private interests came in 1892 with the case of Homer Plessy. When traveling on the East Louisiana Railroad, Plessy, a black man, sat in a car designated for whites only. He was arrested and jailed. In *Homer Adolph Plessy v. The State of Louisiana,* Plessy's lawyer argued that the 1890 Louisiana Separate Car Act violated the Thirteenth and Fourteenth Amendments. The trial ended with a judgment against Plessy, the judge claiming that the state of Louisiana could regulate railroads that ran only within the state. By 1896, the case was taken up by the U.S. Supreme Court in *Plessy v. Ferguson,* where the court upheld the previous rulings and found Plessy guilty. This case would serve to legally justify racial segregation for the next half century.

1922 Charles Carroll, a former U.S. assistant commissioner of education and author of the 1918 book, *Public Education in Rhode Island,* drafted a Rhode Island law aimed at prohibiting commercialization in schools. Carroll argued that schoolchildren should be left alone to focus on education, not on commercial activities in which they would inevitably become involved without legal protection. The law was passed after the Rhode Island Association of Superintendents of Public Schools adopted a resolution stating "the tendency to promote various [commercial] activities through the public schools has become excessive, and if not checked and regulated will seriously interfere with the progress of pupils." The legislation was approved by the Rhode Island state legislature and continues as law today.

1947 The U.S. Supreme Court rendered its first important decision about education in the case of *Everson v. Board of Education.* The case challenged a New Jersey statute authorizing local school districts to make rules and contracts for the transportation of children to and from schools. Under the statute, school boards could authorize reimbursement to parents whose children used public transportation to and from school. A taxpayer filed suit in state court, challenging the right of school boards to reimburse parents of students in parochial schools, contending that reimbursement for religious education violated state and federal constitutions.

When the case made it to the Supreme Court, Judge Hugo Black wrote the majority opinion that the statute violated the First Amendment: "Congress shall make no law respecting the establishment of religion, or prohibiting the free exercise thereof."

1954 The U.S. Supreme Court affirmed equal access to public accommodations, especially schools, in the decision rendered in *Brown v. Board of Education.* The ruling overturned the *Plessy* case of 1896. Immediately after the *Brown* decision, Edward County, Virginia, effectively closed its public schools and attempted to make public funds available for whites who wished to escape forced integration by attending all-white private schools. School boards elsewhere also refused to follow the new ruling against segregation.

1955 The high court ruled in another case titled *Brown v. Board of Education,* which came to be known as *Brown II,* that the rights of black children were personal rights, not general rights belonging to African Americans as a group. The court sent five consolidated cases back to the federal district courts to design a desegregation plan with "deliberate speed." The five cases involved school boards in Kansas, North Carolina, Virginia, Delaware, and Washington, D.C., that refused to live up to the ruling rendered in the first *Brown* case.

The ruling in *Brown II* was a radical shift from the first decision because it allowed each school board to delay the implementation of the court's first decision in *Brown*. In *Brown II* the court established no deadlines for the states to comply with the ruling in *Brown* and allowed each school board to establish its own compliance with the court's decision.

Libertarian economist and noble laureate Milton Friedman argued for private school vouchers. For the first time in modern education history, Americans were introduced to a serious, economic public policy proposal calling for the privatization of public schooling.

1957   After the courts forced Little Rock Central High School to accept the "Little Rock Nine" (the first African American students to attend the racially segregated school) in 1957, voters approved the closure of public schools to avoid integration and concocted a privatization plan to lease the public schools to a private corporation that would maintain segregation.

1961   In a Vermont case entitled *Swart v. South Burlington Town School District*, the U.S. Supreme Court struck down the practice of allowing public school districts to pay for tuition costs at religious schools. The court ruled that this was a violation of the Establishment Clause of the First Amendment.

The Elementary and Secondary Education Act was signed into law, allocating federal funds for education. Traditionally, the bill has financed educational opportunities for poor children and expresses a federal commitment to public education.

In the late 1960s parents and innovative public school educators across the nation joined together to design distinctive educational options, or choices, for students. Metro High School in Chicago, City as School in New York, Parkway in Philadelphia, Marcy Open School in Minneapolis, and St. Paul Open School in St. Paul gave public school teachers the chance to create new kinds of schools that would make sense for a variety of students. Internships and apprenticeships in communities, site-based decision making, and extensive parental involvement were all features of these new and innovative schools. There were no admission requirements, and the schools were open to a variety of students. These schools were designed by groups of parents, educators, and community members, not by central district offices, and they were generally operated at the same per-pupil cost as other, more traditional schools.

1971 The U.S. Supreme Court rendered another seminal judgment in the case of *Lemon v. Kurtzman.* The case involved the use of public monies for parochial and elementary schools and produced the three-prong Lemon test, which continues to be the criteria by which the Court determines religion-state separation issues. The Lemon test includes three criteria that must be used to assess legislation: 1) The legislation must have a secular purpose; 2) the primary effect of the legislation must not advance or inhibit religion; and 3) the legislation must not foster excessive government involvement with religion.

1972 The U.S. Supreme Court handed down a landmark decision in *Brusca v. State of Missouri State Board of Education,* denying the use of public funds to pay private tuition costs and ruling unconstitutional a Missouri statute that authorized public funds for such use. The case involved the parents of children attending religious schools in Missouri. They argued that the Free Exercise and Equal Protection Clauses of the First and Fourteenth Amendments require subsidization, with tax funds, of their children's tuition costs. The *Brusca* decision was used to deny such relief in later decisions.

Parents of parochial school children brought suit against the state of California, arguing that the lack of a system of "tuition grants" for parents who wished to educate their children in non-public elementary and secondary schools violated their rights of free exercise and equal protection stipulated in both the California and U.S. Constitutions. The court rejected the claim.

1983 *A Nation at Risk* was published, providing a strong conservative argument against public education and ushering in an era of calls for school privatization.

The early 1980s witnessed the development of private voucher philosophies as an organizing concept for the conservative wing of the Republican Party. Because the idea appealed to the Christian Right's family values agenda and coupled nicely with the neoliberal belief in the primacy of markets, school choice was held up as a national political, cultural, and economic issue.

1988 Governor Tommy Thompson of Wisconsin introduced Bill No. 816, the first comprehensive private school voucher proposal introduced in a state legislature. The governor's bold first attempt failed to pass the state's Joint Finance Committee. Governor Thompson continued to struggle for the privatization of schools into the 1990s, mounting a successful second attempt to develop and gain passage of a private school voucher proposal. Democratic Representative Annette "Polly" Williams, generally thought of as a liberal legislator, worked to rally the support of her Democratic colleagues for the legislation, which was approved in 1990.

1991 The Milwaukee Parent Choice voucher program in Wisconsin began with ten schools and 341 students.

1992 Milwaukee, Wisconsin; San Antonio, Texas; Atlanta, Georgia; and Battle Creek, Michigan, followed the example of the Indianapolis scholarship program, constructing their own versions of the scholarship plan.

Partners Advancing Values in Education (PAVE), formerly the Milwaukee Archdiocesan Education Foundation, was founded. PAVE provided low-income families in Milwaukee with private scholarships worth half the tuition charged by private religious or nonsectarian schools, up to a maximum of $1,000 for elementary and middle school students and $1,500 for high school students.

1993 Albany, New York; Austin, Texas; Denver, Colorado; Detroit and Grand Rapids, Michigan; Little Rock, Arkansas; Phoenix, Arizona; and Washington, D.C., launched private scholarship programs that paralleled the PAVE efforts and others.

In Wisconsin, Representatives Polly Williams (D) and Scott Jensen (R) introduced A.B. (Assembly Bill) 1266, which was designed to expand the new school voucher plan to include parochial schools. The bill would also have ended the lottery system by which participating students were selected and would have increased the number of participating students from 1,000 to 5,000. The bill did not pass.

1994 A $2 million grant by the Walton Family Foundation launched CEO America, another national private scholarship program dedicated to privatizing education.

The U.S. Supreme Court significantly narrowed the opinion that it had rendered in the 1961 case *Swart v. South Burlington Town School District.* A Vermont statute directed each school district to furnish a high school education to children within the district by either funding the high school or by paying tuition at a school of the student's choice. The statute did not explicitly exclude religious schools from the program, but that is how the Vermont State Board of Education interpreted the statute. A parent in a school district that did not provide a public high school sued the state, arguing that his request for reimbursement of tuition for an out-of-state parochial school was illegally denied. The high court virtually overruled its earlier decision in *Swart* and ruled that the statute did not exclude religious schools from the reimbursement policy. The court went on to analyze arguments that claimed such an interpretation of the statute would violate the Establishment Clause, ruling that allowing tuition grants to the plaintiff in the case did not violate the Establishment Clause.

1995 Orlando and Jacksonville, Florida; Buffalo, New York; Knoxville, Tennessee; and Bridgeport, Connecticut, began private scholarship programs similar to those in other states, adding to a growing national movement to provide private tuition grants to students.

In the 1995–1997 budget bill for Wisconsin, Governor Thompson again proposed expanding the Wisconsin voucher system to include religious schools and to increase the number of eligible students. The proposal was signed into law, and a public interest lawsuit followed, charging that the legislation violated the state constitution. The case was fast-tracked to the Wisconsin Supreme Court, which was deadlocked on a three to three vote. The case was then referred back to the lower court.

1996   Wisconsin Senator Tim Weeden introduced S.B. 565 in the state senate. The bill required schools accepting state vouchers to create governance structures and be more accountable to state government.

Wisconsin Representative Williams introduced A.B. 1008, which would have made all private schools more publicly accountable. The bill failed to pass the legislature.

The Cleveland voucher program began.

1997   The New York City private voucher program began.

On June 23, the U.S. Supreme Court overturned a 1985 decision made in *Aguilar v. Felton.* In the earlier case, the Court had struck down the use of public financing for remedial education services in religious schools. Now, however, the Court noted that decisions made since 1985 made it clear that assistance to students in religious schools was permissible if it did not create an incentive for students to attend those schools.

On November 4, the U.S. House of Representatives defeated H.R. 2746, known by proponents as the Help Empower Low Income Parents Act. At the final vote, thirty-five House Republicans voted against the measure, which would have allowed state and local education agencies to use their Title VI funds to pay for private vouchers to private and religious schools. Title VI, part of the Civil Rights Act, prohibits discrimination on the basis of race, color, and national origin in programs and activities receiving federal financial assistance.

On November 10, the U.S. Senate refused to vote on H.R. 2646, the so-called A+ Education Savings Account Bill. The bill would have created tax-free educational savings accounts for families earning up to $160,000 annually to use for payment of expenses associated with private, religious, or home schooling.

On November 12, the U.S. House of Representatives passed the District of Columbia Appropriations Bill without the controversial voucher language that was contained in the earlier draft.

Nationally, as of November 1997, more than thirty-five privately sponsored scholarships provided nearly 20,000 low-income children with an opportunity to attend any private school of their choice.

1998 Ohio, California, Alabama, Tennessee, Kentucky, Minnesota, and Connecticut created private scholarship programs.

In the spring, school choice advocates spent $2.7 million dollars in the state of Texas on a pro-voucher initiative campaign. Voters failed to pass the initiative.

New Mexico Governor Gary Johnson tried unsuccessfully to push through the legislature an unregulated voucher program for all K–12 students. The voucher bill was defeated by large margins in both houses.

Pennsylvania Governor Tom Ridge failed for the fifth time in his attempts to push private voucher school legislation through the state legislature.

On November 9, the U.S. Supreme Court refused to hear a challenge to the expansion of the Milwaukee Parental Choice Program (MPCP) to include religious schools. The court's refusal to hear the case in effect allowed the state of Wisconsin to provide direct public support, in the form of public funds, to religious schools.

1999 In January, A.B. 116 and A.B. 117 were introduced to the California state legislature. The first bill would limit the amount of corporate advertising and the use of corporate logos in instructional materials approved by the state. It would also call for criteria to be developed that would discourage corporate advertising in textbooks. A.B. 117 would prohibit the governing board of a school district from entering into a contract that granted exclusive advertising rights for the sale of carbonated beverages. The bill would also prohibit the governing board of a school district from entering into a contract that prohibited a school employee from disparaging the goods or services contracted for by a school board.

In February, The Children's Scholarship Fund, underwritten by entrepreneurs Ted Forstmann and John Walton, committed $30 million in new funds for private school scholarships for low-income families in communities throughout the nation. Participating families received partial scholarships at the private school of their choice, paying the balance of the tuition themselves.

On March 25, the Florida House of Representatives handed Governor Jeb Bush a major victory by approving his plan for the nation's first statewide school voucher program, using tax dollars to send children to private schools. Under the program, entitled the A+ Plan for Education, students in struggling public schools (those graded with an F by state auditors for two years in a four-year period on the basis of student test scores and other factors) can receive vouchers for up to $4,000 for private or religious school tuition. Public schools that earn As or show improvement over the years will get incentive rewards from the state of $100 per pupil. It was expected that 169 schools and 156,000 students would be eligible in the 2000–2001 school year for the private voucher program.

On April 23, the Maine Supreme Court found that publicly funded vouchers for private religious schools were unconstitutional.

In May, the Ohio Supreme Court ruled on a technicality and found that the Cleveland scholarship program, a private voucher program, violated the state constitution's single-subject rule because it had been attached to the state's biennial budget. Although the court found the program in violation of the law, it stayed the effect of this ruling, giving the legislature time to reenact the program in a proper manner. When the legislature did so, the original plaintiffs then filed another lawsuit, arguing that the scholarship program violated the Establishment Clause. The plaintiffs asked the court for a preliminary injunction. In August, just before the public schools were to open, the court granted the plaintiff's request. The court eventually modified its original decision and allowed already participating students to continue in the program for another semester while litigation proceeded.

Several education bills were introduced to the U.S. Senate by Georgia Senator Paul Coverdell (R). The most comprehensive, S.B. 277, cosponsored by Trent Lott of Mississippi (R), had many elements of the Republican education agenda, including education savings accounts (ESA), block grants for federal education funds, and for the first time at the federal level, private school tax credits. From the conservative Republican point of view, ESAs were the linchpin of Republican efforts aimed at schools in 2001. If enacted, this bill would be the first step toward direct federal financial assistance to religious schools. Such a step could run counter to the high court's ruling in 1970 in *Liberty v. Nyquist,* which struck down a state law providing tax deductions to parents for the cost of tuition at religious schools. The Supreme Court, in the Nyquist case, characterized the tax credits as "a charge upon the state for the purpose of religious education." They ruled the law unconstitutional.

The Wisconsin state legislature introduced A.B. 103, which would prohibit certain contracts between school boards and commercial enterprises. The bill was designed to prevent schools from entering into exclusive contracts with beverage companies and similar commercial interests. The bill did not pass.

Illinois enacted an educational expenses tax credit designed to provide parents with a tax credit of up to 25 percent of education-related expenses (including tuition, books, and lab fees) exceeding $250, for a maximum of $500 per family. The program is being legally challenged.

In September, U.S. Representative Dick Armey (R) of Texas introduced H.R. 2971, by which state governors could declare "academic emergency areas," somewhat like federal disaster areas. Parents in these areas would be eligible for $3,500 vouchers that could be used in public, private, or parochial schools. Armey attached his bill, proposing the Academic Emergency Act, to the bill reauthorizing the Elementary and Secondary Education Act (ESEA). He also added another provision, called the Safe and Sound Schools Act, to grant vouchers to victims of violence in schools. Nothing in the bill was designed to protect schools or students. The bill did not pass.

Arizona Senator John McCain (R) offered an amendment to H.R. 2971. He proposed to institute a voucher program of $1.8 billion per year. The Senate ultimately rejected McCain's idea.

On September 22, H.R. 2915 was introduced in the 106th Congress. Described as legislation to protect students from commercial exploitation, the bill provided that no funds authorized under the proposed act may be used by an applicable program to allow a third party to monitor, receive, gather, or obtain information intended for commercial purposes from any student under eighteen years of age without prior, written, informed consent of the student's parent. The bill would also stipulate that before a school entered into a contract with a third party, the school must inquire whether the third party intended to gather, collect, or obtain information on students and if so, how this information would be used. The bill also provided for a consent form to be utilized by any third parties attempting to obtain information from students.

In October, the U.S. Supreme Court refused to consider an appeal of the Maine lower court's ruling limiting the voucher program in Maine from covering expenses in private schools. In effect, the refusal prohibited the state from providing direct support to religious schools.

Also in October, the Court refused to consider a similar appeal of a lower court ruling involving a Pennsylvania law, in effect prohibiting the state from giving a tax break specifically to religious publications.

In October, Wisconsin State Representative Christine Siniki introduced a bill in the Wisconsin state legislature that would increase access to voucher schools by the public, including the media. The bill would subject all schools participating in the Milwaukee Parental Choice Program, as well as charter schools, to the state's open meetings and to public accountability and public record laws. Under current law, voucher schools were not required to make public any of their records, nor were they required to conduct their affairs in public.

On October 4, the U.S. Supreme Court stated that it would not consider an appeal of a lower court ruling involving an Arizona law, in effect permitting a tax-break plan that directly and strongly benefited religious schools through direct tax credits.

On October 12, the U.S. Supreme Court affirmed a superior court decision in the state of Maine rejecting a challenge brought by parents against a Maine statute that allowed that children living in an area without a public school could attend a private non-parochial school or public school in another district with the tuition to be paid directly to the school by the state. The parents had argued that the statute excluded sectarian schools and that such exclusion violated the Free Exercise Clause, the Establishment Clause, the Equal Protection Clause, and Maine's constitution.

In December, U.S. District Judge Solomon Oliver ruled that the Cleveland Scholarship Program violated the Establishment Clause of the First Amendment. However, the judge stayed the injunction pending appellate review. In December 2001 a federal appeals court struck down the program as unconstitutional.

In the fall of 1999, A.B. 342 was introduced into the Wisconsin state legislature. It would prevent voucher schools from discriminating on the basis of race, religion, gender, sexual orientation, or disability.

U.S. Representative Buck McKeon (R) of California introduced legislation designed to gut President Bill Clinton's plan to hire 100,000 new teachers nationwide by 2000. The bill, H.R. 1995, would essentially offer block grants to states for programs to train and hire teachers, but it would do so by eliminating current federal programs. The act passed the House but did not pass the Senate.

2000 A number of education-related bills were introduced in Wisconsin in 2000. A.B. 543, known as the Accountability Legislation, requires private schools accepting vouchers to administer uniform tests.

On March 14, Florida Judge L. Ralph Smith ruled that the program authorizing Florida's Opportunity Scholarships was illegal, stating that it violated the Education Clause of the state constitution.

The Children's Educational Opportunity Act (H.B. 68, S.B. 336) was introduced to the Virginia legislature. The bill would have provided Virginia parents of children in kindergarten through high school with state subsidies for tuition payments to private schools. The bill was defeated that same year.

On June 28, the U. S. Supreme Court ruled to allow a Louisiana school district the use of public funds to purchase computers and other "instructional equipment" for private and religious schools. According to opponents of the decision, the court's ruling further blurred the separation of church and state and added confusion to the rights and responsibilities of school districts. The ruling indicated where the court might be going on the issue of private vouchers. According to the People for the American Way, the court's decision revealed the key vote on vouchers came from Justice Sandra Day O'Connor.

In November, school choice initiatives appeared on the ballot in Michigan and California. Financed by multimillionaire Ted Draper and known as Proposition 38, the California voucher initiative failed significantly by a vote of 71 to 29 percent. African Americans voted down the initiative by 68 to 32 percent, and Latinos opposed the initiative by an even higher margin—77 to 23 percent.

    The proposition was designed to give $4,000 to any student in kindergarten through twelfth grade wishing to attend a private school of their choice. This was the second time in seven years that California voters overwhelmingly rejected private voucher proposals.

In the November election, a voucher initiative also failed to win voter support in Michigan, where the vote against vouchers was 75 to 25 percent among African Americans and 59 to 41 percent among Catholics. The plan was opposed by 69 percent of all voters.

On December 11, the U.S. Circuit Court of Appeals upheld a lower court ruling that the Cleveland voucher program violated the First Amendment. The court ruled that the Cleveland program, under which most participating students attended religious schools, was unconstitutional because in effect, it benefited sectarian schools.

The circuit court ruling affirmed a December 20, 1999, U.S. District Court ruling against the Cleveland voucher program. The issue could come before the U.S. Supreme Court in years to come and serve as a test case as to whether public monies should be or can be used to subsidize private schools.[1] According to Clint Bolick of the Institute for Justice, a Washington-based think tank, this is the "test case" that voucher proponents have been waiting for.[2] But according to Barry Lynn, executive director of Americans United for Separation of Church and State, the court's decision reinforces the fact that taxpayer monies cannot be diverted for use by nonsecular schools.[3]

2001   The Elementary and Secondary Education Act, originally signed in 1965, was up for reauthorization by the 107th Congress. There are more than forty programs contained in ESEA. These programs presently receive approximately $12 billion in funding. Nearly every school district in the country receives ESEA funds, which are used to ensure equity in learning.

In February of 2001, President George W. Bush established a faith-based charitable program, with a federal office to be staffed by government employees and subsidized through taxpayer funds. The office coordinates the bidding and awarding of government contracts to faith-based charities that provide public services. The issue promises to be politically incendiary, and many argue that it could lead to support for faith-based vouchers for schools. Bush also promoted a $5,000 dollar tax credit that could be used for charitable purposes.

In late December 2001, the House and Senate reauthorized the thirty-five-year-old Elementary and Secondary Education Act (ESEA), the main instrument through which the federal government funds education for children in kindergarten through twelfth grade. The bill (H.R.1) authorized $26.5 billion in federal spending on elementary and secondary education for fiscal year 2002, $4 billion more than President Bush requested, and $8 billion more than the 2001 spending level. The ESEA was reauthorized through fiscal year 2007. The bill was signed into law on January 8, 2002.

2002 In early January, Rep. Christopher Smith (R-NJ) introduced HR 3685, the Education, Achievement, and Opportunity Act. The bill would provide a refundable credit against income tax for education expenses, including tuition at private schools, for up to $2,500 per year for parents of students in K–8 and up to $3,500 per year for parents of high school students.

President Bush's fiscal year 2003 budget included a tuition tax credit plan in place of vouchers. This credit would refund part of families' private schools expenses, at a cost to the U.S. Treasury of $3.7 billion.

In a 5–4 decision, the U.S. Supreme Court ruled on June 28 that the Ohio law creating a private-school voucher program in Cleveland is constitutional. The Court said allowing parents to use tuition vouchers to send their children to private schools run by religious organizations does not violate the separation of church and state mandated in the Constitution.

In June, People for the American Way Foundation filed a complaint with the Milwaukee County Corporation Counsel on behalf of two city residents, charging that five of the nine members of the Board of School Directors of the Milwaukee Public Schools violated the Wisconsin Open Meetings Law. Under the Open Meetings Law, governmental bodies, including school boards, are required to give advance public notice of their meetings and to conduct their business in open session. The complaint charged that the five board members violated the law by meeting in private as defined by Open Meetings Law. The Milwaukee Department of Instruction found probable cause issued on April 28, 2000. Two schools changed their procedures and settled with DPI.

On August 5, State Circuit Court Judge Kevin Davey ruled that Florida's 1999 "A+" voucher law violates the state's constitution, which prohibits the use of public funds to support religious schools. The decision is likely to be appealed by the state. Although a sharply divided U.S. Supreme Court ruled 5–4 in June that a Cleveland school voucher law does not violate the Establishment Clause of the U.S. Constitution, the Cleveland decision does not bar states, like Florida, from prohibiting the use of state monies to fund religious institutions.

In November Florida voters approved an amendment limiting class size. The Florida State Conference of NAACP Branches, the Florida Education Association, and the Florida State Council of the Service Employees International Union endorsed the amendment.

NOTES

1. People for the American Way. (2000, December 11). "Cleveland Vouchers Dealt Another Blow by Federal Appeals Court." People for the American Way Web site. http://www.pfaw.org.

2. Associated Press. (2000, December 11). "Court Rejects School Voucher Program." SpeakOut.com Web site. http://speakout.com. (Accessed June 3, 2002.)

3. Ibid.

Chapter Three
● Privatization and School Choice

Under the rubric of so-called school choice, educational policy reform efforts have become increasingly tied to the goal of privatizing public education. Although choice advocates have multifaceted agendas and come from diverse ideological backgrounds, both liberal and conservative, most share a neoliberal belief that educational excellence, efficiency, student achievement, and quality will emerge as a result of the educational marketplace, not through public schools. The problem with education, according to the neoliberal educational argument, is that government intrusion and burdensome bureaucratic regulations have created a government monopoly on schools that serves to smother innovation and change. But such attacks on public education are not new.

For example, after a destabilizing defeat at the hands of the Prussians in the 1870s, France faced a period of complex social upheaval. Many blamed the public school system not only for this unrest but for the failure of the military. A reform plan to improve the schools included a parochial school voucher plan strikingly similar to those now recommended in the United States. That the plan was not taken up by the legislature had more to do with the tradition of French anticlericalism than with support for the public schools.[1] As we will see, contemporary support for private school choice is often based on similar dissatisfaction with current conditions and a blanket attack on the public schools as the source of the nation's problems. The twentieth-century version of school choice can be traced directly to the efforts of Milton Friedman, a disciple of Friedrich Hayek and the winner of a Nobel Prize in economics in 1976. In 1955, Friedman argued that every family should be given a universal voucher of equal worth for each child who attended school. Under Friedman's rationale, families would be able to choose any school that met minimal government standards. Parents would be allowed to complement the private voucher with their own resources, and schools would be able to set their own admission requirements and tuition costs.[2]

The central premise underlying the economic theory of private choice is that the provision of education can be understood in the same way as the production and provision of any other good or service. In fact, Friedman likened private school choice to a consumer's decision to select a restaurant. This perspective touts the value of the free educational marketplace, arguing that parents should be allowed to act as rational consumers of education, to "shop around," so to speak. If unsatisfied with the educational product their children were receiving, they could then take their business elsewhere. This would force all schools, public and private, to deliver better educational services more efficiently. The logic of the free market and economic competitiveness dictates that any school unable to compete advantageously with other schools would simply go out of business.

Although much of the rationale for private school choice rests on neoliberal claims of market efficiency, many people have been attracted to the privatization movement by other ideas and concerns as well. The motivating ideas identified by private choice advocates have included belief in individuality, personal sovereignty, religious worship, cultural diversity, and community empowerment, and a desire to dismantle or, at the very least, to reconfigure public bureaucracies.

As we shall examine in more detail, many stakeholders in the privatization controversy have failed to recognize that proponents of private choice are themselves diverse in background and organizational vision, and this failure seriously restricts the current choice debate. Choice means different things to different Americans, and thus does not automatically translate into market-based reform positions, as can be seen in the case of public school choice and the charter school movement. American views about the limits and advantages of government intervention continue to remain mercurial and indistinct.

Another important distinction is one between targeted private voucher proposals that target the poor or other groups and universal private voucher proposals, like Friedman's, that would provide vouchers without considering economic or other factors.

PUBLIC AND PRIVATE CHOICE: IDENTIFYING THE DIFFERENCES

The simple definition of private school choice first advocated by Milton Friedman and ideologically inherited by Christopher Jencks and others generally persists today, and neoliberal advocates of private school vouchers have not strayed far from Friedman's original universal voucher proposal. School choice as proposed by Friedman would be a "private choice," and the difference between private choice and public choice is crucial in understanding the difference between voucher proposals and public choice proposals. Although both private choice and public choice proponents demand parental choice and argue that competition is the key to increased public school performance and accountability, the two movements are significantly different in other respects.

First of all, the public choice plans allow parents to choose the school they wish their children to attend, but their choices are limited to schools within the public school system. This is why the movement is called "public" choice—parents must choose within the public school system. Depending on the school system, parents can choose from a broad range of schools, including charter schools, magnet schools, alternative schools, and home schooling. The charter school movement is a contemporary example of the exercise of public choice.

Under private choice or school voucher plans, families would be given private vouchers for a specific amount of public money that they could then use to pay tuition at their choice of private schools—religious or secular. For example, in Wisconsin, families can use public financing in the form of vouchers to help pay for their children's parochial school education. These schools are sometimes called "public parochial schools." All of the private choice or voucher proposals that have been put forward differ from the public choice proposals in four distinct ways.[3]

First, public choice cannot be used for sectarian schools. Private choice programs allow students to attend either public or private parochial schools, but under public choice programs, public funds cannot be used for sectarian or private religious schools, generally as a matter of constitutional guarantee under the Establishment Clause.

Second, in most states, public school choice consists of a system that does not allow schools to pick and choose among applicants on the basis of previous achievement or behavior. This differs dramatically from many private school voucher plans, which state that private schools may choose their students in any way they wish as long as their criteria are not constitutionally prohibited. (Some states, as we shall see, claim that their private choice plans involve random selection processes). This difference in admission policy has been one of the key reasons that public school choice has been accepted and embraced as an idea for educational reform by many public school defenders. The fear of outright privatization has put many educational policy makers on the defensive, and this fear of losing public education altogether makes them more open to public choice proposals.

Third, public choice cannot be used to send children to schools that require more tuition than the state allocation they receive. By contrast, private choice and voucher proposals permit private and parochial schools to charge as much tuition as they wish, above and beyond whatever public monies are given to parents for their children's education. Parents must then make up the difference in cost with their own private funds.

The fourth and final difference between the private choice and the public choice concepts is the explicit responsibility for documenting student achievement. Public choice schools, whether they are charter schools or home schools, are held publicly accountable to state educational standards and must demonstrate that their students are improving their skills and expanding their knowledge base. They also have public accountability requirements for organizational procedures and records. Private voucher schools, on the other hand, have no public accountability requirements and are not responsible for publicly documenting or assuring student achievement beyond the school's own requirements. This difference is a source of legislative debates in cities like Milwaukee, Wisconsin. As we will see when we examine the MPCP, the Legislative Audit Bureau for the state of Wisconsin, which that oversees the Milwaukee voucher program, has virtually no accountability requirements built into its legal provisions.

A BRIEF HISTORY OF PRIVATE SCHOOL CHOICE

Friedman's proposal was not widely or enthusiastically received by the public when originally proposed in the mid-1950s; the proposal actually surfaced at a time when Americans were more interested in improving public education through the development of academically enriched curriculums and improved access for some students (usually whites) to advanced placement classes.

However, with the 1954 Supreme Court decision in *Brown v. Board of Education*, optimism about and expectations for the promises and possibilities of public education escalated among diverse segments of the American public. In *Brown*, the Court ruled that separate schools for different races were inherently unequal and therefore violated the Fourteenth Amendment to the U.S. Constitution, which guarantees equal protection under the law for all citizens. Henceforth, all public schools would have to be open to all races equally.

School desegregation created the hope that perhaps, for the first time in American history, equality in public education would improve the nation's schools—not just for a few privileged students but also for American children of all races, cultures, linguistic backgrounds, gender, and social classes. Yet ironically, it was desegregation that gave us our first modern historical experience with the Friedman voucher proposal. Not all Americans were pleased with the *Brown* decision, and vouchers promised to provide a way around what many segregationists saw as its infringement on state sovereignty.

Paradoxically, or some would perhaps say "logically," the concept of private school choice was initially used not only as a way around the *Brown* decision but also as an attempt to stop the progress of integration efforts completely and establish "white flight academies." Private choice did not emerge as an ideological attempt to improve public schools or provide unique learning opportunities for all children, as some educational academicians would like us to believe. And although Friedman himself publicly stated his support for racial integration at the time the *Brown* decision was rendered, his political and economic theories regarding the role of government and the markets suggested that federally imposed desegregation attempts were a threat to parental choice in education and also threatened states' rights. He avidly argued against any regulatory impositions on private choice, even in light of racial inequality, and thereby made clear the reactionary nature of his argument at a time when many Americans were attempting to open societal institutions to those historically marginalized and disenfranchised.

Meanwhile, Friedman continued to garner a reputation as a notable neoliberal economic advocate of free markets as a tool for improving the quality of life for all Americans, even though the policies he proposed had done little since Reconstruction to provide equality for African Americans and other communities of color. In practice, hope for equality was kept alive not by free markets, but by the active intervention of the federal courts, a notion antithetical to economic neoliberalism. The Supreme Court, in the form of a federal judicial decree called *Brown*, was eventually called upon to guarantee equal access to public accommodations for all our nation's children.

Unbeknownst to many, yet salient to any understanding of the private choice proposition, is the fact that the nation's first private choice program actually occurred in the state of Virginia immediately after the *Brown* decision. Prince Edward County, Virginia, in effect, closed its public schools to avoid the court-ordered desegregation of schools codified in *Brown II*. Prince Edward County attempted to make public funds available to white students so that they would not have to attend public schools with blacks but instead could opt out of public schools and use tax vouchers to pay for private school tuition.

During the second half of the twentieth century, a large number of Virginians were apparently willing to engage in the wholesale surrender of public education to African Americans to avoid sending their children to public schools with people of color. Many educational stakeholders now wonder if this same sacrifice is being made today in the midst of the resegregation of schools through a multitude of factors ranging from property taxes, to urban flight, to specific zoning laws.

In Little Rock, Arkansas, a notorious battle over desegregation took a similar turn. After the courts forced Little Rock Central High School to accept the "Little Rock Nine" in 1957, voters the following year approved closing the public schools rather than allowing black students to attend. The school board then concocted a privatization plan by which the schools would be leased to a private school corporation that would ensure and maintain segregation. A federal circuit judge stepped in to put a halt to the board's innovative and racist "privatization" efforts and prevented it from implementing the plan.[4]

During the 1960s, the American public continued to express confidence in public education, and American higher education was viewed throughout the world as exemplary—perhaps even the best on the globe. During this tumultuous period, private school vouchers had support in many circles, ranging from progressives, black nationalists, liberal scholars and social critics, and those like Ivan Illich, who argued that current education techniques disempowered students, on the one hand, to conservative political groups and businesspeople, on the other. Voucher proponents on the left were especially enthusiastic about "regulated" voucher plans that would make the size of the voucher dependent on the need of the family. Such plans came to form what is currently known as the targeted voucher approach to privatization.

Practical applications of such plans were slow in coming. The Office of Economic Opportunity (OEO) proposed a federal voucher program during the Johnson administration's War on Poverty, and during the Nixon administration the OEO set up a pilot program to test the proposal. Local enthusiasm for the OEO program was so limited, however, that only one city, Alum Rock, California, agreed to participate in the pilot. The results were disappointing, and the program was discontinued.

In the early 1970s, the Panel on Non-Public Education of the Presidential Commission on School Finance announced its intention to provide public funds to religious schools. At the time, such plans (called "Parochiaid") not only met with public opposition but also faced a long constitutional battle in the courts. In its majority ruling in *Lemon v. Kurtzman* the Supreme Court presented a legal barrier to Parochiaid. The Court interpreted the First Amendment to define three criteria for any school voucher legislation: "First, the statute must have a secular legislative purpose; second, its principal or primary effect must be one that neither advances nor inhibits religion...; finally, the statute must not foster an 'excessive government entanglement with religion.'"[5]

Remarkably, despite this setback, the idea of providing public funds to families in order to send their children to parochial schools continued to find support. Indeed, the debate over Parochiaid set the stage for today's school privatization debate. In the mid-1980s the Reagan administration tried to pass voucher legislation. Although this effort failed, it is significant for its argument that vouchers would "empower" the poor. This was the same argument that had attracted progressives to the school voucher idea in the 1960s and 1970s, providing impetus for the "reform" of Chapter 1 of the ESEA to provide individual vouchers to poor families.

Yet by the 1980s, with the publication of *A Nation at Risk*, a report by the National Commission on Excellence in Education concluding that the U.S. public education system was a catastrophic failure, confidence in American education was silently being eroded and many Americans were beginning to develop and hold the quiet conviction that public education was becoming increasingly mired in bureaucracy and inefficiency and that U.S. students—particularly students in urban centers—were falling behind their international counterparts.

THE ACADEMIC FAILURE OF AMERICAN STUDENTS: FACT OR MYTH?

Valid or not, the belief that public schools are failing continues to prevail among a great number of Americans and is responsible for much of the wide appeal of private choice among many diverse constituents. Somehow, a conventional wisdom has been uncritically established and is now taken for granted: American students are falling behind, and they cannot hold their own against their international counterparts. They can't read; they can't do math; they are incapable in science; and they are undisciplined in both mind and body. And this sad state of affairs, we are told, is due to a disabled and decrepit public education system that allows students to fall further and further behind and is responsible for any economic difficulties that the nation has faced in the past or may face in the future.

Gerald Bracey, noted research psychologist for the Educational Testing Service, associate director of the Institute for Child Study at Indiana University–Bloomington, and for many years the director of research, evaluation, and testing for the Virginia Department of Education, argues that student achievement may provide a long-term contribution to economic health but that the schools are not responsible for the fluctuating state of the economy.[6] Bracey cites educational historian Lawrence Cremin, author of *Popular Education and Its Discontents,* who argues that the competitiveness of the U.S. economy in world markets has more to do with fiscal, trade, and other economic policies and programs than with educational reform. Cremin writes: "Therefore, to conclude that problems of international competitiveness can be solved by educational reform, especially educational reform defined solely as school reform, is not merely utopian and millennialist, it is at best a foolish and at worst a crass effort to direct attention away from those truly responsible for doing something about competitiveness and to lay the burden instead on the schools."[7]

It is true that the globalization of the marketplace has added a new twist to the debate over educational reform, among other things. It is also true that over the course of the last half century, the ability of the United States to compete in the global economy has not always been outstanding. For example, measures of U.S. competitiveness fell during the mid-1990s. The Global Economic Forum, which provides an annual ranking of the world's countries in terms of international economic competitiveness, placed the United States first among twenty-five countries in 1994 and 1995, a position that had fallen to fourth by 1996.

A related measurement of U.S. success is provided by the International Institute of Management, which provides access to some of Europe's best systems of education in management programs of the British Open University School. The institute has been deeply involved in ranking students from various countries in terms of performance on educational examinations.

In 1996, eighteen of the twenty-five countries ranked by the Global Economic Forum participated in the institute's Third International Math and Science Study (TIMSS). According to measures of statistical association between the forum's competitiveness rankings and the TIMSS rankings in math, there was no relationship between the two measurements.[8] So what do the other studies about student performance tell us?

According to Gerald Bracey, it depends on what is being tested. The major study of reading, conducted in 1992 among thirty-one countries, ranked U.S. students second only to students in Finland, a small, homogeneous country with significantly higher tax rates than the United States. Schools in the United States, unlike those in Finland, receive thousands of new immigrant students each year, who speak nearly 150 different languages. So the reading scores reveal, not that the U.S. educational system is in dire shape, but that U.S. students are doing well. In fact, the top U.S. students were ranked higher in reading than the top students of any other country, including Finland, when tested at ages nine and fourteen.[9]

However, according to Empower America, an educational foundation headed by former Labor Secretary Jack Kemp and former Education Secretary William Bennett, American eighth graders scored nineteenth in mathematics and eighteenth in science out of thirty-eight nations in 2000. The U.S. students in this study were compared to students from other nations, excluding eleven Western European countries. Furthermore, the eight graders tested at levels far below what they had accomplished as fourth graders in the same subject four years earlier. From the point of view of Empower America, the longer one stays in public school, the more obtuse one seems to become. Although it may be upsetting and unpleasant, they argue, admitting that there is a problem with public schools is the first step toward launching authentic educational reform.[10]

FACTORS INFLUENCING PUBLIC OPINION ABOUT THE IMPACT OF PRIVATE VOUCHERS AND PRIVATIZATION AS AN EDUCATIONAL CONCEPT: THE ROLE OF THE MEDIA AND SPECIAL INTERESTS

Does the media drive public opinion regarding privatization or simply report the facts? Any interested reader can see how the issue of assessment and student achievement has been communicated by neoliberal analysts simply by looking at the media coverage of the 1992 study by President George Bush's Department of Education. First, the department called a press conference to announce the poor results of testing in science and mathematics. But later, when reading scores were tallied, the department did nothing to publicize these scores, which were quite good. Nor can the media be held blameless for this bias in coverage. Perhaps not surprisingly, it was not until two months after the report was issued that anyone noticed the positive study of reading scores. When *Education Week*, the newspaper read by most educators, finally reported on the reading score, *USA Today* followed up with a front-page article. But the coverage was not entirely positive; it quoted a Bush administration official who dismissed the study as irrelevant. No other media outlet covered the story.

Television political ads and infomercials consistently maintain that despite increased funding for public education (a fourteen-fold in inflation-adjusted spending since 1920), test scores have fallen and our international counterparts far exceed U.S. students in math and science. In fact, U.S. students are claimed to be at the bottom among industrialized nations.[11]

Amidst the cacophony of claims regarding low student achievement, many progressive policy makers argue that the media's concentration on public school deficiency and failing standardized test scores has in many, if not most, cases fabricated a legend of national educational apocalypse, a myth that is without substance. Critics argue that demagoguery and propagandistic characterizations of public schools as failure factories have painted an unreasonable portrait of what is actually taking place within U.S. public education and the daily lives of schools and those who work in them.

Progressive educators and policy makers argue that although it is true that U.S. schools can certainly be much better than they are, it is downright untruthful and damaging to distort the data, looking for sensationalist and nightmarish stories in every educational setting, mentioning only the problems associated with public education and not the successes, and emphasizing low test scores without analyzing what these tests purport to test and why. A spurious and unquestioned demonization of public schools has been the source of concern not only for authors such as Gerald Bracey, but also for noted scholars David C. Berliner and Bruce J. Biddle, who grappled directly with the issue of student and school performance in their seminal book, *The Manufactured Crisis*.[12] In the book, Berliner and Biddle discredit statistics about the decline of U.S. students and claim that SAT scores are rising for many segments of students. They analyze proposals for correcting problems in education and offer solutions.

John F. Witte, official state auditor for the Milwaukee private voucher program, also claims media coverage of the voucher movement has concentrated on the virtues of the free market while at the same time condemning public education. He believes that the answer has to do with the nature of educational policy and the dramatization of schooling issues as reported in the national media.[13] In fact, Witte describes the meteoric development of the private choice debate as "theater." He identifies the epicenter of the debate as the Milwaukee Parental Choice Program, enacted in 1990. Once the Milwaukee plan was initiated, entrepreneurs, politicians, private interest groups, religious constituencies, and other national and state actors could scarcely wait to climb aboard the privatization bandwagon and wholeheartedly embrace the idea.

The more the voucher principle was described as a market solution to the troubles of public education, the more the media concentrated its efforts on private vouchers as a symbolic antidote for an allegedly failing public school system, suggesting entrepreneurs, faith-based solutions, and private choice as a way out of the public school "dilemma." Free markets became the new public mantra, continuously glamorized and reinforced by an eager, ratings-driven, profit-making media industry that was emerging at a time when all public institutions were under scrutiny. According to Witte, when the Milwaukee bill passed in 1990, business interests also began to line up behind the idea. Publications like the Wall Street Journal eagerly jumped on the bandwagon, attacking any opponents to the idea as impediments to change.[14] In fact, in 1990 the Wall Street Journal published more than a dozen stories and editorials supportive of the Milwaukee plan. In Wisconsin, the most powerful state business organization, the Wisconsin Association of Manufacturers, also supported the program.[15]

What Witte suggests is that many of the important and reasonable arguments against vouchers and private choice have been purposefully demonized as un-American or trivialized by the media as little more than absurd attempts to support a faltering public school system. Opponents of vouchers have increasingly become typecast as being associated with "failing government schools" and the retention of an antiquated status quo. Phrases like "powerful teachers' unions" and "unworkable governmental experimental educational reforms" have been used to implicate unions and educational policies as impediments to educational improvement, and their supporters have actually been described as selfish antagonists—educational Benedict Arnolds who are more concerned with maintaining an educational monopoly that supports their own self-interests before those of the children and the nation they are intended to serve.

According to Bracey and other individuals and watchdog groups that monitor claims about voucher plans, these stories are extensive, numerous, crafted for target audiences, and far too often blatantly false, or at the very least, incomplete. Bracey argues that the U.S. public school system ranks better in comparisons with other countries than these stories claim. And he points out that in any case, whether the schools have succeeded or failed, education is not a significant factor in measurements of U.S. competitiveness or economic health.[16] He recalls that in 1983, when *A Nation at Risk* maintained that the failure of the schools was causing the nation's economic woes, the economy was indeed suffering. However, a decade later, when the U.S. economy was booming, few claimed that the strength of U.S. education was the cause. Further, those countries identified as having first-class schools, including Germany, Japan, and Korea, have in the meantime suffered from long-term economic crises.[17] So we are still left asking, what is the relevance of the school performance to economic performance?

Bracey and other progressive educators are honest; they certainly do not think that U.S. public schools are perfect and would agree that they are in need of hefty reforms. However, Bracey is concerned with moving public dialogue about education beyond the misconceptions and downright distortions that have been identified and analyzed through his organization, America Tomorrow. Bracey and others work to analyze such controversial claims, and Bracey hopes to continue to provide "the story behind the story" in many media reports in the interest of enhancing public dialogue.

Nationally known as a policy analyst, Bracey may be best known as a target of the wrath of the first Bush administration and for his refutation of statements made in the controversial publication *A Nation at Risk*, a national education report issued by the Bush administration. Although Bracey is critical of many news stories about public and private schools and is skeptical of arguments that tie economic productivity to educational gains, he is optimistic when it comes to the task of structuring public schools that work. He acknowledges that student achievement could be improved, but he argues that such improvement would take little effort. According to Bracey, the problems of public education can be better addressed without the unwarranted attacks on public schools.[18]

As Bracey notes, the "golden era" of U.S. education to which many of these attacks wistfully refer never really existed. Rather, the history of public education in the United States is the story of steady, hard-fought accomplishments, many of them made by the poor and the disenfranchised. It is a history of increasing diversity. Amidst the assimilation of countless immigrants, the inclusion of thousands of mostly illiterate freed slaves, and the ever broadening participation of the nation's poor, levels of educational attainment have continued to increase. Improved educational outcomes have consistently accompanied expanded educational opportunities. Critics of privatization argue that this legacy of diversity and quality can best continue without the unwarranted attacks of critics and the unfounded fears of economic disaster. There is no doubt that U.S. public schools can be improved and that there is much to learn from the experience of other countries. But is scrapping our whole system the real answer?[19]

Bracey is not alone in his critique of the media's coverage of voucher stories. Witte asserts that from 1990 to 1995, the number of stories sympathetic to private choice and vouchers soared astronomically. The CBS show *60 Minutes* ran two episodes favorable toward voucher programs in 1999, and the *McNeil/Lehrer News Hour*, the NBC *Nightly News*, and *Nightline* ran favorable feature stories on them. Milwaukee private choice schools were visited by President Bush and Vice President Dan Quayle, and Milwaukee private voucher schools were visited several times by Education Secretaries Lamar Alexander and William Bennett and the 1996 Republican presidential nominee Robert Dole.[20]

According to Witte and other interested educational stakeholders, with the passage of private choice in Milwaukee began a torrential media coverage of private choice that highlighted entrepreneurial solutions to "failing schools." The change in news coverage was accompanied by a shift in the community dialogue on schools, with more of the dialogue being controlled by the media. For example, criticisms of programs in Milwaukee and Cleveland were covered very little, if at all, in the mainstream press. The more dramatic and usual approach was to run uncritical television programs that opened with Dickensian depictions of children of color in dilapidated schools and then shifted to cast aspersions on public schools, followed by interviews with private choice proponents and neoliberal policy pundits, who were quick to offer the nostrums of deregulation and outright privatization. Along with the diatribe were the omnipresent "800" numbers for those wishing to volunteer or donate funds.

Witte describes the typical media coverage of vouchers and private choice. The scene is something like this: The report opens with a tragic set of circumstances, depicted visually in pathetic educational settings such as deteriorating buildings with metal detectors. The bleak conditions are then overlaid by a small but poignant set of statistics demonstrating public school failure, usually test score comparisons to national averages or dropout rates. After the scene is set, the tragedy is given a human face with the introduction of one or two families-usually single-parent families of color living in poor economic conditions and struggling against long odds to help their children to escape their impoverished lives. The difficult social and personal conditions these families suffer are quickly correlated with the failure of the schools in the minds of the viewer by highlighting the poor performance of the children and the anger of the parents at those schools.[21]

In many ways, critics argue, the press has done more to conceal than to reveal the issues behind private choice. This is a tragic failure at a time when public education arguably finds itself in need of radical reform. Yet so much of the debate regarding school choice has taken place within a cacophony of rhetoric, partisan infomercials, misinformation, and vapid, cliché-driven language. Many critics maintain that the media effort seems designed to create nightmarish metaphors that have little or no relevance to the real performance of schools or the lives of people in the inner city, where private choice is most often touted as an educational panacea. The media coverage only fuels the widespread and growing belief among many diverse communities and political persuasions that private choice may be the way to solve the financial and student achievement crisis in our nation's schools, particularly in our inner cities. And some privatization proponents argue that private choice may actually end class divisions and racial segregation in schools.

According to Amy Wilkins, a principal partner in Education Trust, a nonprofit group based in Washington, D.C. that works to close the achievement gap between low-income minority students and more affluent white students while also raising achievement for all students, this pro-voucher media coverage makes it more essential that advocates of public education face facts about the health of U.S. schools: "The first thing we need to do is admit to the failures of public schools. The schools are underserving important populations of kids, primarily kids of color and low income kids." Wilkins argues that in midst of the undeniable need to reform public education, those on the left have been on the defensive, claiming that public education is improving, that SAT scores are rising, and that more people are going to college. [22]

Wilkins stresses that this claim that everything is fine does not address the serious problems plaguing public schools, such as "the problem of the wide and growing achievement gap that separates low-income students and students of color from others."[23] From Wilkins's point of view, this facile argument for business as usual produces a sense of disconnect among U.S. citizens, who know that schools need improvement. Parents see what is going on in the schools and then they hear educational establishment voices crying that schools are fine, and they ask, "What schools are they talking about?"[24]

For activists like Wilkins, this state of denial among well-intentioned constituencies who support public education has allowed more sophisticated conservative electorates and corporate media outlets to capitalize on poor public school performance for their own self-interests and personal agendas. The answer, she and other progressive educators posit, is to embrace and fix public schools, not to surrender them to a host of private consortiums or profit-driven companies. She is adamant that the first step is to admit that problems in public education exist. This will allow the public to see that those who oppose private vouchers understand the problems associated with many public schools, empathize with families, and are attempting to address these needs with requisite vigor.

POLITICS, MARKETS, AND AMERICA'S SCHOOLS: MAKING THE CASE FOR PRIVATE SCHOOL VOUCHERS

In 1990 the first scholarly validation for private vouchers appeared with publication of the book *Politics, Markets, and America's Schools* by John Chubb and Terry Moe.[25] Chubb and Moe, sensitive to the criticisms levied against public schools, especially urban schools, concluded that the academic quality of the public schools was unacceptably low.[26] The book was released with all the media fanfare of a highly publicized sports event when Wisconsin State Representative Annette "Polly" Williams, a Democrat, traveled to Washington, D.C., as a guest of the Brookings Institution. The visit of Williams, who sponsored the Milwaukee Parental Choice Program, and the publication of the highly controversial book by Chubb and Moe supporting the 1955 Friedman proposal, coincided to form a key event in the debate over what has become the most publicized and perhaps most important major educational public policy issue facing citizens today.

For Chubb and Moe, the problem is one of bureaucracy and politics. According to their thesis, public bureaucracy is the culprit in the poor academic performance of students in public schools, and politics and the organizational development of schools in turn serves to create an ever more onerous bureaucracy.[27] Chubb and Moe point to numerous maladies afflicting public education—maladies they claim render our schools incapable of providing quality education to our children. Their arguments are not simply relegated to conservative educational agendas or privatization proponents; they resonate with many parents, students, and educators.

The authors note, for example, that principals cannot fire or hire teachers. Under such a system, poorly performing teachers cannot be removed. They also point to the fact that teachers are forced on the one hand to comply with irrelevant and bureaucratic teacher certification requirements while on the other hand they may lack knowledge about the very subjects they teach. Chubb and Moe discuss the lack of teacher autonomy in the classroom and the paucity of collegiate collaboration; they also point to lack of parental involvement in schools, especially in the decision-making process and agenda setting.

However, the main point of *Politics, Markets, and America's Schools* is not to empathize with the plight of public schools and those professionals and students who labor in them. Chubb and Moe's point is loud and clear: reform efforts that are imposed by government regulation are doomed to fail. For Chubb and Moe, government bureaucracy is the malefactor tormenting American schools because bureaucracy smothers the capacity of educational stakeholders to participate creatively in linking effective instruction with effective learning. Therefore, they claim that the future of educational reform should not be to increase governmental reform efforts but to allow the private marketplace to achieve excellence through the elimination of bureaucratic controls and the privatization of parental choice. Whereas government encourages bureaucracy, privatization and the free market are autonomous, uninhibited, and therefore less bureaucratic.[28] The answer, they announce, is simple: only private choice has the capacity to offer real educational reform; all other efforts are merely perpetuating an ineffective system.[29] And Chubb and Moe are in no way alone in their critique of public school reform efforts; their public school reform assessments and privatized solutions are shared by a wide range of U.S. educational analysts and decision makers.

IMPLEMENTING PRIVATE SCHOOL CHOICE IN MILWAUKEE, WISCONSIN: A BRIEF HISTORY

Polly Williams, sponsor of the Milwaukee Parental Choice Program (MPCP), first pushed for a parental choice plan in Milwaukee out of intense frustration with its public school system. The African American grade point average was a D, and parents were vocalizing loudly for change. Williams was no Republican free marketeer. An outspoken liberal, she was twice the manager of Jesse Jackson's presidential election campaign in Wisconsin. She took her own children from the public school system in the 1980s, placing them instead in an independent urban school called Urban Day and beginning the long road to legislate private school choice.

In June 1990 the experiment in private choice finally became a reality. Implemented in a district that enrolled nearly 100,000 students, the MPCP was the nation's first real experiment in private choice. It provided public funds for private education, originally through targeted vouchers to 1,000 low-income Milwaukee students. Each voucher was worth approximately $2,500, so that each student would be able to attend a nonreligious private school of his or her choice. In the first school year, 1990–1991, 558 students applied and 341 ultimately enrolled in the seven schools that took part in the program.[30]

The Milwaukee experiment in vouchers served as a controversial first step in an effort to reconstitute and reform educational services through privatization and parental choice. Milwaukee, some thought, was a harbinger for privatized educational reform nationwide. Indeed, as a result of the successful passing of the MPCP legislation, initiatives supporting tuition vouchers that would allow parents to spend public money on private and parochial schools mushroomed nationally over the next three years and were supported in more than thirty states.[31]

It is clear, however, that although proponents of private voucher initiatives depict the movement as a grassroots, parent-led expression of democratic activism, the initiatives have not proven popular enough to succeed. In November 1993 Californians were asked to consider a voucher program in an initiative entitled Proposition 174. If passed, this legislation would promote a universal school voucher initiative under which private schools would be supported by taxpayers' dollars, much like the Milwaukee program. This was not the first time Californians had been asked to support a voucher program. Targeted voucher initiatives had already been defeated twice, in 1980 and 1982. This time, the outcome was the same: the measure was strongly opposed by the California Teachers Association and was soundly defeated by 70 percent of California voters in 1993. Voucher proponents in the state did not give up; they proposed another voucher initiative in November 2000, when once again voters rejected it.

Similar efforts were defeated by large margins in Oregon in 1990, Colorado in 1992, Michigan in 2000, and California again in 2000. In New Jersey, support for Governor Christine Todd Whitman's voucher proposal also proved weak, despite her popularity, and she decided to withdraw it.

WHAT FORCES HAVE FUELED THE
PRIVATE CHOICE MOVEMENT?

The idea that schools should function as free-market providers of a commodity is attractive to many different constituencies for many reasons. Indeed, there are strange bedfellows and unusual alliances within the private voucher movement. In this section, we look at some important motivations for the private voucher movement.

Neoliberalism, the Educational Maintenance Organization, and the Emerging Educational Industrial Complex

Efforts to privatize education, much like efforts to privatize Social Security, are based on specific neoliberal economic assumptions, which we outlined briefly in chapter 1. One champion of the idea, Milton Friedman, continues to this day to make the neoliberal economic argument very explicitly. Never one to remain silent on the issue, Friedman believes that the only way to make major improvements in the U.S. educational system is through a rigorous privatization reform through which a substantial fraction of all educational services is rendered to individuals by private enterprises. His point of view, echoed for close to fifty years, is that nothing but private choice will destroy or even greatly weaken the power of the educational establishment. Nothing else will provide the competition needed to force schools to improve, thereby maintaining their student bodies, or what Friedman refers to as their "clientele."[32]

But what is the real goal of neoliberal efforts to reform education? Is it to provide public schools with competition through vouchers, so that they might improve? Or is it to incrementally dismantle all public educational institutions, replacing them with a private educational system supported by a loose consortium of private schools beholden to consumers and private vouchers? The answers vary, but the significance of the question cannot be underestimated.

The neoliberal polemic against "government schools" is really an argument against government involvement in any form of social policy—public educational institutions are simply one expression. In 1892 Herbert Spencer, like Adam Smith a "liberal" economics philosopher, embraced similar ideas. He believed that the growth and expansion of public institutions creates among the populace the idea that the government will do everything for them—what has been referred to as the "entitlement" mentality. For Spencer, the more active government becomes, the more people become accustomed to government problem-solving, and the less they understand the process by which they themselves, or private groups, could set and reach goals. Finally, after generations, people will see the government as the only viable actor through which to solve individual and social problems and design social systems.[33] One hundred years later, Friedman continued to voice agreement with Spencer's antigovernment rhetoric. In an interview in 1992, Friedman once again advanced the idea that the government is too big: "the government performs [its] basic function poorly today, precisely because it is devoting too much of its efforts and spending on things which are harmful."[34]

However, the neoliberal argument for the privatization of schools is not made on purely economic grounds. Many supporters, concerned with what they see as a moral and political dilemma fostered by the public schools, point to the words of John Stuart Mill, who believed that a state education operates as a contrivance for molding people to be exactly like each other. This "despotism of the mind" leads to control over the body and over social and personal actions.[35] Thus, classical neoliberals would argue that in order to develop a high-quality educational system that reflects the values of citizens, rather than the values of government, we must eschew any form of government involvement in schools as educational tyranny, as little more than the public subsidization of propaganda. Guided by this assumption, among others, the neoliberal argument for the privatization of education has one unambiguous goal—"the complete separation of school and state."[36]

Certainly some of the most prominent advocates of private school vouchers—from concerned pubic policy makers to average citizens whose children must attend less-than-adequate public schools—have a genuine concern for public school reform and see vouchers as a way to strengthen public schools. However, vocal neoliberal proponents of private vouchers and educational privatization measures as vehicles to dismantle public schools (including think tanks like the Cato Institute, the Heritage Foundation, and other conservative institutions) understand all too well the political, economic, and ideological agenda and implications that are at stake in this public policy controversy, and they are quite open about their positions and goals.

David Harmer and Douglas Dewey, two prominent Cato Institute fellows and supporters of the privatization of education on neoliberal grounds, are refreshingly candid when they admit that "even voucher advocates who are not committed to the complete separation of school from state believe vouchers would lead to a major contraction of government-run schooling."[37] Yet they also admit that these advocates rarely make this point in open political parlance. Because of the controversies surrounding vouchers, voucher supporters attempt to hide their real agenda. Yet Blast and Harmer note that most voucher proponents would say, off the record, that although some state-run schools would survive under a voucher system, many would go out of business.[38] In other words, the real neoliberal goal is the demise of all public schooling; it would be naive to believe otherwise. And the Cato Institute candidly declares that this is the only way that the "current socialist regime" behind schools can be dismantled.[39]

For advocates of the privatization of education, government involvement in schooling is not only economically unsound, it is also ideologically insidious because it gives the government the ability to manipulate and manage people's thoughts. It sets in motion what neoliberals see as the entitlement mentality first described by Herbert Spencer, whereby the individual loses personal freedom to governmental agencies and bureaucrats. Neoliberal voucher proponents argue that when the government is in charge of education, politicians can manipulate the curriculum for their own political benefit, and this manipulation inevitably inhibits the production of knowledge and politicizes its dissemination; the threat to learning and to liberty, they claim, is obvious.[40]

Interestingly, privatization proponents go so far as to claim that the gravest threat facing American democracy is what is currently transpiring in American "government" schools. From this point of view, students in public schools are being poorly educated and so are ill-prepared to contribute to society as adults. Furthermore, they argue that public education inculcates our children with values and ideology that run counter to the values of parents and communities. High school and even elementary students are indoctrinated, they argue, with radical views about the environment, politics, diversity, sex, and other sundry "reforms." Couple this, they say, with the fact that our children attend public institutions where drugs are sold and guns are found on campus, and we have a large problem. Instead of offering a safe environment for learning, many inner-city public schools seem more like war zones.[41]

Are these critiques justified? For those groups, like the Cato Institute and Heritage Foundation, that are opposed to any government involvement in schools, private vouchers represent a firm moral, ideological, and economic argument for the full dismantling of public education. They would agree with Friedman that the voucher must be universal, available to all parents, and large enough to cover the costs of a high-quality private education. As Friedman writes, "No conditions should be attached to vouchers that interfere with the freedom of private enterprises to experiment, to explore, investigate, and to innovate."[42]

This freedom would not be limited by social concerns that constrain the public schools: most private voucher proponents would not require voucher schools to renounce racial, religious, or gender discrimination, and many would oppose a firewall of separation between church and state, arguing that parents should be able to choose where to send their children to school, without restriction. Although private choice advocates agree that schools should serve the public interest, they think that these interests are minimal compared with the notion of competitive individualism. They oppose public enforcement of educational policy as an impingement on parental choice, individual liberty, and free markets—which for them is a primary concern.

Furthermore, many voucher proponents maintain that the present system, by which the government fully funds public schools while granting only tax exemptions and smaller subsidies to private schools, is simply unfair to parents who send their children to private schools. After all, they contend, these parents are simply paying for other people's children to attend public schools (to which they would not want to send their own children). The sole role of government in educational policy, according to private marketeers, should be to inspect schools to ensure that they meet minimal curricular standards and building codes, much as the government inspects restaurants to ensure that they maintain minimum sanitary standards and codes.

Yet on full inspection, the idea of competition and free markets as a panacea for the organization of schooling deliquesces. Making schools compete so that "all ships rise" resonates well at first glance, but as John D. Witte asks, where else has competition worked in inner-city neighborhoods? For example, he asks, has it worked in housing, grocery stores, health care, retail clothing, and the like? For Witte, the problem is that most Americans take many things for granted in their communities that cannot be taken for granted in most inner-city communities. For example, in the inner-city one probably cannot buy a new car and maybe not even be able to get a used one. One probably cannot buy a bicycle or even get a hinge for a door at a local department store. One cannot see a movie that is not X-rated or shop in a large, well-stocked, modestly priced grocery store. And discriminatory lending practices by financial institutions, called redlining, has decimated real estate opportunities in poor communities. On the other hand, as Witte notes, inner-city residents can buy any liquor, albeit at inflated prices. If the free market is so superior to government provisions, why does it fail to provide basic services and commodities in these communities? Does the government have a monopoly on movies, for example, or on car sales, or grocery stores?[43]

Amy Wilkins of Education Trust makes this same observation: "We've never seen market forces really work well when it comes to people of color and low-income people."[44] After all, she maintains, if market forces work so well, why are so many people poor? For Wilkins, the market is an utter failure for people of color and the poor; it is not simply a matter of individual choice. And if this is true, she asks, how will the market bring quality education to kids?[45]

The Educational Maintenance Organization and the Educational Industrial Complex

It would be a mistake to think that an ideological opposition to public schools per se is all that animates neoliberal proposals for market-based educational reforms. Venture capitalists and investors foresee attractive rewards in privatization, whether it take the form of vouchers or other forms of contracting out vital educational services. As in the early days of the HMO movement, when private health care ushered in a virtual billion-dollar industry, now investors and capitalists are poised to profit from a similar billion-dollar bonanza by opening up the private educational marketplace. The expectation is that a for-profit EMO, dependent on government subsidies, will develop around the principles of privatized education.

Should the educational industrial complex emerge, it will create a huge new market, providing a tremendous profit motive for school privatization. Entrepreneurs, brokerage houses, Wall Street investors, and other speculators are simply waiting for the for-profit opportunities to emerge from privatization. Add to this the transnational corporations—from soft drink companies to clothing industries—that are targeting children with sponsorships, brand-name advertising, and commercials aimed at students directly in the classroom, and another more economically striking picture of privatization efforts emerges.

Close scrutiny also reveals that many voucher proponents are leading businesspeople interested in the promise of a flourishing educational marketplace. Ted Draper, the multimillion-dollar Silicon Valley entrepreneur who in 2000 engineered the unsuccessful Proposition 38 in California, which would have implemented private vouchers, has frankly stated that he sees a growing trend in investment opportunities in entertainment and educational content.[46] John Walton, son of the founder of Wal-Mart, Sam Walton, not only directs CEO America and co-founded the Children's Scholarship Fund but he is also a primary sponsor of TesseracT (formerly Education Alternatives Inc.), a for-profit corporation that manages public schools. Businessman David Brennan, one of Ohio's biggest backers of the Republican Party at the state and the national levels, is a strong supporter of vouchers and operates two voucher schools in Cleveland. Part of the funding for establishing these schools came from John Walton Family Foundation.

Supporting private vouchers is consistent with the neoliberal ambition of ending public support for public education in any manner and by any means, or separating schools from the state. As such, it truly offers a new, if little-understood, shift in the economic and social relations of U.S. society.

Impetus from the Religious Right

The so-called religious right is inarguably the most visible participant in the campaign to privatize education through school vouchers and choice; both private and public choice have become the centerpiece of the religious right's education agenda. The religious right would benefit greatly from private school vouchers because they would allow the various religious advocates who comprise the religious right movement to gain public financing for instruction in their private religious views. Eighty percent of the private schools in America are operated by religious groups, and these religious schools would be among the most significant beneficiaries of voucher programs.[47] And the religious right's support for diverting public monies to religious schools also couples nicely with ideological attacks on public schools in general.

Just who makes up the religious right? According to the People for the American Way (PFAW) Foundation, the religious right is a loose consortium of various organizations, including the American Family Association, the Christian Coalition, Citizens for Excellence in Education, the Eagle Forum, Focus on the Family, the National Right to Life Committee, and the Traditional Values Coalition, to name just a few. Catholic schools, many of which have served the inner cities for years, are also among those that stand to gain from voucher programs, as public funds would become available to subsidize private tuition for existing and new students. What these institutions and organizations have in common is their unwavering support for religious instruction and religious ceremonies in schools, along with their resolute opposition to secular public schooling.

The religious right conducts unrelenting attacks on public education, capitalizing on problems of organization in public schools and casting the blame on "government schools." The religious right is especially critical of public education, challenging state and national reform efforts, battling for "back to basics" in instruction, fighting against "outcome-based education" (where students discover knowledge and apply it to everyday life), and denouncing the very notion of a public common school for U.S. citizens. In many ways, groups of the religious right are the architects of the public relations and organizing network that has pushed the voucher idea into the political forefront and public arena.

Many conservative religious leaders make it clear that they would not mourn the loss of the public school system. As Pat Robertson, founder of the Christian Coalition, explained to his followers at the Christian Coalition's national conference in 1993, "You give every parent a voucher for $2,500 or $3,000 or whatever the cost of education is and you say to them, 'You may spend this on the best education you can get for your child—you pick the school.' And if the public schools do not deliver quality education, let them go out of business and nobody would miss them."[48] Jerry Falwell, another religious right leader, was equally if not more candid when he said that he hoped to "see the day . . . when churches will have taken over [public schools] again and Christians will be running them."[49]

According to PFAW's president, Carole Shields, the religious right has shaped educational discourse by gaining political clout through Congress and at the local level. According to Shields, this clout has shifted the debate about public education: where once Americans debated how best to improve public education, now, as a result of the religious right's political movement, many Americans are debating whether public education should exist at all. Many think this shift may pose frightening consequences for our children.[50]

After years of attempting to force public schools to teach theology in science classes and abolish the teaching of evolution, to remove literature they find morally offensive from school libraries, and to exclude sex education classes and the dissemination of any information regarding sexual orientation or abortion, the religious right may have found in school choice a priceless nostrum. They have wisely concentrated their political efforts on inner cities, where religious schools are typically less expensive than most nonreligious private schools. In this way they specifically target poor children and their parents, who are themselves too often the victims of inadequate public schools and thus an eager audience for promises of meaningful change in educational policy.

Other proponents of private school vouchers and the religious right share many goals and perspectives, and they have become accommodating, if not comfortable, bedfellows in their mutual quest to end public schooling. As we shall see, through their founders, board members, donors, advisors, regional think tanks, local affiliates, and networking opportunities, both neoliberals and members of the religious right have mounted an admitted attack on public education. For many supporters of public education, the by-product of this effort has been the wholesale abandonment of discussion regarding meaningful public school reform; for others, it has meant a new beginning in the fight for what they see as private, quality education based on an individual's right to choose religious or nonreligious private schools.

No matter where one finds oneself on the issue, it cannot be understated that any effort to either realize or resist private school choice programs must reckon with the religious right and its immense political power, organizational abilities, and sizable infrastructure. As many are now finding, any effort to combat the idea of school vouchers will of necessity have to confront a diverse coalition of religiously inspired and tremendously well-organized nonsecular public policy think tanks.

Parental Dissatisfaction with the Status Quo

Many parents and citizens favor privatization efforts and voucher plans. Very little of the public support for private school vouchers is due to a strong philosophy or ideology regarding government-neoliberal or otherwise; nor is it a result of hidden business interests or even a certain religious orientation. Private school vouchers enjoy a great deal of support among parents because they offer the promise, if not the reality, that their children might escape what they believe are failing public schools. This is especially true in inner cities, where the state of public schools, along with public life, is deteriorating and the level of educational neglect is glaringly apparent, even to the staunchest critics of private school vouchers. The voucher idea is very appealing to disenfranchised parents whose children are trapped in deteriorating schools. Many parents think that vouchers would finally free their children to go to the best schools, which until now have been reserved for the more affluent.

So it is important that we do not lump all voucher proponents in the same category. Many supporters of private vouchers, such as diverse groups of parents, do not even care if the vouchers come with government regulations and restrictions or if they are "neoliberally correct." These parents are simply looking for the way to provide their children with the best education. Luis Garden Acosta—founder, president, and CEO of El Puente, a community public school in New York—concurs and suggests that we avoid overgeneralizing when discussing why parents might support private vouchers. Educational policy makers need to avoid labeling supporters of vouchers as extremists, says Acosta, because even parents who sound radical really have deep-seated concerns about their children's education. Repudiating parents for their support of vouchers can often backfire, whereas appreciating parents' concerns can provide common ground between progressive educators and parents.[51]

The Applied Research Center (ARC), a think tank based in Oakland, California, concluded in its latest report that racial discrimination has not abated in public schools, but on the contrary, continues to pervade education. ARC released a "Racial Justice Report Card" as a result of its research on schools across the nation. It found that minority students were more likely to be disciplined in schools than white students. In Chicago, where African Americans make up 53 percent of the student population, the study found that they constitute 63 percent of those suspended and expelled from public schools. Regarding other indicators of racial equality, the study determined that public schools should get very low marks. Among the twelve cities ARC researched, only in Los Angeles was the number of African American teachers proportionate to the number of African American students. Further, the study found that in Rhode Island, where Latinos constitute almost half of the student body, only 5 percent of the teachers were Latino.[52]

Parents' dissatisfaction with what they see as intolerant bureaucracies, racism in education, violent campuses, inadequate resources, and uncaring teachers is also prevalent and increasing. And parents in inner cities, especially African American parents and other people of color, are appalled at low student performance and achievement as measured on standardized tests. At a 1997 Brookings Institution conference on school choice, Lawrence Stedman, professor of education at State University of New York, described the distressing state of education in the African American community. He stated that black students lag four or five years behind in every area of educational endeavor—from math to reading—so that some twelfth-grade black students perform at lower levels than middle-school white students. Racial gaps, he claimed, are larger than they were a decade before, and a generation has passed since *Brown vs. Board of Education,* and the achievement of educational equity still seems a dream. Schools, like other social realms, remain broken into two separate and unequal realms, black and white.[53]

The National Assessment of Educational Progress (a U.S. Department of Education agency) has also established a gap between the academic performance of white students and black students. In reading, math, and science, white students had more "proficient" or "advanced" scores than did black students. In math, for example, 18 percent of whites had proficient scores, compared to only 4 percent of black students. The gap is even worse in reading and science.[54]

One of the most eloquent advocates of vouchers and school choice is Polly Williams, the liberal Democratic state representative from Wisconsin and supporter and champion of the Milwaukee choice legislation. Besides being a representative from the state of Wisconsin, Williams is also an African American mother. In a charismatic speech made to the Heritage Foundation in the early 1990s, Williams summed up in straightforward terms some of the concerns and frustrations expressed by African American parents regarding their children's education. She pointed to the fact that in her local public school, there is a 90 percent failure rate among African American children—and this is in spite of the fact that taxpayers spend $6,000 per year to educate each of these children. Some 14.9 percent of Milwaukee freshmen who enter Milwaukee high schools do not graduate. Williams added that of those who remain in school and walk across the stage to pick up their diploma, only 10 percent are able to read it.

From Williams's point of view, the fault lies not with the parents, but with the system. If children come from a family where divorce is prevalent, where there is one male in a household of four or five women, then the system says they are doomed, according to Williams. She went on to note that her son is thirty-five years old, that all her children have successfully finished school and are doing well, and have never been in trouble with the law. Yet, she notes, she is one of those people who are supposed to be very ignorant because they are black, live in the inner city, are poor, and have raised their children in a single-parent home. Williams rejected this assumption outright and declared that the only thing different about the constituency she described is that they have been deprived of resources and access. Her answer at the time was targeted vouchers for those kids who have been labeled as failures.[55]

There is little to argue with in Williams's descriptions, and many progressive educators agree with conservative claims that more money for public schools is not necessarily the only answer, that there are structural changes, both material and ideological, that must be made. The question is whether the schools so supported should be public or private.

African American support for some sort of choice, be it private or public, has been noticeably rising in the last decade. Many African American parents think it is unfair that white, rich, or upper-middle-class parents can opt out of the public education system while poor parents of color must send their children to failing and deteriorating public schools. Far too often, inner-city parents cannot find satisfactory educational opportunities in urban public schools, and this fact along does much to explain the appeal of the voucher idea. As of 1997, a majority of grass-roots organizations supporting educational vouchers and private school choice programs hailed from black communities. This should not be surprising.

A study conducted in 1997 by the Joint Center for Political and Economic Studies, an international nonprofit established by black scholars, professionals, and elected officials that studies issues of concern to blacks and other minorities, found that support for vouchers among blacks increased by ten percentage points between 1996 and 1997. Nationwide, 57 percent of blacks purportedly supported school vouchers for public, private, or parochial schools, and support for vouchers was strongest among blacks thirty-five years old and younger. This is astonishing because in 1992 barely one-third of blacks had even heard of educational choice.[56]

The support for some sort of privatization in education is not simply limited to support for private school vouchers. A 1999 survey of more than 700 Georgia parents found that more than half of all African American parents with children in public schools supported the idea of allowing private companies to run public schools. Yet the same study found that only one-third of white parents were willing to turn their campuses over to private companies.[57]

The Joint Center for Political and Economic Studies reported in 1997 that nationally 70.4 percent of African Americans who earn less than $15,000 per year supported school choice. In addition, the survey found that 86.5 percent of African Americans aged twenty-five to thirty-five supported school choice—up from 61 percent in 1996.[58] It is important to mention that the study asked if parents supported "choice," not specifically "private choice." However, even in light of this fact, it is clear that African American support for radical changes in the delivery and form of schooling is growing.

Yet many others in minority communities are far less willing to embrace privatization efforts. They argue that school vouchers play on the fears of minorities and that the relationship between privatization proponents and those parents who truly wish a better education for their children is perfidious, at best. Luis Acosta of El Puente argues that the private voucher movement deceives parents and community leaders and cripples public education while claiming to assist poor people. Acosta argues that politicians want to dismantle public education and replace it with a segregated private school system that is even more discriminatory and inadequate than the current public school system.[59]

Sherry Posnick-Goodwin of the California Teachers Association agrees. She believes that vouchers will hurt minority communities because they create false hope for minority parents who want the best education possible for their children.[60] And according to Esteban Ramirez, a member of the Windsor District Educators Association in Windsor, California, proponents of vouchers make it sound as though vouchers are created to help poor, minority students, but in reality vouchers are about expanding tax breaks for the rich because tax money will go to private schools.[61]

Are private vouchers a cruel hoax perpetrated on a marginalized segment of American society? Are they a panacea for failing public institutions that manage children as opposed to teaching them? Of course, the answers are complex and depend on one's perspective. Yet despite the criticism of private voucher plans, private school choice continues to be embraced by many diverse constituencies of parents-not just African Americans. According to a study launched by Public Agenda, a nonprofit research organization, support for vouchers is strong among all parents with children in school; nearly seven in ten (68 percent) favor the proposal.

Public Agenda asked parents the following question in a survey of national public opinion: "How much do you favor or oppose the following idea? Parents are given a voucher or certificate by the government to pay for all or part of tuition if they decide to send their child to a private or parochial school." Of the participants who answered the question, 29 percent of the general public favored the proposal, while 40 percent of the parents favored it; 23 percent of the general public opposed the idea, while only 17 percent of the parents opposed it.[62] Yet when parents in the same study were asked: "If money were not an issue, where would you prefer to send your child to school?" Forty-two percent of the respondents favored public schools, while 34 percent favored religious schools, with 21 percent favoring nonreligious private schools and 2 percent remaining undecided.

However, many analysts argue that once parents understand the ramifications of the privatization of education through private choice, support for private vouchers goes down. According to the Phi Delta Kappa/Gallup Poll in 2000 of the public's attitude toward the public schools, support for private vouchers has actually plummeted in the past three years, from 44 percent of respondents supporting vouchers in 1998 to 39 percent in 1999. And when asked to identify the biggest problem facing public schools, the largest proportion of respondents—18 percent—cited a lack of financial support. From this study, it appears that a decline in support of public education is basically a myth. The poll, in its thirty-second year, was based on telephone interviews conducted in June 2000 with 1,093 randomly selected adults. The margin of error reported was 4 percent.[63]

Many progressive educators are quick to point out that when we consider the debates about vouchers and private choice, especially in the media, one central topic is missing. There is a connection between poorly performing schools and other socioeconomic factors that is experienced by parents and families in the inner city every day. The

cumulative effects of economic and political decisions in the larger urban and rural context have, over time, severely constrained the current
ability and actions of educators in inner-city schools. Missing from the
dialogue are issues of race, culture, linguistic diversity, gender, and socioeconomics. And these economic and cultural constraints have im-
peded efforts to achieve meaningful school reform, according to some
public policy makers. For these educators, the cumulative effects of previous decisions are embodied in institutional poverty, racism, deteriorating infrastructure, lack of affordable public transit, low-paying work,
and the social isolation of neighborhoods in urban centers. The solution, they claim, is not private choice and marketplace control of education but a comprehensive social movement that confronts the totality
of the urban environment itself—a massive social and economic program on par with the Marshall Plan enacted after World War II, a societal commitment that confronts disintegrating cities, poverty, racism,
gender discrimination, and unequal opportunities. Jean Anyon, a highly
distinguished educational researcher, postulates that if society can provide the conditions for a reduction of anger and a resurgence of hope in
decimated urban centers by launching an aggressive assault on urban
poverty and racism, we will begin to see positive changes in schools. Reform proposals that separate schools from the socioeconomics of society are simply disingenuous.[64]

Is Anyon right? If she is, can private school vouchers accomplish
her lofty mission, or should they even try? Is the answer a radical agenda
for urban renovation that involves government as well as private concerns?

Teachers' Dissatisfaction with the Status Quo

Besides parents, many teachers also experience deep frustration with
the current public school system, especially in inner cities.

Teachers in all environments encounter intense bureaucratic
control, increasing levels of paperwork, time-consuming clerical duties,
overcrowded classes, poverty, and racism. Many argue that their schools
offer no educational leadership, lack a vision of what students should be
doing and what they should know, do not provide meaningful professional growth opportunities, and fail to adopt innovation and creativity
as the cornerstone for educational reform and improvement. Much like
the frustrated parents discussed above, some teachers also discover that
impersonal administrations, coupled with inadequate teaching strategies and large class sizes, have reduced the effectiveness of public
schools.

One experience from the nation's huge public school system provides a good example of this frustration: A talented black high school educator in Brooklyn, New York, explained that he had filed a grievance over what his supervisor had termed an "unsatisfactory" lesson in his global social studies class. According to the teacher:

> The facts are that the day after the attorney general released a report concerning racial profiling by the cops, I taught a lesson entitled, "Are Black Youths an Endangered Species?" The supervisor rated it as unsatisfactory because it was not part of the state-mandated curriculum. There I was, in a room with the supervisor, hearing officer, and union rep, all white—and both the principal and supervisor argued strenuously that what I discussed in class should not be discussed in Global History since it was not part of the state-mandated curriculum. They put forward the argument that only what is stated in the curriculum should be discussed. From the questions asked by the hearing officer, an eminent doctor of social studies education, it was obvious that she was partial to the supervisor's position. Perhaps it's me, but I couldn't understand how "educators" would claim that students' lived experiences are not relevant to their education. It is not that I am frustrated with the outcome; rather, it's a sense of sadness to know that these are the types of clowns we have running our educational systems.[65]

Some teachers see the idea of private school choice, or privatization through vouchers, as a real possibility for positive change, while others see vouchers as a disaster. Many other teachers remain undecided.

Business and Political Dissatisfaction with the Status Quo

Another significant impetus for the private school choice movement can be found within the business community. Arguing that U.S. schools are not preparing students for the productive necessities of the twenty-first century, business leaders such as John Sculley, former Apple Computer CEO, and Joseph Alibrandi, CEO of Whittaker Corporation and chairman of the Excellence through Choice in Education League (ExCEL), have bitterly complained about public education. Alibrandi, sponsor of the Parental Choice in Education initiative that was defeated by California voters in 1994, maintains that the U.S. education system is a monolithic monopoly, driven by rules rather than by outcome. The world economy is demanding a workforce with much higher skill levels. As a country able to compete in the world, Alibrandi says we are sinking rather than gaining.[66]

Sculley made similar remarks in 1992, when he argued that a highly skilled workforce must begin with a world-class public education system. From Sculley's point of view, low-skilled manual work will be paid less in the so-called new economy. For Sculley, education reform is about aligning the educational system with the new economy and providing a broad educational opportunity for everyone.[67]

These business leaders agree that education must be restructured to meet the new global demands of production and consumption. With production and consumption changing globally and the new economy emerging, many business leaders argue that what is needed is a first-class educational system that prepares people for the postmodern exigencies of an emerging technological society—one that replaces the factory model of education with a more modern approach. They look at teaching and learning as preparation for a new economic order, whereby citizens become loyal consumers and hi-tech producers in a new era of globalization. With public education steeped in antiquated notions of learning, they claim, private choice offers a chance for America to continue its competitive economic and social edge as we move into the new millennium.

SUMMARY

Although it would be a mistake to conclude that support for private choice represents a consensus among diverse political forces, one thing is for sure: the issue of privatization of education through the provision of vouchers is becoming the primary public policy issue affecting schools and school reform efforts today. But, as we will see, educational privatization is a far more complex issue, extending far beyond parental choice. More and more school boards and local and state governments are contracting out vital public educational services in another type of educational privatization. Recent privatization developments have included awarding franchises to private firms to operate government programs, selling public assets to the private sector, and contracting out with a private corporation to provide services such as management of public schools, Title I remedial educational or custodial services, along with transportation and food services. And as we will see, the role of faith-based charities in public debate and idiom is due to expand now that President George W. Bush has made this concept part of his new administrative vision. As a result, many teachers, paraprofessionals, and support personnel in K-12 education face what they see as the threat of the private, for-profit management of schools and the contracting-out of what were once seen as indispensable government assistance agencies that provided livable salaries and learning centers.

Most education stakeholders, as we have seen, believe that there is a need to alter radically the way we organize, deliver, and develop educational opportunities for our children. In the past, a radical restructuring of our educational priorities and systems of learning has correlated with significant changes in how we organize our productive and consumptive lives. However, many citizens and policy makers believe it would be a mistake to simply reduce the parameters of educational reform to the productive exigencies of the new economy. Educational reform asks us to consider how we will identify our private selves through the public policies we employ and the consequential legal and political actions we take. People go to schools to learn how to live, not just to learn how to make a living.

The disagreement regarding privatization and school choice in the United States will continue to fuel educational policy debates well into the future. Whatever the outcome, there is little doubt that these debates bring forth new ideas, new shifts in thought, and new political and social agendas that will refigure education and educational policy for years to come.

NOTES

1. Molnar, A. (1996). "School Choice." Wisconsin Education Association Council (an affiliate of the NEA).

2. Friedman, M. (1955). "The Role of Government in Education." In: *Economics and the Public Interest,* edited by Robert A. Solow. New Brunswick, NJ: Rutgers University Press.

3. Nathan, J. (1996). *Charter Schools: Creating Hope and Opportunity for American Education.* San Francisco: Jossey Bass, p. 5.

4. Johnson, T., L. Piana, and P. Burlingame. (2000). *Vouchers: A Trap, Not a Choice.* Oakland, CA: The Applied Research Center, p. 6.

5. *Lemon v. Kurtzman,* 403 U.S. 602. (1971).

6. Bracey, G. (1998). "Are U.S. Students Behind?" *The American Prospect Online.* http://www.americanprospect.com. (Accessed June 21, 2002)

7. Cremin, quoted in Bracey, "Are U.S. Students Behind?"

8. Ibid.

9. Ibid.

10. Koonce, M. (2001, January 3). "Poor Math Scores Multiply." *Washington Post.*

11. Mathews, J. (2000, December 12). "Class Struggle: U.S. Schools Not as Bad as Portrayed." *Washington Post.*

12. Berliner, D., B. Biddle, and J. Bell. (1996). *The Manufactured Crisis: Myths, Fraud, and the Attack on America's Public Schools.* Cambridge, MA: Perseus Press.

13. Witte, J. F. *The Market Approach to Education,* p. 172.

14. For example, see Grover, B. (1990, June 27). "Blocking the School House Door." *Wall Street Journal,* editorial page.

15. Witte, J. F. *The Market Approach to Education,* p. 173.

16. Bracey, "Are U.S. Students Behind?"

17. Ibid.

18. Ibid.

19. Ibid.

20. Witte, J. F. *The Market Approach to Education,* p. 173.

21. Ibid., pp. 173–174.

22. Wilkins, A. (2000, June 5). Quoted in "Forum—School Colors: The Racial Politics of Public Education." *The Nation,* 270, no. 22 (special issue).

23. Ibid.

24. Ibid.

25. Chubb, J., and T. Moe. (1990). *Politics, Markets and America's Schools.* The Washington, DC: Brookings Institution.

26. Ibid., p. 6.

27. Ibid., pp. 26–27.

28. Ibid.

29. Ibid., p. 216.

30. Lowe, R. (1996). "The Hollow Promise of School Vouchers." In: *Selling Out Our Schools: Vouchers, Markets, and the Future of Public Education,* edited by Robert Lowe and Barbara Miner. Milwaukee, WI: Rethinking Schools.

31. Bastian, A. (1994). "Lessons from the Voucher War. In: *Selling Out Our Schools: Vouchers, Markets, and the Future of Public Education,* edited by Robert Lowe and Barbara Miner. Milwaukee, WI: Rethinking Schools, p. 18.

32. Friedman, M. (1995, June 23). "Public Schools: Make Them Private." Briefing Paper No. 23. The Cato Institute. Available at: http://www.cato.org.

33. Spencer, H. (1960). *The Man versus the State.* Caldwell, ID: Caxton, p. 37.

34. Friedman, M. (1992, June). "Interview with Milton Friedman." *The Region* (journal of the Federal Reserve Bank of Minneapolis). http://minneapolisfed.org. (Accessed June 25, 2002)

35. Mill, J. S. (1947). *On Liberty.* Northbrook, IL: AHM Publishing, p. 108.

36. Bast, J. L., D. Harmer, vs. D. Dewey. (1997, March 12). "Vouchers and Educational Freedom: A Debate." Cato Policy Analysis No. 269. http://www.cato.org. (Accessed June 25, 2002)

37. Ibid.

38. Ibid.

39. Ibid.

40. Ibid., p. 4.

41. Ibid., p. 17.

42. Friedman, M. "Public Schools: Make Them Private."

43. Witte, J. F. *The Market Approach to Education.*

44. Wilkins, A. "Forum—School Colors: The Racial Politics of Public Education."

45. Ibid.

46. People for the American Way. (1999, April 20). "Privatization of Public Education: A Joint Venture of Charity and Power." People for the American Way Web site. http://www.pfaw.org. (Accessed June 25, 2002)

47. Ibid.

48. P. Robertson. "The Privatization of Public Education." http://www.pfaw.org.

49. Falwell, J. (1979). *America Can Be Saved.* Lynchberg, VA: Liberty University, p. 53.

50. *People for the American Way.* (1997, September 4). "A Right Wing and a Prayer: Report Reveals Religious Right's Attack on Schools." Press release. People for the American Way Web site. http://www.pfaw.org. (Accessed June 25, 2002)

51. Acosta, L. G. (2000, June 5). Quoted in "Forum—School Colors: The Racial Politics of Public Education." *The Nation* 270, 22 (special issue), p. 13.

52. Applied Research Center. (2000). "Racial Justice Report Card." Oakland, CA: Applied Research Center.

53. Stedman, L. (1997, April 16). "An Assessment of the Contemporary Debate Over U.S. Achievement." Binghamton, NY: School of Education and Human Development, SUNY. Presented at the Brookings Institution, May 1997.

54. Fuller, H. (2000). "The Continuing Struggle of African Americans for the Power to Make Real Educational Choices." Presented at the Second Annual Symposium on Educational Options for African Americans. The Center for Education Web site. http://edreform.com.

55. Williams, P. (1992). "School Choice Promotes Educational Excellence in the African-American Community." Speech delivered to the Heritage Foundation and reprinted in *Voices on Choice: The Education Reform Debate.* (1994). San Francisco: Pacific Research Institute for Public Policy, p. 4.

56. National Center for Policy Analysis. (1997). "Blacks Support School Choice." Dallas, TX: National Center for Policy Analysis.

57. Salzer, J. (1999, October 1). "Faith in Public Schools Fades: Growing Support for Privatization." *Florida Times Union* (Jacksonville).

58. Shokraii, N. (1998). "School Choice Programs in 1998." The Heritage Foundation. Available at: http://www.heritage.org.

59. Acosta, L. G. "Forum—School Colors: The Racial Politics of Public Education."

60. Posnick-Goodwin, S. (2000, October). "School Vouchers Play on the Fears of Concerned Minority Communities." *California Educator* 5, no. 2: 7.

61. Ibid., p. 9.

62. Public Agenda. (1999). "On Thin Ice." New York: Public Agenda, p. 14.

63. ReThinking Schools. (2000, October). "Decline in Support of Vouchers." *ReThinking Schools* 15, no. 1: 13.

64. Anyon, J. (1997). *Ghetto Schooling: The Political Economy of Urban Educational Reform.* New York: Teachers College, Columbia University, pp. 181–182.

65. Winthrop Holder of the New York City Public School System. (2000, October 14). Interview by author. New York.

66. Alibrandi, J. (1994). "The Real Issue." In: *Voices on Choice: The Education Reform Debate.* Edited by K. L. Billingsley. San Francisco: Pacific Research Institute for Public Policy, p. 69.

67. Sculley, J. (1992, December 15). Remarks by John Sculley, chairman and CEO of Apple Computer, Inc., to President-elect Bill Clinton's Economic Conference, Little Rock, AR.

Chapter Four

⚫ The Privatization of Education: Arguments and Controversies

One could argue that even without private school choice, parents have all sorts of choice when it comes to the education of their children. As Bruce Fuller, Gary Orfield, and Richard Elmore point out in their book, *Who Chooses, Who Loses?*, families exercise choice when they decide where they will live, when they choose care for their preschool-age children, when they decide whether to send their children to private or public schools, and when they sign up their children for places in specific public high schools or magnet schools. Yet, as with private school choice, these choices are not equally distributed but are instead shaped and constrained by economic, ethnic, cultural, and social factors.[1]

Very few people would argue that parents should not have choices about where their children attend school. After all, the freedom to choose is quintessentially American, and virtually everyone agrees that in a democracy parents should be free to choose the school they believe is best suited for their children. The real issue is not whether private choice should exist, for it does. A better question is what kind of choices should public policy support, and how should these public policies be formulated. Basically, the public policy query we face is how are we as a nation going to provide the best quality education for our children, and what role, if any, should the government and the marketplace play in this provision.

Choice sounds like a good idea to many, but ironically, despite all the continued controversy surrounding private school choice, there is a pervasive lack of awareness among many American citizens regarding school vouchers and private choice. A study conducted in 1999 by Public Agenda, a nonprofit research organization, found that the vast majority of the U.S. population knows very little about proposals to implement school vouchers, charter schools, or for-profit schools. Moreover, this lack of familiarity is pervasive across regions and across demographic groups.[2]

In its survey of parents across the nation, Public Agenda found that 63 percent of the general public knew very little or nothing about vouchers and private choice proposals. Furthermore, the study conıded that 66 percent of parents knew very little or nothing about the propositions on their own state ballots that supported vouchers for schools. And according to the study, when asked if they needed to learn more about vouchers, 80 percent of the general public and 81 percent of parents responded that they believed they needed to learn more.[3] This humble admission from our nation's citizens speaks volumes about the role of the media in public policy debates and educational democratic discussions. Yet even in light of the public's general ignorance and confusion regarding private school choice and the voucher movement, many pundits from all political persuasions continue to make boastful claims regarding the public's support for or opposition to the idea.

In the same study conducted by Public Agenda, it was discovered that 11 percent of the respondents described school vouchers as a good idea that promises to solve the nation's education problems, 67 percent described school vouchers as a good idea that cannot solve the nation's education problems, and 17 percent described school vouchers as a bad idea that will make the nation's education problems worse.[4] If the majority of the public does not see school vouchers as either salvation or destruction, it would be reasonable to infer that many Americans see vouchers as a limited education reform attempt to try to improve, not destroy, public education. The public's response is far more tentative and inconstant than claimants on both sides of the issue would concede. In fact, it might be said that many segments of the public are more curious about the issue of private choice than supportive of the idea.

With parents and the general public admitting little knowledge of vouchers and their implications, it is difficult to gauge public judgment on the issue. Perhaps part of the problem lies with the level and depth of media reporting on vouchers and private school choice. If the issue of private choice continues to be framed as an either/or proposition, more molded by media spin and cleverly contrived sound bites than explicated by in-depth coverage, the school voucher debate will continue to elude public understanding.

Chapter 1 looked briefly at some of the factors behind the growth of the private choice/pro-voucher movement, couching the issue of privatization within broader ideological and socioeconomic concerns—from public dissatisfaction with the quality of schooling to ideological critiques of the fashion and methods by which educational services are organized and delivered. This chapter looks specifically at some of the general claims and arguments for and against private choice and private school vouchers. By critically examining the polemics regarding private choice and private school vouchers from multiple frames of reference, this chapter provides the reader with a more expansive understanding of the fundamental issues involved in the ongoing debate.

THE LANGUAGE OF CHOICE

A further issue for readers to ponder is the unique linguistic form the educational privatization message has taken within the last ten years. According to some voucher opponents, advocates of an educational marketplace have won a significant ideological victory by successfully labeling their program "choice" rather than favoring the more ideologically suspect term "voucher." Certainly no one in their right mind would deny families educational options, and the label "choice" promises more options while obscuring the reality that those who come from economically empowered families are those most likely to be chosen by good schools. Furthermore, the language of private choice proposals seems to convey the idea of private school choice as a way of improving public schools, not destroying them, by using phrases that elevate the voucher proposals with such sanitized and generalized euphemisms as "private choice," "opportunity scholarships," "charitable choice," "education reform," "parental choice," "Samaritan project," and "straight As," among others. Barry Lynn, of Americans United for Separation of Church and State, noted that the second Bush administration has sought to play down the contentious aspect of its educational voucher plan by referring to vouchers as "scholarships," even though it is obvious that vouchers are not scholarships.[5] At the same time, the language used demonizes public schools, calling them "state-controlled monopolies" and "government schools," in order to resonate among people opposed to government involvement in daily life. Proponents of the neoliberal idea attempt to create a benign language to describe voucher proposals and a malign language to describe public schools, thereby obfuscating the real issues inherent in the public policy controversy. Feel-good phrases conveniently substitute for real in-depth debates over concrete details and innovative visions, and consequently an entire language wedded to the idea of private choice has emerged. Add to this the use of public discourse to denigrate public institutions and we find new ideological boundaries and political realities.

The language of choice is the result of astute public relations efforts on behalf of voucher proponents. They are aware that they must shape and define the ideology of competition and privatization as a concept grounded in the public benefit. Vouchers and private choice must be viewed as "innovative opportunities" for constituents who have

traditionally been marginalized; this, of course, necessitates a more benign language of charitable subterfuge.

But are vouchers really the ruse progressives claim they are? Is the
American people's thinking affected by a language of choice that seeks
to define its own terms, create its own sets of assumptions, and convey
its own set of ideological images? The answers are difficult to surmise at
this point. Whatever the intent of this language, the public response has
been less than enthusiastic. In November 2000, voucher proposals in
both California and Michigan were defeated, even though they were
both portrayed by their supporters as "scholarship plans." And exit polls
indicated that opposition to these plans existed across the board,
among voters from all racial, religious, and socioeconomic groups. The
outcome of these and other voucher proposals suggests that the public
is not yet sold on private vouchers. However, how the issue of school
vouchers is presented will have a tremendous effect on the discursive
outcomes and ideological positions we can expect.

In light of the mixed and often contradictory messages of pro-
voucher groups regarding the role of competition in public education
reform, citizens must seriously inquire whether competition is being
proposed to strengthen the effectiveness of public schools, as many
conservatives claim, or whether it is being advanced as a mechanism to
eventually replace public schools with a privatized system wherein
market-driven choices are subsidized by the state. Furthermore, how do
we assess the legitimacy of claims about privatization and identify the
varied public policy implications that the innumerable ideas might have
for our nation's children and for the essence of our democratic ideals?

ARGUMENTS FOR AND AGAINST PRIVATE CHOICE
AND SCHOOL VOUCHERS: WHAT ARE THE ISSUES?

In chapter 1 we discussed various arguments for and against neoliberalism as a political economic theory. It is important to engage in this inquiry because the movement toward private vouchers and private
school choice can only be fully understood within the context of neoliberal economic and political theory and practice.

In this section, we examine some of the neoliberal contentions
regarding claims to market superiority in educational reform. The following questions are important to consider:

What ideological positions should shape educational policy—
those of consumers in the marketplace or those of mutually

agreed upon collaborative public purposes and democratic
citizenship? Are these two alternatives mutually exclusive?
Can we as a nation agree on the purpose of education?

Are Americans comfortable with allowing federal funds to be
used by those who wish to attend schools that are racially
specific, that discriminate against other religions, or that
practice forms of gender discrimination such as all-girl or
all-boy schools?

Should we publicly subsidize schools that practice specific
forms of religion?

Should we subsidize with public funds any nonsecular
institution?

Will school vouchers provide excellent schools for the poor and
disenfranchised or simply accomplish the public funding and
subsidization of private schools, thereby financing elite educational enclaves for those more well-off?

Will vouchers take monies from public schools? If so, can these
public schools hope to compete for educational excellence
with private schools when they are asked to do more with less?

If poor children attend bad schools, does this have anything to
do with the fact that they live in poor neighborhoods, perhaps because their parents lack decent jobs with livable
wages? Does it have anything to do with the fact that they
lack adequate provisions for child care, available and low-
cost transportation, and satisfactory health insurance? Or is
the supposed failure of public schools due to a lack of personal responsibility and faulty choices among our citizens,
which produce social dislocation and individual oppression?

What is the role of social organizations and institutions in analyzing educational policy, or is there a role at all?

Are troubled public schools really an isolated problem of inadequate and/or bureaucratic public control of educational institutions? Or can issues of educational policy be understood
only within a larger context of socioeconomic disorganization
and disintegration, including problems such as lack of affordable health care, insufficient affordable housing, lack of
meaningful work for living wages, and disenfranchised
neighborhoods?

With these questions in mind we begin by focusing our attention
on the basic neoliberal arguments for the privatization of schools
through private school vouchers.

Neoliberalism and the Primacy of Markets: The Argument for Private Choice and School Vouchers

Noted neoliberal economist Friedrich Hayek, in his seminal work entitled *The Constitution of Liberty,* argued that a "free economic market" in the field of education was necessary for many reasons. Hayek was a proponent of compulsory education, claiming that "educational consumers" (students and their parents) are basically ignorant, and that children must be compelled to attend school. Yet Hayek also supported a private voucher system to avoid what he considered a government monopoly over the provision and control of the content of education. His argument basically advocated and called for a compulsory private education.[6]

Andrew Coulson, author of a new and controversial book, *Market Education,* agrees wholeheartedly with Hayek's positions. Coulson argues that long-standing support for state-controlled education has blinded citizens to other ideas for improving education. This support began with the efforts of dedicated reformers some 150 years ago, when schools were private and decentralized. Their work resulted in a central system of tax-funded schools that were felt to be superior to a loosely associated system of private education existing at the time. The idea of this "common school" promised to shift the reins of education from the anarchy of the market to public hands, thus yielding far better teaching methodologies, organizational patterns, and efficiencies. Moreover, this common school would be better able to provide aid to the poor, and would thus create a stronger nation. According to Coulson, this shift from private to public education created an almost calcified popular belief in the institution of public schooling and the ideals of public education. As generation after generation attended public schools, and especially with the explosion of student populations in public schools directly after the Civil War and at the turn of the twentieth century, fewer people were able to discern between the notion of education and the idea that it should be public. From Coulson's point of view, Americans' historical experience with public education has created the unconscious assumption that only the state can supply educational services.[7]

Coulson and like-minded neoliberal proponents of private school choice feel that this seemingly unbreakable ideological link between the ideals of public education and the very notion of schooling has served to smother any alternative thinking that would assist in challenging current public school dogma. The idea that one must support public schools if one is concerned about public education, Coulson argues, is part and parcel of the government-controlled propaganda responsible for demagogically leading people into unquestioning acceptance of failing public school systems. From Coulson's perspective, the narrowing of educational vision is due to the public's acquiescence and acceptance of the public school paradigm. This has resulted in a virtual inability to conceive of educational improvements outside of current reform efforts, which merely tinker with the restructuring of public institutions. Is Coulson right? Has our dependence on public schools shrouded our thinking about the best and most innovative way to design and deliver quality education?

Coulson's admonition, shared by many like-minded thinkers, is both comprehensible and controversial. Basically, the argument states that competitive educational markets have consistently done a better job of serving the public than have what he terms "state-run educational systems."[8] After 150 years of U.S. public schools, Coulson and other proponents of school privatization believe it is now time to consider a radical restructuring of educational systems through market-based reforms—specifically, the privatization of public schooling through private educational vouchers. Their critiques and solutions call into doubt the entire notion of a public common school and question whether we as a nation can or should continue to support and maintain public education.

Not surprisingly, the original promoter of the private voucher idea, economist Milton Friedman, continues to concur with the belief that privatization can be best accomplished through private school vouchers that are universal and obtainable by all citizens. Pointing to a need for radical improvement in education, Friedman stated as recently as 1995 that the solution is to privatize the current system to a marked degree, so that a good number of educational services currently provided through the government are supplied by private business.[9]

Friedman's contention is interesting in that he seems to agree that maintaining and improving public schools is necessary even while he proposes private vouchers as a means of accomplishing this. This apparent contradiction aside, Friedman's historical record and actual public policy positions are remarkably transparent and convey his genuine economic and social agenda. For Friedman, the voucher proposal is not an end in and of itself but rather a means for transforming "government-run schools" into a market-based system of education. For Friedman and other neoliberal proponents of private choice, vouchers are simply an instrument toward a greater ideological objective—getting government schools and their bureaucrats off the backs of ordinary citizens while simultaneously freeing up their children's educational opportunities through the introduction of a host of market-based educational reforms and incentives.

However, Friedman is an astute politician, and he is quick to counsel voucher proponents that politically, the acceptance of private vouchers is an evolutionary and gradual process that cannot be foisted upon the public. From his point of view, to get the majority of people to support private choice and the voucher system of education, two important issues must be kept in mind when structuring the proposals. First, any proposal for vouchers must be straightforward and simple, so that it is comprehensible to the voter. Second, voucher proposals must not require an increase in taxes but rather should promise a reduction in government education spending.[10] In keeping with Friedman's counsel, many state voucher initiatives are springing up. California's recently defeated Proposition 38 and the defeated Michigan initiative, "A Proposed Amendment to the Michigan Constitution to Provide for Guaranteed School Funding, Teacher Testing, and Choice," both in 2000, offer the latest, albeit unsuccessful, examples.[11]

The argument that privatization proposals exist to improve public schools must be considered with hearty skepticism and subjected to critical scrutiny. As Friedman astutely reminds us, the objective of private vouchers and private choice is not the improvement of schools, but the development of an ideology connected to entrepreneurial educational innovations. But Friedman is also wise enough to note that only a widespread switch to private schools will produce the privatization many voucher proponents are seeking, and such a switch is possible only with universal vouchers. Friedman also argues that the individual vouchers must be big enough to support for-profit schools. Universal, financially adequate vouchers, he argues, will allow many families to make their own contribution to the cost of education to provide their children with even better schooling. And this will create the competition necessary to improve all schools, as the advances made by the higher quality schools are embraced by other schools as well.[12] Friedman's perspective basically supports a form of trickle-down educational economics, under which innovations filter down to basic schools once they have been institutionalized for those who can initially afford them. Thus, according to the theory, the luxury for a few will eventually become the norm for the many.

In their work *American Education and the Dynamics of Choice,* scholars James Rinehart and Lee Jackson wholeheartedly concur with Friedman's assessment. They even go so far as to maintain that it is useless to create choice among public schools because the government is bureaucratic, inefficient, and costly. For Rinehart and Jackson, the answer is the free market and the eventual replacement of public schools with a conglomerate of private schools. The authors echo the argument that if parents are allowed to shop around for the best schools for their children, all schools will improve the quality of education they provide precisely because they will be driven to do so by competitive market forces. Furthermore, they also claim that choice within the private market will desegregate education, as inner-city students will be able to spend the voucher monies they receive outside of the confines of the inner city. Carpooling, special busing, and transportation monies will be available and abundant, they contend, to enable both rural and inner-city students to travel wherever they need to go to find the best education.[13] How these services will be provided is rarely, if ever, mentioned.

The neoliberal justification for private school choice is unambiguous: it breaks up the educational monopoly that is controlled by government. From this perspective, as long as education is financed through public monies, education will be reformed only at the whim of political power brokers, not consumers. And from the neoliberal position, only consumer choice within the privatized free market will serve to radically restructure education and make the ideological break in what they see as a dismal link between the public's commitment to democracy and its commitment to public education.

Therefore, poor student performance, a lack of teacher accountability in public schools, ridiculously high prices in the form of more taxes for schools and annual bonds, and a lack of concern for the demands of the consumer (parents and students)—all of these problems will be solved once the free market is interposed to end government involvement in educational policy and once and for all "fix" the schools. The demand is unequivocal, even next to the claims that private vouchers will improve public schools: public education must be replaced with private choice and market-driven imperatives.

But Paul Starr, a noted author on educational and privatization affairs and leading contributor to the *Yale Law and Policy Review,* asks a salient question that must be considered when looking at the privatization of education. By moving public services into the free market, will privatization also shield these services from open public scrutiny and access? And if so, will this narrow the interests, visions, ideologies, and activities that constitute a good society and a good life?[14] Starr's concern is that the ideology of privatization will become omnipresent, eventually shaping the public mind and vitiating independent thinking as it narrows public debate and questioning through private concealment and lack of accountability. His concerns may be well founded.

The argument against any public involvement in education does not simply stop with calls for private vouchers. The pro-privatization movement is far more complicated. In fact, many neoliberals are at odds on basic issues. For example, many classical neoliberal thinkers, including some staunch libertarians, argue against the entire notion of private vouchers. Their opposition to government involvement in education goes so far as to argue that public funding of private schools through government scholarships (private vouchers) will result in unacceptable government controls over education. One concern they have regarding the notion of vouchers is that these publicly financed scholarships, or government-funded private choice vouchers, would produce a vast system of government contractors who, along with parents, would become dependent on vouchers as a form of "school stamps" or "educational stamps," much like food stamps. This, they contend, would create a massive Medicare-style lobby, dependent on ever-increasing subsidies funded through taxation and controlled by Washington power brokers, teachers unions, and other special interest groups. The voices of parents who pay for their children's tuition privately, they argue, would be suffocated and compromised by government contractors and parents groups, who would band together and demand more public subsidies for education.

In short, these critics maintain that vouchers would bring us back to government control of the educational financing and distribution processes and that, as a result, public education and its associated problems would continue to exist—albeit in a unique and distinctive form. For this reason critics of private vouchers, such as some members of the Cato Institute and the Libertarian Party, advocate the abolition of income taxes as a way to privatize schools, rather than providing government vouchers. According to these critics, abolishing the income tax would give families the money necessary to pay for any kind of education they wish to pay for in the private market.[15]

To buttress this libertarian claim, Andrew Coulson argues that state subsidies in K-12 education have historically led to the pervasive regulation of schools. Arguing that from Rome to the medieval Muslim empire, from England to Canada and the United States in the nineteenth century, state subsidies have been used as an instrument of government to control schooling. He applies the same criticism to today's public education system. "If public funds flow to private schools there will be a demand for regulations to ensure public accountability, and these regulations will limit the very freedom that defines a true marketplace."[16] As we shall see in chapter 6, what some conservative critics of private school vouchers promote as an alternative to public education and private vouchers is a huge network of private scholarships designed to move students from public to private schools, financed by corporations and faith-based charitable contributors.

Clearly, anything that interferes with the smooth operation of the free market is suspect to classical neoliberals. Neoliberal philosophy embraces private school choice, arguing that the private voucher movement promises to help families precisely because it is private and therefore, according to neoliberal economists, owes no allegiance to the state.

Furthermore, in a privatized system of education, the neoliberal argument steadfastly maintains there is greater parental responsibility, involvement, and participation in a child's education. After all, the educational marketplace forces parents to see how much the education of their children really costs. Forcing parents to become more conscious as consumers, the argument claims, would thus lead to better parenting, more rational choices, and more effective decision making. In other words, when parents have to pay for educational services, much as they do any other product, they operate far more responsibly and effectively as consumers of education than when the government controls and organizes their choices. Responsibility on behalf of all educational stakeholders—from parents to principals—becomes tied to, accountable to, and held in check by the rigors of the marketplace. The privatization of schooling, maintain advocates, would allow for an active participatory process among parents that would replace the current "entitlement" philosophy, which neoliberals argue has ruined the political, intellectual, and social landscape, depriving many parents and ordinary citizens of intellectual imagination and the capacity to form alternative educational visions.

This argument appears somewhat ironic at first, as many of those who argue that public schools promote a form of "social engineering" also advocate their own form of social engineering through market-based educational reforms. And although the term social engineering is not found in privatization debates, the implications of the public policies that we may adopt in regard to education will no doubt serve to engineer new choices and responsibilities, both socially and individually.

THE INTERNATIONAL EXPERIENCE WITH VOUCHERS

To support their argument that the demand for educational services is satisfied by private school choice—a kind of "demand-side" financing of schooling—many defenders of private vouchers point to international experiments with the idea throughout history.

For example, in a 1997 pamphlet, *Decentralization of Education,* the World Bank points to the Dominican Republic and Pakistan to make the case for private choice and school vouchers. It claims that the practice of providing private vouchers to parents is universal and effective in these countries, reaching even the poorest families. Their conclusions are optimistic and upbeat, promoting the idea that we have much to learn from other international experiments in privatized schooling.[17] That we have much to learn is certainly undeniable.

James Tooley, a leading advocate of private vouchers and author of the book *The Global Education Industry,* agrees. Traveling throughout the world—from Brazil to Zimbabwe—to study the merits of competitive, private educational businesses, Tooley and his colleagues concluded that the private schools they studied were dynamic and innovative, bolstering the argument for private schools and private school vouchers in developing countries.[18] As a result of his investigations, Tooley was moved to question why the state even needs to be involved in education. Let the market have a free rein, he argues, and competing chains of high-quality schools would emerge that would eventually be affordable enough to appeal to the poor. He fondly points to Brazil, where this privatization is currently happening. In Brazil, he argues, the private school system is accompanied by a social safety net funded by philanthropy or the state for those children who really need it. From Tooley's frame of reference, just because there are some parents who are too poor to feed or clothe their children doesn't imply that we have to have universal soup kitchens for all. This same principle should apply to education as well.[19]

Tooley's argument seems to callously promote the idea that public schools should be a last resort for the poor and disenfranchised, much as K-Mart provides an alternative to those who cannot shop at Nordstrom's. Yet what Tooley leaves out of his analysis is the fact that Brazil, his example of neoliberal success in education and his model for school reform, is itself considered one of the most unequal societies on earth. In Brazil the income of the highest fifth of the population is thirty-two times that of the lowest fifth. In Brazil 28.7 percent of the population live below the international poverty line, and 24 percent lack access to safe drinking water. This compares with 25 percent and 22 percent, respectively, worldwide.[20] It is difficult to imagine how the Brazilian experience with the privatization of schooling would offer any healthy recommendations for the United States, or any other country for that matter. Furthermore, to extrapolate privatization lessons from a country like Brazil, a country so socially, economically, and racially stratified, seems unjustifiable and irrational.

Other proponents of school vouchers have studied and point to the market system of education prevalent in nineteenth-century England in an attempt to make their case for the privatization of education in the United States. They argue that literacy and school enrollment rates in England during the 1800s were high and continued to advance and grow rapidly.[21] Although this may be the case, objectors argue that nineteenth-century England was a highly agrarian society experiencing a radical shift to manufacturing. It had little resemblance to the postindustrial England of today, and thus it would be difficult to extrapolate the nineteenth-century British experience to advance an understanding of today's educational reality. And this reveals the real weakness of these arguments from historical authority: for neoliberal educational policy advocates, the competitive marketplace appears to stand outside of history, unaffected by historical transformations and shielded from never-ending cycles of boom and bust.

An alternative assessment of the historical experience is provided by George Whitty, who reviewed the literature on school choice in the United States, Great Britain, and New Zealand. Whitty argues that the privatization of education in these countries did little to improve student achievement. In fact, he concludes that school choice programs are more likely to exacerbate existing inequalities in education.[22] Martin Carnoy, a professor at Stanford University, came to a similar conclusion in his study of school privatization in Chile and elsewhere.[23] In chapter 5 we look specifically at Carnoy's critical analysis of the twenty-year-old voucher experiment in Chile. It offers some profound data leading to critical questions that we should be asking before we embark on experimental policies with unimaginable implications.

Neoliberalism and the Inadequacy of Markets: The Argument against Private Choice and School Vouchers

Not everyone agrees with the neoliberal perspective relative to the privatization of our nation's schools and its alleged benefits. Many critics of privatization point to growing public sentiment against public-sector solutions to broad-based social problems, arguing that these solutions are a reflection of the success of powerful economic interests over the last fifteen years in pushing their agenda with the help of partisan media outlets. Some maintain that these powerful economic, media, and political interests have redefined the notion of public good as personal as opposed to social responsibility. Critics claim that conservative foundations and think tanks like the Olin Foundation, the Heritage Foundation, the Cato Institute, the Hudson Institute, the Eagle Forum, and countless others have enlisted the support of right-wing political pundits and the religious right in an effort to redefine public accountability as individual responsibility and personal choice.

Opposition to this concept of public accountability maintains that what is conspicuously absent in the debate over private choice is the awareness that public schools are not merely service providers, product distribution centers, restaurants, or places where individual or social economic needs are met. Instead, public schools have a special status as coproducers of values and of a shared sense of citizenship—public schools are places to exchange diverse perspectives, where knowledge and skills that are fundamental to democracy, community, and civic health are fostered and developed.

Many would assert that the language of choice, which favors consumer analogies and promises individual customer satisfaction over the public good, has reconfigured the debate over educational reform. The focus of this language—the market—has been pronounced the sole bedrock of major public policy considerations.[24] Progressive critics of neoliberalism are basically concerned that in the minds of many, citizenship has been replaced with little more than consumerism. They also disfavor the language of choice, which they claim emphasizes schools merely as preparatory sites where students acquire the knowledge necessary for the maintenance of specific social and economic business relations.

Preoccupied that overreliance on individualism through private choice will isolate Americans from each other, critics of neoliberalism contend that the real questions ask: education for what and education for whom? If the answer is that education is important for crystallizing the public good and strengthening democracy, then it should be available for each and every child regardless of class, gender, race, religion, or culture. Progressive educational analysts argue that this cannot be accomplished by market-based educational reforms, which they claim actually produce greater class stratification and racial and cultural segregation because private economic funding promotes the discriminatory distribution of educational opportunity.

Progressive educational analysts also maintain that if education is viewed as a separate variable—that is, an institution divorced from democratic ideals and attached only to individual competitiveness and economic production—then democracy itself will be jeopardized in favor of market needs. When schooling is judged by how well it satisfies marketplace imperatives and the individual consumer, the collective public good is lamentably abandoned in favor of an insipid individualism divorced from community.[25]

But proponents of the school voucher idea insist that they too believe education should be offered to every American citizen regardless of race, culture, linguistic capabilities, or special needs. They maintain, however, that today's public schools do not do what progressive educators say they should do and that the system is organizationally incapable of fixing itself. Furthermore, they declare, many public school teachers have enrolled their own children in private schools rather than allow them to attend the same public schools they supposedly champion and defend. Should not all parents be able to do what many middle- and upper-middle-class parents are doing—that is, send their children to a private school that works rather than a public school that does not?

Opponents of private school vouchers claim the controversy regarding privatization is really over two primary questions: First, should American citizens view themselves as merely an atomistic collection of unattached, competitive individuals and consumers attempting to create the best economic lives for themselves in social isolation? Or should they see themselves as citizens who possess the right and duty of self-governance not merely as competitive individuals but as a collective of individuals connected to a larger community? And second, if this latter description is accurate, then what type of community do Americans seek to construct, and what might it look like? Clearly, for many private voucher opponents, the real debate is about this fundamental public policy question: What kind of community do we want to create and for whose purposes?

Deborah Meier, a critic of neoliberal theory and a well-recognized educational reformer and educator, conceptualizes the progressive educational concern much differently. She believes that the concept of public education is sacrosanct and rests on the assumption that the way we educate our youth is connected to the collective future we as citizens hope for. So if, for example, we believe that children have a better future and educational experience if they meet other children from different socioeconomic, religious, linguistic, and cultural backgrounds, then a certain policy follows from that assumption. From Meier's point of view, the presumed advantage of the marketplace is that one does not have to consider or even think about anyone else when one makes one's educational decisions. Under a neoliberal, market-based approach to schools, the only people who have a voice are parents as consumers. Educators like Meier rigorously question the idea that when parents make individual decisions about what's best for their children, then we get what is best for society. Meier and others fear that in the long run, privatization of schooling will undercut the needs of the larger society by substituting collective decision making and open and public debate with private individual decision making.[26]

Amy Gutmann, a respected researcher and author on educational policy affairs, agrees with Meier. She argues that Friedman's comparison of one's choice of restaurants with one's choice of schools is troubling, if not obfuscating. Is the public's interest in schools and restaurants really so similar? If it were, then according to Gutmann and other progressive educators, this would imply that we have no obligation as a society to pay for other people's schools, just as we have no obligation to pick up their restaurant tabs. Would this then mean that the public would have no obligation to ensure equality in opportunity, universal access to schools, and the development of accountability procedures?[27]

Progressive opponents of the privatization of education maintain that primary and secondary schools are quite dissimilar to restaurants—they serve as locations of public community interest that are involved in the development of personal and social identity. One of the duties of education, they claim, is to ensure that all children, regardless of their socioeconomic class, ethnicity, religion, gender, culture, or race, receive an education that prepares them to live wisely in a democracy, while at the same time preparing them for the exigencies of productive life. By downplaying the public purposes of education and arguing that "he who pays the piper picks the tune," proponents of vouchers and private choice reduce education to a individual consumer choice.[28]

The Carnegie Foundation, a distinguished think tank, has also expressed concern with private school choice and larger conceptual issues of community. In its seminal book on the subject, *School Choice,* the foundation criticizes placing the claimed benefits of competition at the center of current school reform efforts. The book argues that competition is the wrong paradigm to use to examine what ails public education. It goes on to support the idea of public community and citizenry as the metaphor for discussing needed changes in schooling. The Carnegie Foundation contends that advocates of private choice have overemphasized the market and its alleged benefits to individuals. In the process, these privatization proponents have paid little or no attention to how education benefits public, civic, and communal purposes and experiences. The Carnegie Foundation exhorts the public to adopt a more ethical and inclusive language regarding the public goals of education instead of the language of competition and choice that has fueled current educational debate.[29]

Neoliberalism, according to its critics, really questions the basic meaning of civic community and challenges the legitimacy and utility of any government action. And from this point of view, education becomes less a social venture than an individual investment. The result, opponents claim, is an insipid social Darwinism whereby social mobility for those privileged enough to have the power and affluence to choose is guaranteed, while others who are less fortunate simply fall by the educational wayside with nobody to "vouch" for them.

The real problem, according to voucher opponents, is not that market-based proposals for private choice will allow some students to attend private schools, but that privatization in general will erode democratic and public forums by reducing education and educational issues to purely consumer choices that are socioeconomically, sexually, and racially organized by market forces. And this, they maintain, will eventually undermine democracy in general. American citizens once believed in the primacy of government to solve all their problems, or at the very least believed in a partnership or social compact between the public and private sector, but this conviction has radically shifted. Many Americans have now been convinced that the answer to social and individual problems and dilemmas is the wholesale abandonment of government—that the public sector is inefficient, threatens individual liberties, and is intrinsically immoral and therefore cannot solve *any* problems.

Opponents of neoliberal efforts to privatize schools specifically question the assertion that increased competition will provide the impetus required to improve schools. They argue that many of those who oppose current public school systems are not interested in actually fixing public schools, but in eliminating them. In regard to those private voucher advocates who genuinely believe that competition will fix public schools, opponents answer that real competition among schools would require a level playing field.

The People for the American Way (PFAW), a public interest group devoted to critiques of conservative agendas in education, recently made the point that by their very definition, publicly funded vouchers present a powerful redistribution of resources. Arguing in a compelling study that this shift in resources is unwarranted and in fact harmful to our nation's children, they point to the emergence of what they term "many classes of losers" where vouchers have been tried:

> Students who want a voucher but never get one.
> Students who are happy in public schools but see them weakened by diverted funds.
> Students in schools that would receive substantial help from proven reform efforts if the money had not been diverted to a few students under the rubric of vouchers.

> Students for whom all available private schools are inappropriate and do not meet their needs because of religion, lack of special programs (including free lunches for the poor and remedial instruction), or other factors.
>
> Students who live where private schools are unavailable or are no better than public schools.
>
> Parents who lack an informed choice because private schools are not required to release information about the quality of education they provide or the progress or regress of students in their care.
>
> Students who do not succeed in private schools, and who then must return to public schools that have lost money and community support.
>
> Students who must remain in those public schools regardless of the school's ability to attract funds to replace those lost due to vouchers.
>
> The community whose public institutions shrink and are fewer and weaker, and whose tax investment has gone to build capital for profit-making businesses.
>
> Taxpayers whose money has been separated from public accountability.
>
> Anyone who believes the argument that financially strapped public schools, which must serve all students, will be in a position to compete with moneyed investors equipped with access to capital, venture or otherwise, and have the flexibility to lower costs and restructure programs.[30]

If public funds were bequeathed to private schools, PFAW argues, private schools would most certainly have access to entrepreneurial venture capital or seed monies, while public schools would quickly see needed monies and crucial resources virtually vanish. Competition between public and private schools could not possibly work, these progressive education analysts argue, simply because the market concept creates a win-lose situation in which public schools would be left bereft of funds while private schools would enjoy private infusions of public and private venture capital. And while public schools that are forced to educate all students will be saddled with the problems outlined above, private voucher schools will face no such problems.

Critics of the private choice idea also argue that taking a handful of students out of an urban school district does not reduce the district's fixed costs, such as building maintenance, employee salaries, school supplies, and administration costs. They maintain that this shift in student population instead reduces funds from already impoverished schools currently unable to afford capital improvements. If true, this would undoubtedly cripple serious educational reforms in the public schools, not enhance them.

Finally, opponents of vouchers and private choice point to the fact that private schools, as businesses dependent on private and public capital, have the ability to simply leave a location or municipality when it becomes unprofitable or difficult for them to educate children. The owners of the new voucher schools, argue progressives, not only have capital readily at their disposal but, like any other business, they can relocate and abandon their clientele whenever they see fit. The argument is that they are less accountable to students than they are to their economic bottom line. Public schools, on the other hand, must be available and accessible to all students all the time and do not operate for a profit, but for a human bottom line—the benefit of students. They cannot simply decide to relocate when profit margins necessitate it.

As we mentioned earlier, progressive public policy makers agree with many outspoken voucher advocates that the true goal of privatization is not to ensure educational equality for all our nation's children by improving public schools. On the contrary, the voucher effort and the notion of private school choice are being utilized to privatize the entire educational system through disciplined and patient attrition. The Milton and Rose Friedman Foundation actually sees means-tested vouchers as a virtual beachhead in a war to privatize education through private school choice.[31]

However, Henry Giroux, a leading educator at Pennsylvania State University, noted author on education, and vitriolic opponent of educational privatization, proposes that there is more at stake in the voucher privatization controversy than we have thus far considered. For example, the issue of how individual achievement is measured and weighed must be scrutinized, and this in turn involves issues of social equity and public good. How will teaching be defined under privatization? What will learning look like, and what sort of identities will our students and teachers create for themselves? Will their experiences, values, and social class be defined through corporate control of education as opposed to public control?

As a society, we must answer many questions to critically evaluate how educational privatization efforts affect our educational institutions and our nation's citizens. The educational future of U.S. society in many ways reflects the pedagogical possibilities we choose to design and the educational opportunities we wish to furnish our nation's children.

POLITICS, RELIGION, AND THE EMERGENCE OF THE PRIVATE VOUCHER MOVEMENT

In this section we look more specifically at the social, political, and economic issues that impact the school voucher movement. This section examines the ideological arguments for and against vouchers as they relate to important nuts-and-bolts topics such as the separation of church and state, student admission policies, public funding of education, student achievement, and current efforts to reform schools.

It is important to remember that not all supporters and opponents of school vouchers base their position on a particular philosophy regarding government, religious freedom, or free enterprise. Many school voucher advocates simply want the best education for their children, and they see the problems in the public schools as proof that public schooling is failing, especially in urban centers. Also, some parents see public schools as too coercive or too liberal, particularly in the controversial areas of sex education and moral and ethical development. Many parents argue that these subjects are family and private matters and that the role of schools is to teach their children the basic academic skills they will need to operate in larger society—nothing more, nothing less. Still others believe that religion should be the basis for a strong, moral education, and they see public schools as godless institutions that discriminate against those who hold religious beliefs.

On the other hand, many critics of private school vouchers are not suspicious of or opposed to the private market per se. These critics simply believe that privatized education will not work and, in fact, will end up creating more problems than it solves. They point to the separation of church and state as one troubling issue and argue that financing sectarian schools with tax dollars is patently unconstitutional and inherently antithetical to the principles of American democracy. They also claim that private school vouchers are segregationist in their practical applications, arguing that private choice will not fix schools but instead will inevitably contribute to a further stratification of citizens through class- and race-based discriminatory admission policies. Critics also adamantly argue that private school vouchers will serve to bleed public school budgets by confiscating public tax monies from general education funds and essentially turning these funds over to private, for-profit schools in the form of voucher subsidies.

The opposition to school vouchers, much like the support for them, is not monolithic or homogenous. However, opponents to school vouchers generally share the following sentiments:

Vouchers threaten the wall of separation between church and state. Opponents claim that our tradition of constitutional protections has protected religious freedom and has prevented the outbreak of factionalism and ethnic strife.

Vouchers accelerate the right-wing agenda: to reduce social services, roll back worker protections, reduce the role of government in enhancing the social welfare, and limit the accountability of private schools.

Vouchers change the direction of educational reform. In terms of admission policies, voucher schools are free to discriminate and "skim the cream" of the best students from the public schools, and this is precisely what they do. Nor are they required to provide special services, provide open enrollment policies for all applicants, or even protect rights of free speech and freedom of religion.

Vouchers are not an educational answer to the problems experienced by our nation's schools. Vouchers threaten support for poor inner-city school districts, and they ignore other reform options such as reduced class size, improved facilities, more support for new teachers, and relevant and renewed curriculums. In short, vouchers exacerbate educational problems— they do not fix them.

Supporters of school vouchers and private choice vehemently maintain that these claims are false.

Should School Vouchers Be Used for Private, Religious Schools?

The answer to this question depends on one's point of view. Nationwide, religious schools account for 79 percent of all private schools and 85 percent of all private school students.[32] This fact seems astonishing, as the implication is that vouchers could and probably would be used primarily to offset the costs of religious schools. Indeed, much of the opposition to vouchers focuses on the use of public monies to fund religious schools. Many progressive activists and other civil libertarians opposed to vouchers believe that the required separation between church and state, as embodied within the U.S. Constitution, will in the end force states and municipalities to abandon their support for private choice. They ardently maintain that if the church-state separation argument against vouchers can be made successfully within the judicial system, then much of the privatization sought through the voucher movement will not need to be confronted politically; the issue can simply be left to the courts for judicial determination. The underlying assumption, of course, is that the courts will agree with anti-voucher advocates on religious and constitutional grounds.

However, according to Corporate Watch, a nonprofit watchdog group, opponents might wish to reconsider their political assumptions and consequent strategy. The church-state separation objection is becoming weaker and weaker, especially with the new Bush administration's creation of an agency to nurture cooperation between government and faith-based charitable agencies. Further, the judicial precedents do not bode well for those who believe that the judicial branch will protect the separation of church and state. The federal government already subsidizes religion with billions of dollars annually. In 1995 about 57 percent of the $144 billion made in tax-deductible charitable contributions went to churches, which, using conservative estimates of average marginal tax rates, implies indirect subsidies of about $16 billion.[33]

Corporate Watch could be right. Between 1947 and 1971, the Supreme Court rendered three seminal judicial decisions that set the groundwork for today's laws regarding the separation of church and state. With the current Supreme Court so divided and with many new Supreme Court appointments anticipated in the near future, the issues these three decisions generated have now been subject to further debate and interpretation. We look at two of these three decisions, as they impact directly on the issue of utilizing public funds for private parochial education.

The Court rendered its first important decision regarding the separation of church and state in the 1947 case of *Everson v. Board of Education*. The issue in the case was whether to uphold a New Jersey statute authorizing the use of public funds to pay for the transportation of children attending religious schools. The opinion, written by Justice Hugo Black, set forth the constitutional doctrine that continues to govern the Court's interpretation of the First Amendment provision, "Congress shall make no law respecting the establishment of religion, or prohibiting the free exercise thereof."[34]

In the *Everson* case the Court upheld the New Jersey statute allowing the use of public funds to provide transportation to private religious schools. When Justice Black expressed concern for the safety of children walking on the highways, the concept of "child benefit" arose. This argument claims that public assistance to religious schools may be allowed if it serves to benefit the child in ways that do not involve religious inculcation—for example, by promoting the child's physical safety or the study of content-neutral academic subjects. Child benefit provided the first judicial argument not only for noncontroversial forms of government aid to parochial schools, such as providing police and fire protection, but also for more contentious forms of public assistance. The decision ushered in such public policies as the issuance of publicly supported bonds to be used to finance the construction of facilities at church-related colleges and universities. The *Everson* decision was eventually used to allow the public purchase of accoutrements for diagnostic and remedial services in religious schools, such as private technology, private remedial programs and curriculum, and provided that sundry forms of teaching aids be made available to parochial schools using taxpayer funds.[35]

But the *Everson* decision did something even more controversial than merely allowing for public funds to be used for various forms of economic aid to parochial schools: it indicated that the denial of certain public benefits to parochial schools might be interpreted as a deprivation of the students' constitutional rights under the Equal Protection Clause of the Fourteenth Amendment to the U.S. Constitution. If this was the case, it could be legally argued that a state's refusal to offer public aid to parochial schools would abridge the parochial school students' rights to receive the same treatment as public school students, as well as their right to the free exercise of religion guaranteed by the First Amendment. A new day in judicial interpretation was dawning.

In 1971 the Supreme Court rendered another seminal judgment regarding the separation of church and state in the case of *Lemon v. Kurtzman*. This case dealt with public financial aid to parochial elementary and secondary schools. In the decision written by Chief Justice Warren Burger, a three-part test was developed by which to decide church-state separation issues. Although it has since been mutated, reinterpreted, and criticized, it continues to be used for legal analysis in virtually all church-state cases.[36]

Under the three-pronged Lemon test, any legislation regarding public monies and religion must first have a "secular legislative purpose." Second, the effect of the statute must neither advance nor inhibit religion. Third, the statute must not foster disproportionate "government entanglement" with religion. The Lemon test has subsequently been used to examine the constitutionality of a host of actions by governmental bodies, including the purchase by the state of educational equipment for parochial schools, the use of public funds for "remedial" programs in parochial schools, and the use of public funds to help handicapped or disabled students attending religious schools.

The separation of church and state was a central issue to our nation's founders. The founders wanted the new democracy to refrain from giving money to support any institution—any church, mosque, synagogue, or the like. James Madison, for one, was adamant that a fire wall between church and state be constructed and remain permanent and absolute. The first sixteen words of the First Amendment read, "Congress shall make no law respecting any establishment of religion, or prohibiting the free exercise thereof."

Yet the majority of private voucher proposals advocate that parents wishing to send their children to religious schools be afforded tax monies to pay for tuition. They seek to allow parents to use public funds to enhance and advance their religious doctrines and teachings. School voucher proponents assume that providing tax monies in the form of vouchers constitutes the free exercise of religion as provided for in the First Amendment and therefore is far from unconstitutional.

With the future clouded by proposals for government support of so-called faith-based charities, an idea President George W. Bush touted in his campaign for president and a movement he intends to support with an office in the executive, it had to be simply a question of time as to when the issue of voucher programs would once again fall into the lap of the U.S. Supreme Court. Prior judicial decisions pave the road for the U.S. Supreme Court decision.

For example, on March 14, 2000, Florida Judge L. Ralph Smith ruled that the lower court ruling authorizing Florida's "opportunity scholarships," the country's first and most ambitious statewide school voucher program, was unconstitutional because it violated the Florida constitution. The judge's ruling against the voucher program was based solely on his interpretation that the state constitution's mandate regarding the separation of church and state would be violated by the provision in the program allowing for state spending of public dollars on private schools. The state court of appeals heard oral arguments on August 16, 2000. On August 5, 2002 the State Circuit Court Judge Kevin Davey ruled that Florida's 1999 "A+" voucher law violated the state's constitution, which prohibits the use of public funds to support religious schools. Even though a sharply divided U.S. Supreme Court ruled 5 to 4 in June that a Cleveland school voucher law did not violate the Establishment Clause of the U.S. Constitution, the Cleveland decision did not bar states, like Florida, from prohibiting the use of their own monies to fund religious institutions. In his ruling, Judge Davey recognized that the court had no authority to abandon the "clear mandate of the people as enunciated in the Constitution." Judge Davey's decision was based on a provision of the Florida Constitution that expressly declares that no revenue of the state or any political subdivision or agency shall ever be taken from the public treasury directly or indirectly in aid of any church, sect, or religious denomination or in aid of any sectarian institution.

Another important case began in Ohio in 1995, when the state passed a voucher proposal for the city of Cleveland. The program involved religious schools. In response, the Ohio Education Association, the ACLU, Americans United for Separation of Church and State, and People for the American Way filed suit on behalf of several parents and community members, alleging that the voucher program violated the Constitution under the Establishment Clause. The Ohio Federation of Teachers also filed suit against the program, and the two cases were consolidated.

In July 1996, the lower court upheld the Cleveland voucher plan, but in May 1997 the state court of appeals reversed the ruling, a reversal that the Ohio Supreme Court affirmed. The higher court's ruling was not based on the program's unconstitutionality, but on a technicality: the voucher proposal had been improperly added to another bill.

In June 1999 the state reenacted the voucher program, this time according to the rules set out in the state constitution. Again, the program was challenged in court on behalf of the same plaintiffs in *Simmons-Harris v. Zelman*. In August 1999 the court granted a motion by the plaintiffs to stop the program from functioning until the case was decided. In December 1999 the court ruled that the voucher program was unconstitutional because it effectively advanced religion, failing the Lemon test. The judge stayed his ruling pending review by the Sixth Circuit Court of Appeals. Ohio has filed an appeal that is pending, and the Sixth Circuit is likely to hear oral arguments in spring or summer of 2001.[37]

The U.S. Supreme Court decided the case on June 5, 2002 and allowed parents to use tuition vouchers to send their children to private schools run by religious organizations. The Court overturned the lower court decisions, and ruled that the Ohio aid program did not violate the separation of church and state mandated in the Constitution. The conservative majority of justices said that use of vouchers for religious schools did not violate the Constitution because the parents, not the state, select the schools. This ruling is seen as one of the biggest church-state decisions in 50 years because of its potential to reshape U.S. education.

The U.S. Supreme Court has also weighed in on school voucher programs, issuing sometimes vague and contradictory rulings. And because the Court has given mixed signals regarding the impact of private choice programs on the separation of church and state, various choice programs within different states have been left subject to different rulings of law. It is not unreasonable to expect that this will change as new appointments are made to the Court.

In 1999 the Supreme Court declined to consider an appeal from a lower court's ruling in Maine that limited a voucher program covering expenses in private schools within the state. The ruling effectively prohibited the state from providing direct support to religious schools. Yet, in its prior opinion of November 9, 1998, the Court had sent completely different signals. In that ruling, it decided it would not consider an appeal of a Wisconsin Supreme Court ruling on Milwaukee's private school choice program. The effect was to allow that state to provide direct support to religious schools.[38]

The impact of the high court rulings on the Wisconsin and Maine private voucher programs is that these states have opposing policies regarding the use of public monies to pay the expenses of students attending religious schools. Complicating the Court's seemingly contradictory position was its 1999 decision not to take an appeal from New York State involving the creation of a school district that, in practice, would serve only disabled children from a community of Hasidic Jews. This refusal to hear the case meant that New York laws governing vouchers remain intact and New Yorkers have no choice but to see their tax dollars used for private schools.

Within all the contradictions inherent in recent court rulings regarding vouchers and public monies, one pertinent point can be ascertained: this extensive legal experience has left many school voucher proponents more astute and better able to design and draft private school voucher programs that will withstand myriad court challenges. The following section addresses some of the issues that have arisen in the legal debate regarding the separation of church and state and private school vouchers. The issues promise to become crucial indicators of the directions that future private voucher programs might take.

Parochial School Vouchers and the Establishment Clause of the U.S. Constitution

According to the Establishment Clause of the First Amendment to the U.S. Constitution, government cannot support or advance religion, and it must not force religion on anyone. The high court has ruled that including religious schools in a school voucher program would violate the Establishment Clause because it would constitute direct aid to these schools. This introduces a key point in school voucher cases: the difference between direct aid to a religious school and indirect aid. Direct aid directly supports and advances religion with federal or state monies. Indirect aid has been distinguished by supporters who argue that there's no advancement of religion when public monies are used for bussing to religious schools, religious services within public schools, and private religious curriculum. Navigating the line between these two types of aid has been a recurring challenge in applying the Establishment Clause to these cases.

An example of this can be found in the high court's reasoning in *Helms v. Mitchell,* a case that originated in Louisiana. The Court, in its final 1999–2000 session, upheld the implementation of part of a federal educational program under which computers, library books, and other instructional equipment could be purchased with public tax monies for religious and other private schools in one Louisiana school district. In their decision, Chief Justice William Rehnquist and Justices Antonin Scalia, Clarence Thomas, Sandra Day O'Connor, Stephen Breyer, and Anthony Kennedy indicated that they would uphold virtually any public aid to religious schools as long as the material provided was not religious in nature and would be provided equally to nonreligious schools. The Court majority ruled that the aid sought was "supplemental" (thus not direct) and was not actually going to be "diverted to religious uses."[39]

What the Court did in this case was to reinterpret, in effect, the *Lemon v. Kurtzman* decision. The justices reasoned that the state statute allowed direct financial aid to religious schools under the theory of "neutrality," which viewed the aid as part of a broad educational assistance program. However, it appears that the "neutrality" doctrine was uniquely designed to assist religious schools. Clarence Thomas's reasoning in the matter, which ultimately prevailed, was that the aid follows the child rather than going to the religious institutions themselves, and therefore it is "neutral" and does not violate the First Amendment. Given this clever reasoning, one could have expected the Court to find voucher programs that allow parents to use federal and state funds to send their children to religious schools constitutional, as they did in Ohio.

The Supreme Court has ruled that the government neutrality toward religion described by the Establishment Clause does not require the government to treat religious institutions the same as it treats public institutions. Thus the government is prohibited from giving *direct* support to religious institutions, and when the Court has supported the granting of public money to religious schools, that support has always been described as *indirect* or targeted. For example, monies might be used to pay for computer equipment at private secular schools. Monies would not be allowed to directly subsidize religious instruction. However, given the Supreme Court decision regarding the Ohio voucher plan these issues now seem mute. Moreover, the Court has stated that the Establishment Clause may be invoked only as a defense against state subsidies of religious activity; it cannot serve as a justification for religious groups that are seeking state subsidies. In other words, one may not argue that government's refusal to give subsidies to religious activities amounts to the "establishment" of a religion—in this case, the "religion" of nonreligion.

However, one dexterous argument for reasonable alternatives to direct funding of religious schools has surfaced in the form of the creation of educational tax credits. Under such a plan, families would be able to use federal tax credits to defray the costs of tuition and other private school-related expenses. This would mean that parents could send their children to any school they wished, religious or nonsectarian, and still be eligible for the tax credit. In such a plan, following the logic of the U.S. Supreme Court, there would be no direct aid to religious schools. Would this mean that a student could use voucher funds, charitable contributions, tax credits, and private scholarship funds to pull out of public schools in favor of private schools? If so, how does this fit with the argument that all these proposals are designed to create competition among public schools? Are not these really incentives to abandon public schools through private and public subsidization?

Supporters of educational tax credits claim that these credits provide many advantages over government-funded scholarship programs, including private vouchers. One advantage they cite is that tax credits provide a way around the Establishment Clause, which separates religion and the state. A nonrefundable tax credit, they argue, simply allows the taxpayer to keep more of his or her earned money, which therefore is never actually collected by the government in the first place. Thus it does not constitute a direct government subsidy to private religious schools. Therefore, claim voucher supporters, even though parents sending their children to parochial schools would be eligible to receive the tax credit, any argument that these tax credits would directly support religious schools is simply not true and would fail as a legal challenge.

One of the first states to pass such an educational tax credit law was Arizona. Challenged legally by the state and national teachers unions, the tax credits were ruled constitutional in 1999 by the Arizona Supreme Court, and the Arizona tax credit law was upheld. Currently, Michigan is proposing such an initiative, and the idea is spreading, with more states planning to follow suit.

For example, a similar tax proposal has recently surfaced in Virginia. Known as the Children's Educational Opportunity Act (2000), H.B.

68 and S.B. 336, the bill would provide Virginia parents of children in kindergarten through high school with state subsidies for tuition payments, generally to private schools. The subsidies would be as much as $2,500 per child and would be structured as credits against Virginia income taxes that these taxpayers would otherwise owe. These credits could be used for either religious or nonreligious private schools and thus, proponents maintain, would not be the subject of constitutional challenges on religious grounds.[40]

The Institute on Taxation and Economic Policy analyzed the Virginia bill and found that if implemented, the plan would distribute most of the tax credits (75 percent) to the small number of Virginia families (24 percent) who make more than $75,000 annually. More than half (55 percent) of the tax credits would go to families who make more than $100,000. In contrast, 24 percent of families in the state who make $20,000 or less would receive an average of only 5 percent of the maximum credit allowed. Most families in Virginia would receive no or little benefit from the program.[41]

Such analyses suggest that programs like the Virginia tax credit program may result in a top-heavy distribution that benefits high-income families who can afford to send their children to private schools even without the tax credit. PFAW certainly thinks so. It organized its southern field office to mobilize opposition against H.B. 68, which would have authorized the tax credits. Arguing that the richest families would reap over $100 million from the proposed legislation, PFAW officially lobbied to kill the tuition tax credit scheme for Virginia. However, with a new administration in the White House and the development of national policies breaking with the past, it is likely that we will see similar proposals submitted into the legislatures of various states.[42]

Parochial School Vouchers and the Free Speech Clause of the U.S. Constitution

The Free Speech Clause of the First Amendment states that "Congress shall make no law respecting an establishment of religion, or prohibiting the free exercise thereof; or abridging the freedom of speech . . ." Many promoters of public funding for religious schools have seized upon this clause to claim that they have a right to utilize public monies for private religious activities. After all, they claim, their religious viewpoint is simply that—a viewpoint. They argue that failing to fund private religious schools with private vouchers funded by public funds actually constitutes discrimination against a specific viewpoint and violates their right to free speech.

From this point of view, the First Amendment was intended to protect a right to freely practice religious faith. Conservative arguments claim that the First Amendment was designed to secure the blessings of liberty to our posterity and ourselves. Those who argue that the First Amendment has been interpreted to discriminate against religion state that it is quite clear from the historical record that the founders of American government intended to encourage religion, not discourage it, and that they simply wanted to ensure that the power of the federal government would never be used to favor one denomination over another. From this frame of reference, the First Amendment does not prohibit the encouragement of religious belief and morality. It does prohibit an establishment of religion—that is, the creation of an official state church—but this prohibition applies solely to the federal government. So far the Supreme Court has rejected this claim, ruling that "parents cannot assert that they have been denied a forum for any type of speech" when proposing that religious schools be funded through public funds.[43]

School Vouchers and the Free Exercise Clause of the U.S. Constitution

Under the Free Exercise Clause of the Constitution, every American citizen has the right to exercise any religion he or she wishes. In a famous case, *Brusca v. Missouri,* parents argued that the Free Exercise Clause requires public subsidization of their private tuition costs. In reviewing the case, the court held that even if sending a child to a Catholic school is central to Catholic religious beliefs or practices (which the court refused to decide), the failure to allocate payment for the exercise of this practice does not impose a substantial burden on religious parents and their children and therefore is not a violation of the Free Exercise Clause.[44]

In a similar Wisconsin case, parents of children attending sectarian schools argued that the exclusion of sectarian schools from the school voucher program denied them equal access to a government benefit, and that this denial was based upon a religious belief. This, they claimed, violated their right to free exercise of religion and their right to equal protection under the law. The district court rejected the free exercise claim, reasoning that the request to subsidize private religious schools violates the Establishment Clause, which prohibits the government from giving direct economic benefits to private religious schools. This, too, can be expected to change as we gear up for a new lineup on the Supreme Court in the not-too-distant future.

Do School Vouchers Lead to Better Schools and
Higher Student Achievement?

In the foreword to the Heritage Foundation's 2000 report on school choice, Florida Governor Jeb Bush adds to the claim that school vouchers will advance student achievement across ethnic and class lines. He argues that school choice is not a prerogative of the wealthy and elite alone but that choice focuses on ensuring that all students will be afforded access to the best schools possible.[45] His argument is simple: Private choice and vouchers will reinvigorate public schools and improve the quality of education and student achievement.

From the point of view of Jay Greene of the Manhattan Institute, a think tank devoted to market-oriented reform in education and other arenas, Bush is correct. Vehemently arguing against the view that private choice will drain monies from public schools, he asserts the contrary: "Vouchers, instead, motivate schools to rise to the challenge" of competition and efficiency.[46] According to Greene, a longtime partisan of conservative issues, the threat of vouchers is enough to trigger improvements in standardized test scores—the official and only measure Greene and his colleagues use to calibrate what they call "student achievement."

Greene recently studied Florida's so-called A+ Program, which assigns each public school in the state a grade from A to F. Greene concluded that the schools that received a failing grade from the state in 1999, whose students would be offered private vouchers to opt out of public education if they failed a second time, achieved an eighteen-point gain on the Florida Comprehensive Achievement Test (FCAT). Schools that had a C grade in 1999 saw gains in the FCAT of 4.5 percent. The report is based on the assumption that the FCAT is a viable and responsible means of assessing student achievement, intellectual growth, emotional health, and ability to think critically. As we shall see when we assess the Milwaukee Parental Choice Program in chapter 5, the notion of student achievement as measured by standardized tests is challenged by many scholars and educators. However, according to *USA Today*, which reported on the Greene study, Greene hoped that the study would motivate the Bush administration to push for a universal voucher plan nationwide.[47]

In their work *Politics, Markets, and American Schools*, John Chubb and Terry Moe also argue that the privatization of education in the form of vouchers will enhance student achievement. Their analysis argues that private control over schooling actually increases student performance, and that choice "has the capacity all by itself to bring about the kind of transformation that, for years, reforms have been seeking to engineer in a myriad of ways."[48]

Not surprisingly, opponents disagree. They argue that Chubb and Moe have overstated the advantages of private schools in boosting student achievement. Although private school principals do have greater power to set policies, opponents argue that this hardly translates into an advantage, nor does it mean that teacher professionalism is encouraged. In fact, with most voucher programs leaving teachers unprotected by teachers unions, voucher opponents argue that this leaves educational workers vulnerable, and this vulnerability has a great impacts on teachers' autonomy, work conditions, incentive, and ability to afford learning opportunities to all their students. Most progressive educators and supporters of public schools agree with neoliberals that overblown bureaucracies plague public schools, and that because the compensation provided by private choice is so limited, the vouchers are used mostly by the wealthy, members of the clergy, and families with more than one wage earner. This, they argue, can hardly serve to benefit all of our nation's children.[49] Or can it?

In 1997, the Department of Education analyzed the impact of private and public school choice programs on student achievement. The department's research findings demonstrated that existing private school voucher programs have not shown substantial improvement in student achievement. In fact, according to the department, most of the differences between performance in public and private schools can be traced to:

> factors related to student background (family income, parents' educational attainment)
> self-selection bias
> prior achievement of the student
> the choice of courses taken by the student
> academic standards and expectations[50]

John Witte, Albert Shanker, and Bella Rosenberg, all esteemed academic researchers, also argue that when students' background characteristics and the courses they take are taken into consideration, private schools do not outperform public schools. Their findings demonstrate that private schools are no more able to undo the lock between social class, race, and achievement than are public schools.[51]

The People for the American Way Foundation claims that vouchers have drained needed economic resources from public schools. Looking at Milwaukee and Cleveland, the foundation claims that $22 million dollars allocated for 6,000 voucher students in Milwaukee alone has been diverted from public school coffers. The foundation maintains that in Cleveland the amount drained is $5.25 million, with the likelihood of an increase to $25.4 million by 2001.[52] Such statistics have led many public policy pundits to question the claim that private vouchers will enhance public school performance. As funds leave school districts, how will these districts do more with less?

As we shall see in chapter 5, where we examine specific voucher programs, the claims and interpretations are mixed when it comes to higher student achievement, increased professionalism, and streamlined bureaucracy in voucher-supported schools. Whether voucher programs actually result in these improvements and provide better and more effective learning environments remains unclear. Many opponents of vouchers argue that if there is increased student performance at voucher schools, it is a result of smaller class sizes, personalized learning, and greater resources, not the fact that these schools are privatized.

The Economic Policy Institute (EPI), a nonpartisan, nonprofit think tank contends that by focusing on the differences between private and public schools, we actually obfuscate the real issues of educational reform. According to the EPI, the most significant variations between schools derive from social, cultural, racial, and economic differences, not from the status of the school as private or public. In *Can Public Schools Learn from Private Schools?* EPI Research Associate Richard Rothstein, Stanford University Professor Martin Carnoy, and Luis Benveniste of the World Bank present case studies of public and private elementary schools in California to identify any practices in the private schools that could be used by public schools to improve student performance.[53] The report concludes that private schools do not define student outcome expectations any more clearly than do public schools, and that innovations at private schools do not always serve to motivate nearby public schools to improve their own practices. Furthermore, none of the schools in the study, private or public, utilized formal assessment, supervision, or mentoring of teachers to measure their experience. And finally, the study suggested that school personnel at private schools are not necessarily more accountable to parents than those at public schools.[54] These observations should be important to anyone who champions or considers private choice and privatization of schools as an educational reform. Indeed, they should be of interest to parents of school-age children.

The authors of the EPI study concede that fully examining the complex issue of private school choice and school vouchers is beyond the capacity of any single study. They caution the public to be mindful and prudent before hurriedly implementing any program designed to fix our schools. They implore us to consider significant issues of race, gender, and social class when assessing any educational reform efforts. They argue that the issue of private choice should be met with a healthy skepticism and a critical scrutiny of public policies and proposed solutions. And they argue that such a thorough examination must be part of any process that we as citizens employ in the debate over private choice and public schooling.

The Problem of Accountability

In most states private schools operate outside the scope of public authority and therefore have no public accountability; they are not required to substantiate that they provide a quality education to all students. And because many states do not demand that private schools follow open-meeting laws and do not require them to subject their students to state-mandated tests, claims of heightened student achievement remain questionable. According to the People for the American Way Foundation, this lack of accountability might explain why voucher supporters in Cleveland and Milwaukee have failed to provide evidence showing that their voucher programs have improved student performance or have spurred the public schools to greater achievement. Neither of these voucher programs requires that its voucher schools hold open meetings or make their records, test scores, and attendance data public.[55]

The lack of public accountability and full disclosure seems to vitiate the argument made by neoliberals and other voucher proponents that vouchers allow parents to make informed choices from among the many schools within a free market. If parents are to make informed consumer choices within the market-based model of education, then as conscientious consumers they would need information that would allow them to compare and contrast educational services in the interest of the best choice for their children. However, with laws in Ohio and Wisconsin that actually shield voucher schools from critical scrutiny by potential consumers and interested citizens, it is difficult to imagine how parents can make informed decisions regarding the schools they want their children to attend.

The Problem of Admission Practices

Many concerns about private school vouchers have to do with admission policies. According to Delaine Easton, former state representative of the twentieth legislative district and current superintendent of schools in California, vouchers allow private schools to discriminate against students on the basis of physical disability, gender, religion, or economic status—all at taxpayers' expense.[56]

Research does suggest that private school voucher programs do encourage participating schools to favor more advantaged students—those whose parents have more education and higher incomes and place more value on education. This seems to happen even in targeted voucher programs restricted to low-income families. One study in San Antonio, Texas, for example, concluded that low-income mothers of voucher students were much more likely to have had some college education than were low-income mothers of public school students.[57]

The Institute on Taxation and Economic Policy arrived at similar conclusions, finding in their study of the proposed Virginia Children's Educational Opportunity Act 2000 that better-off Virginia families are much more likely to send their children to private schools than are other families.[58] This is the case in other countries as well. For example, research in England research found that parents who preferred to send their children to schools outside their neighborhood tended to have more education and more income than those who preferred their local schools. Moreover, in areas with the most inter-school competition schools choose students more than students choose schools.[59] Thus, those opposed to private school vouchers claim that the freedom to choose becomes the school's, not the parent's, and this choice takes the form of discriminatory admissions policies.

Discrimination in admissions can occur on many levels. It can occur in the admission requirements of each specific school, such as academic achievement or religious affiliation, and in the actual services that voucher schools provide. Often the extent of educational services and programs offered at a school site silently determines which students will apply. For example, many private schools refuse to serve children with special needs or to provide some of the other programs and services that the public generally associates with schools. This is why opponents of private vouchers argue that the real "choice" of which students attend which school is made by the schools themselves, not by most parents and students.

In 1998 a U.S. Department of Education study found that a minority (less than 25 percent) of the nation's private schools offer facilities or programs for children with disabilities or government-subsidized, reduced-price lunches for students, whereas the vast majority of public schools do. Only a minority of private schools provide medical services, such as school nurses, whereas nearly three-fifths of public schools do.

The study reveals that almost half of the nation's private schools provide no remedial academic services for students who need extra help, whereas some 83 percent of public schools do. About 86 percent of religious schools indicated that if a voucher program required them to permit student exemptions from religious instruction or activities, they would opt out of the program. Finally, the study concluded that one-third to one-half of religious schools would not participate in voucher programs if they had to accept randomly assigned transfer students from public schools, and only 15 percent to 31 percent would participate in voucher programs if they were required to accept students with special needs, such as those with learning disabilities, limited English proficiency, or low achievement.[60]

Another surreptitious way that schools can select students is by their locality. For example, many private schools are located in suburban settings where public transportation is limited, and thus low-income students who wish to attend these schools are disadvantaged by lack of transportation outside their immediate neighborhoods.

Take the Montgomery (Alabama) Transit System, for example. The city that owes its civil rights legacy to the bus boycotts for racial desegregation in the 1950s scarcely has adequate transportation today. "Public transport" here has become a euphemism for poor peoples' transportation. Currently, only one bus line in the city has a dedicated route into the inner city. Montgomery is just one example of the inadequacy of public transportation that is occurring nationwide. Lack of public transportation makes it difficult, if not impossible, to travel to many voucher schools. In cities with populations of 1 million or less, more than half the people who use the public transit make less than $15,000 per year and nearly 60 percent of transit riders are minorities.[61]

How will a faltering public transportation system transport children to voucher schools outside of their immediate neighborhoods? Are primary school students attending kindergarten or first grade expected to use public transportation to travel several miles to voucher schools? And if the answer is that the transportation system cannot and should not be required to handle these issues, then what are voucher schools doing to augment benefits for transportation expenses—especially for low-income citizens who often have no access to dependable automobiles or private forms of transport? The answer is: very little. With more and more cities experiencing the development of two-tiered transportation systems—public systems that serve the poor and private systems, including the use of autos, that serve the more affluent—it is difficult to see how many minorities and low-income residents of neighborhoods will be able to transport themselves to the actual voucher school sites.

Interestingly, according to a recent California study, private schools may have little capacity to absorb the substantial number of additional students they might receive due to the passage of private choice voucher plans. According to the study, existing private schools in California would be able to accommodate less than 1 percent of the state's public school students. The study found that most private schools that had expressed an interest in accepting school vouchers were already operating at 85 percent capacity.[62] Opponents of vouchers thus argue that currently there are simply not enough private schools to educate the 46.5 million students across the nation. And if most of the private schools that do exist refuse to participate in voucher programs if the government imposes conditions on them, it is doubtful that all students who wished to attend private schools could do so. School voucher proponents, on the other hand, are quick to point out that once voucher programs are working, the guiding hand of the market will intervene to provide the needed schools. Entrepreneurs, they say, will fill the deficit, just as the need for any product creates producers. This may or may not be true, but at this point the promise has failed to materialize.

Some important questions to think about when analyzing specific voucher program admission requirements might be:

> Should private schools that attract a more select student body be required, as public schools are, to serve all students?
> Should public schools be able to select students like private schools do? Or should public schools be required to serve all students?
> Should there be some measure of protection for those public schools that have established high standards and innovative programs but cannot compete with highly successful private schools?
> Will voucher programs lead to an inequitable situation in which the best students attend a few select schools?
> Should we consider the needs of the most successful students when developing educational policy, or those of the least successful students?
> Will the voucher program be equitably administered in terms of students' race, gender, and socioeconomic status?
> Will the voucher program provide clear guidelines to ensure that the rights of students with special needs are fully respected?
> Will the voucher program prohibit participating schools from using entrance requirements to exclude students whose primary language is not English?[63]

Opponents of voucher plans contend that it is in the interest of private schools to choose students who are already high achievers. It is also in their interest—especially among smaller schools—to accept those whose families can supplement their voucher with additional funds. Once again, many voucher opponents would claim that the private choice engendered would belong to the schools, not to students and their families. They would also be quick to point out that Milton Friedman's universal voucher plan, which would allow individual families to add their own cash to a private voucher, would further stratify society by ensuring that families who could afford to pay more and thus afford higher tuition would have access to private schools of their choice, while those confined to public schools would have no choice at all. However, privatization proponents have no problem with this conception, arguing that the market is the arbitrator of social and individual good. Chubb and Moe even go so far as to propose that local school districts should augment the value of vouchers through increased taxation.

Opponents of the voucher idea also worry that school voucher programs will lead to resegregation of schools because for many poor and minority families, the baseline vouchers would be difficult if not impossible to supplement. This could create a situation reminiscent of Southern Jim Crow education, where vast differences existed between per pupil expenditures for black and white schools.[64]

ReThinking Schools (RTS), a public interest organization opposed to vouchers and private choice, is concerned about privatization and its historical propensity to discriminate. For example, under Jim Crow it was not uncommon for African Americans to supplement insufficient public funding by constructing schoolhouses with their own donated labor and to pay teachers out of their sparse incomes. As the scholar W. E. B. DuBois maintained, some of these starved schools managed to achieve excellence through unusual efforts, and greater funding would have made such excellence far more widespread. However, the notion that private choice would create a nation of small, effective schools is a mythical construction similar to the argument that the free market can maintain a nation of shopkeepers. There is little doubt that a tremendous level of capitalization and economies of scale would be necessary to construct buildings, to conduct advertising campaigns, to maintain staffing, and to prevent a situation whereby those with an unsupplemented voucher and without wealth would basically be excluded from quality voucher schools. Without capitalization, how would poor students be able to afford privatized schooling? In fact, according to ReThinking Schools, a more likely scenario would emerge: one whereby educational conglomerates requiring orchestrated, standardized teacher behaviors and offering a "fast-food" menu of educational services would emerge, similar to the standardization of companies like McDonald's. Like nineteenth-century charity schools, such schools would compose the bottom tier of an educational hierarchy based on cultural, racial, gender, and class differences. Aside from the inequities associated with a market-based approach to schooling, such a strategy raises fundamental issues of educational purpose.[65]

Yet is this a fair characterization of what might transpire if vouchers became a reality across the nation? Voucher proponents certainly do not think so. They point to U.S. Department of Education studies of twelfth graders, which reveal that voucher students at private schools are more likely to be in racially heterogeneous classes than are public school students. These studies showed that only 17.8 percent of public school students were in diverse classrooms. More than half of all seniors in public school (54.5 percent) were in classes with minority populations of either more than 90 percent or less than 10 percent. Only 41 percent of students in private schools were in similarly segregated classrooms. Proponents of vouchers also cite studies that indicate that racially heterogeneous classes are more likely to be found in private schools.[66]

But is this a salient argument? Do private school vouchers cause discrimination, racially, culturally, or otherwise, in our nation's schools? Do they lead to further stratification along racial and class lines? In an attempt to answer these and other questions, in chapter 5 we look closely at the nation's oldest voucher program in Milwaukee, Wisconsin, and focus on another program in the country of Chile.

The Problem of Restoring Public Schools

Proponents of school vouchers and educational private choice argue that vouchers would not take needed monies from public schools but would actually save the public money. Claiming that it costs far less to give children a fantastic private school education than to give them a substandard public school education, private voucher defenders claim that vouchers would bring enormous savings to public school systems and taxpayers. How? The answer, they argue, is relatively simple. These savings accrue because it simply costs less to run private schools. For example, if a district spends $10,000 per student and a private school spends $4,000 per student, and the district gives parents a voucher for $4,000, then the school district saves $6,000. Is this arithmetic correct or simply "fuzzy math"?

Opponents think that such arguments don't add up. Pointing out that 90 percent of all students, and an even larger percentage of minority students, currently attend public school, they argue that private choice programs will actually serve to disinvest public money from public schools that need it, and that vouchers really represent a form of public divestiture. This, they say, is the real agenda of privatization pundits and politicians. Voucher advocates counter this reasoning by arguing that private choice would give money to kids, not schools. However, opponents maintain that if voucher programs were to be implemented across the board, we would hear a great sucking sound as public school funds were diverted to private schools, thereby disemboweling public school districts, whose costs would not diminish simply because some children left to attend private schools. The result: Kids with no one to "vouch" for them would be left in underfunded public schools, while those with parents able and eager to use private vouchers would enjoy publicly funded, private educational benefits. The effect would be compounded each year, with further cutbacks in school funding for the remaining public schools and a continued diversion of public funds to private schools. In the eyes of voucher opponents, this would assign lower-income students who could not augment their vouchers to meet higher tuition costs to failing public schools and a second-class educational system. Proponents of vouchers are quick to counter by simply stating that this is already happening under the highly stratified public school system that rewards suburban schools while penalizing children at inner-city public schools. Certainly vouchers would not create a worse situation than the one suffered by many parents and their children now. Or would they?

The American Federation of Teachers, a strident opponent of all private voucher proposals, makes the argument that in places like Florida and Milwaukee where vouchers have been studied, money to pay for vouchers comes directly out of local school district budgets. In 1998–1999, the Milwaukee voucher program took $22 million from the local public school budget. In Cleveland, the cost of transporting student to voucher schools took $1.4 million from public school funds. And as we have seen, there is evidence that voucher programs allow private schools to "skim" higher-achieving students and more involved parents, leaving the resource-poor public schools with a doubly disadvantaged student body.[67]

PFAW argues that money spent on voucher programs, currently in the millions of dollars, could be more effectively used to reform the public schools, where the vast majority of students remain. For example, in Milwaukee the funds spent on the voucher program could have been used to create smaller class sizes for 13,000 students. Likewise, of the $10 million spent annually on the voucher program in Cleveland, $4 million could have brought an effective reading program to all eighty of the city's public elementary schools, with plenty of money left over for other improvements.[68]

Voucher opponents are also eager to point out that the radically unequal allocations of funds to public school districts are based on regressive property taxation, especially in inner cities, putting these school districts at a severe disadvantage. They argue that urban districts, which are essentially colonized, economically impoverished communities, harbor the real problems that face public schools, and that a new, progressive system of financial support, a virtual Marshall Plan for our nation's inner cities, not just our schools, must be invented.[69]

CONCLUSION

The controversy over private school vouchers and the impact of these proposals on current public school policies, as well as on parents, students, and teachers, will remain the subject of rigorous debate for some time. Advocates of private choice and school vouchers are educational reformers concerned with transforming the nature and composition of American education. And like all reformers, they make strong claims and passionately advocate specific public policy proposals. However, as we have seen, the issue of private choice is complicated. It deserves intense critical thinking and a more cautious view of what such reform might mean.

According to authors Richard Elmore, Bruce Fuller, and Gary Orfield, there is only scant evidence that private choice triggers the educational improvements in the public schools that its proponents promise. Nor is there much evidence that participants in private choice applicants programs base their choices on the quality of the educational programs. when they make their choices.On the contrary, more evidence suggests that the effects of private voucher programs are shaped more by cultural and political contexts—a potentially important but little understood factor.[70]

Our nation's system of public education has been the bedrock supporting our nation's success and democratic identity for more than 150 years. At a time when privatization is being offered as the answer to everything from fixing our nation's highways to educating our country's citizens, the controversy over privatization and school vouchers deserves more debate than media sound bites can offer. Broad controversies over the role of government and the purposes of schooling have always engendered debates about specific educational content and policy. However, as we enter into a new millennium, when the prescription for all that ails us seems to be the proliferation of markets and market-based reforms, American citizens are being asked not just to reform the existing public education system but to replace systems with new, privatized ones. The new economic and social systems and the new policies being advocated are based on and designed in accordance with the logic of the market. It is important, as we go forward, to understand the perplexing task of developing an effective and equitable educational system. As citizens, we must ask the necessary, fundamental questions to ascertain the tremendous effects of private choice policies on our nation's schools and on our democracy. As citizens we must continue to demand the hard evidence needed to make wise judicial, social, and personal judgments regarding difficult educational public policy issues that have high-stakes implications for society, families, and individuals.

The debate over private school vouchers, and privatization in general, can be taken as a hopeful sign. It promises to bring a new generation of Americans into the discussion regarding the purpose, role, and development of educational policy and purpose. This kind of discourse is healthy and represents the type of learning conversation, as opposed to a quarrelsome argument, a democracy and its populace need. The result of these debates promises to have tremendous ramifications for the potential of our nation and the future of our children.

NOTES

1. Elmore, R., B. Fuller, and G. Orfield. (1996). *Who Chooses? Who Loses?: Culture, Institutions, and the Unequal Effects of School Choice.* Sociology of Education Series, vol. 2. New York, NY: Teachers College Press. http://www.schoolchoices.org.

2. Farkas, S., J. Johnson, and A. Foleno. (1999). "On Thin Ice: How Advocates and Opponents Could Misread the Public's Views on Vouchers and Charter Schools," p. 9. A report by Public Agenda. http://www.publicagenda.org.

3. Ibid., p. 10.

4. Ibid., p. 17.

5. Americans United for Separation of Church and State. (2001, January 23). "Bush School Voucher Plan Poisons the Well of Education Reform." Press release. AUSCS Web site. http:www.au.org.

6. Hayek, F. A. (1960). *The Constitution of Liberty.* London: Routledge.

7. Coulson, A. (1999, April 7). "Are Public Schools Hazardous to Public Education?" *Education Week.*

8. Ibid., p. 2.

9. Friedman, M. (1995, June 23). "Public Schools: Make Them Private." Briefing paper number 23. The Cato Institute. http://www.cato.org.

10. Ibid., p. 5.

11. Ibid., p. 2.

12. Ibid., p. 5.

13. Rinehart, J., and L. Jackson. (1991). *American Education and the Dynamics of Choice.* New York: Praeger.

14. Starr, P. (1988). "The Meaning of Privatization." *Yale Law and Policy Review* 6:6–41.

15. Browne, H. (2000). *Harry Browne's Views on Education.* Washington, DC: The Libertarian Party.

16. Coulson, A. (2000). "Criticism of Government Vouchers." School Choices Web site. http://www.schoolchoices.org.

17. Ariasingam, D. (1997). *Decentralization of Education: Demand-Side Financing.* Washington, DC: The World Bank.

18. Tooley, J. (1999). *The Global Education Industry.* Newcastle, England: Institute for Economic Affairs.

19. Tooley, J. (1999, May 11). "Should the Private Sector Profit from Education?" Keynote speech delivered to the Business of Education Forum. Washington, DC.

20. United Nations Development Program. (1999). *Human Development Report.* Oxford: Oxford University Press, p. 146.

21. West, E. (1994). *Education and the State.* Indianapolis, IN: Liberty Fund.

22. Whitty, G. (1997). "Creating Quasi-markets in Education: A Review of Recent Research on Parental Choice and School Autonomy in Three Countries." In: *Review of Research in Education,* edited by Michael W. Apple. Washington, DC: American Educational Research Association, p. 22.

23. Carnoy, M. (1995, July 12). "Is School Privatization the Answer? Data from the Experience of Other Countries Suggest Not." *Education Week* 11:16.

24. "Private School Vouchers." WEAC Research Paper. Wisconsin Education Association Council Web site. http://www.weac.org.

25. Weil, D. (1998). *Towards a Critical Multicultural Literacy.* NY: Peter Lang; Noble, D. "Digital Diploma Mills." http://www.firstmonday.dk

26. Meier, D. (1996). "The Debate Is about Privatization, Not 'Choice.'" In: *Selling Out Our Schools: Vouchers, Markets and the Future of Public Education,* edited by Robert Lowe and Barbara Miner. Milwaukee, WI: ReThinking Schools, p. 7.

27. Gutmann, A. (2000). "What Does School Choice Mean?" *Dissent* 70(no. 2): 21.

28. Ibid., p. 22.

29. Boyer, E. (1992). "School Choice." In Collected Speeches, 1979–1995. Princeton, NJ: Carnegie Foundation for the Advancement of Teaching, p. 86.

30. People for the American Way. (1999, April 20). "The Privatization of Public Education: A Joint Venture of Charity and Power." PFAW Web site. http://www.pfaw.org.

31. "The Voucher Threat." (1998, Fall). ReThinking Schools 13 (no. 1): 16–21.

32. U.S. Department of Education. (1997, September 23). "Impact of Vouchers on Schooling." http://www.ed.gov.

33. Brighouse, H. (1999, September-October). "USA: What Should the Left Learn from School Choice Debates?" *Against the Current* 14(no. 4):4. http://www.igc.org/solidarity.

34. Redlich, N. (2000, October 9). "Is the Wall Crumbling?" *The Nation.* http://www.thenation.com.

35. Ibid., p. 27.

36. Ibid.

37. People for the American Way. (2000). "Religious School Vouchers and Tax Credits." PFAW Web site. http://www.pfaw.org/courts/education. Accessed July 24, 2002.

38. Borsuk, A. (1999, October 12). "Non-rulings Leave States with Different School Choice Laws." *Milwaukee Journal Sentinel,* p. 46.

39. Ibid.

40. Institute on Taxation and Economic Policy. (2000, February). "An Analysis of the Proposed School Tuition Subsidies in the Virginia Children's Educational Opportunity Act 2000 (H.B. 68 and S.B. 336)". Citizens for Tax Justice Web site. http://www.ctj.org.

41. Ibid., p. 2.

42. People for the American Way. (2000, March). *Victory in Virginia.* Washington, DC: People for the American Way. http://www.pfaw.org.

43. Americans United for Separation of Church and State. (2001). "Voucher Case Summary." AUSCS Web site. http://www.au.org.

44. Ibid.

45. Bush, J. (2000). "Choice Leaves No Child Behind." *School Choice 2000.* Washington, DC: The Heritage Foundation.

46. Henry, T. (2001, February 16). Quoted in "Florida Schools Shape Up amid Voucher Threat." *USA Today,* p. 1D.

47. Ibid.

48. Chubb, J., and T. Moe. (1990). *Politics, Markets, and American Schools.* Washington, DC: The Brookings Institution, p. 217.

49. Cookson, P. (1985). *Preparing for Power: America's Elite Boarding Schools.* New York: Basic Books.

50. U.S. Department of Education. (1997, September 23). "Impact of Vouchers on Schooling." http://www.ed.gov.

51. Cookson, P. (1985). *Preparing for Power: America's Elite Boarding Schools.*

52. People for the American Way Foundation. (1999, April 20). "Grand Illusions: A Look at Who Backs School Vouchers, Who Profits, and the Dismal Performance of Vouchers to Date." PFAW Web site. http://www.pfaw.org.

53. Rothstein, R., M. Carnoy, and L. Benveniste. (2000). *Can Public Schools Learn from Private Schools? Case Studies in the Public and Private Nonprofit Sector.* Washington, DC: Economic Policy Institute.

54. Ibid.

55. People for the American Way Foundation. "Grand Illusions." http://www.pfaw.org.

56. Easton, D. (1994). "A Worm in the Apple: How Vouchers Would Undermine Learning." In: *Voices on Choices: The Education Reform Debate,* edited by K. L. Billingsley. San Francisco, CA: Pacific Research Institute for Public Policy, p. 37.

57. U.S. Department of Education. (1997, September 23). "Impact of Vouchers on Schooling." Department of Education Web site. http://www.ed.gov.

58. Institute on Taxation and Economic Policy. (2000, February). *An Analysis of the Proposed School Tuition Subsidies in the Virginia Children's Educational Opportunity Act 2000.* Washington, DC: Institute on Taxation and Economic Policy, p. 1.

59. U.S. Department of Education. "Impact of Vouchers on Schooling."

60. U.S. Department of Education, Office of the Undersecretary. (1998). "Barriers, Benefits, and Costs of Using Private Schools to Alleviate Overcrowding in Public Schools. Final Report of Analysis and Highlights." Washington, DC: U.S. Department of Education, p. 3.

61. Wypijewski, J. (2000, December 25). "Back to the Back of the Bus." *The Nation Magazine* 271 (no. 21): 18.

62. U.S. Department of Education. "Impact of Vouchers on Schooling."

63. ReThinking Schools. (1997/1998, Winter). "MPS Admission Policies Reward Privilege: A ReThinking Schools Editorial." http://www.rethinkingschools.org.

64. Ibid., p. 2.

65. Ibid., p. 3.

66. The Center for Education Reform. (n.d.) "School Choice Promotes Integration and Tolerance, It Doesn't 'Skim' Students." CER Web site. http://www.edreform.com.

67. American Federation of Teachers. (2000, Fall). "Back to School 2000: What You Need to Know about Vouchers, This Year's Hottest Education Campaign Issue." AFT Web site. http://www.aft.org.

68. Ibid.

69. Kozol, Jonathan. (1996). "The Market Is Not the Answer: An Interview with Jonathan Kozol." In: *Selling Out Our Schools: Vouchers, Markets, and the Future of Public Education,* edited by Robert Lowe and Barbara Miner, section I. Milwaukee, WI: ReThinking Schools.

70. Elmore, R., B. Fuller, and G. Orfield. (1996). "Empirical Research on Educational Choice: What Are the Implications for Policy-Makers?" In: *Who Chooses? Who Loses?*

Chapter Five

•❖ Vouchers and the Law: Drawing Conclusions from Research

In this chapter we will look critically at two well-established voucher systems: the Milwaukee Parental Choice Program (MPCP), and the private national voucher policy in Chile. Our aim is not only to evaluate these experiments, but also to identify the questions we must address as we decide whether voucher programs should be implemented in other locales.

The ten-year-old MPCP, the most systematically studied of the voucher programs, provides an ideological and practical template for other jurisdictions—for those that either have already adopted private voucher programs, such as Cleveland, Washington, D.C., or New York City, and those that have attempted to pass voucher initiatives, such as California and Michigan. The private school voucher experiment in Chile provides an interesting perspective from which to assess the private choice controversy for two reasons: Chile's entire school system has been privatized for more than twenty years; and the neoliberal economic policies of Milton Friedman and the Chicago School of Economics were consciously, copiously, and swiftly implemented there after the military coup in 1973.

EVALUATING RESEARCH ON VOUCHERS PROGRAMS

How does one sort through all the conflicting evidence and claims made by partisan policy makers when attempting to critically examine private choice?

Although analysis of the voluminous data from the scholarly research regarding the MPCP is beyond the scope of this book, we can establish that private voucher opponents and supporters arrive at conflicting results for a few basic yet significant reasons.

→ researchers use different definitions of the "control group" or "set" to which they compare the performance of voucher program participants.

→ researchers use different methodologies to account for socioeconomics, race, gender, culture, linguistic background, family environment, and students' abilities, and unfortunately, many researchers do not consider these variables at all.[1]

→ mainstream researchers believe they can use the same positivistic research methods to study the social and educational world of human beings that scientists employ when they seek to understand the physical world.

Positivism, the basis of the scientific method, postulates that truth arises only from scientifically produced knowledge of a material nature. Positivistic researchers study human beings and their actions much as they would geography or chemical elements, paying little attention to the cultural and social fundamentals that configure the complexity of the human educational experience. They prefer to focus their priorities on "hard evidence" derived from the scientific method.

Joe Kincheloe, noted scholar and director of the Urban Educational Project at City University of New York (CUNY), has pointed out the shortcomings of the positivistic tradition of epistemological research. It assumes that *things* can be isolated and studied as individual fragments, numerically quantified, and understood as parts—of society, race, culture, gender or linguistic background. "When applied to psychology and education," Kincheloe writes, "physical science methods apply tools to control human beings." Thus students as research subjects are "used and controlled just like any other *thing*. Positivism loses sight of the idea that . . .humans possess a special *complexity* that sets them apart from other objects of study."[2] Kincheloe refers to the tendency of scientific modernism as a technical research tool—and specifically positivistic modernism—to devalue human beings by treating them as objects to be scrutinized and quantified—not as subjects with varied degrees of complexity who need to be understood compassionately and contextually. Unfortunately, the positivistic thinking that Kincheloe describes is prevalent in most research studies of the MPCP and is responsible for their definitions of student achievement and research methodology. But human beings, Kincheloe argues, are not like products to be tested by the quality assurance department. They cannot be studied simply as de-contextualized objects to be numerically understood and categorized.

If Kincheloe is right—if a positivistic approach is invalid for research on humans as social beings—then what are the implications for scholarly research based on positivistic theory, especially regarding student achievement?

With some of these considerations in mind, let us begin to examine the Milwaukee Parental Choice Program.

MILWAUKEE'S VOUCHER PROGRAM:
THE HISTORICAL AND SOCIAL CONTEXT

Milwaukee is the largest city in Wisconsin, with a population of over one million. Originally a city of primarily white European immigrants, it has undergone dramatic ethnographic, economic, and social transformations in the last three decades. Beginning in 1970, Milwaukee was hit by a series of economic recessions that nearly doubled the poverty rate over the next thirty years—from 11.4 percent of residents with incomes below the poverty level in the 1970's to 22.2 percent by the end of the millennium.[3] As a result, the number of poor students also increased dramatically. In 1970, 15 percent of public school students qualified for free or reduced lunch fees; by 1997 the number had risen to 68.8 percent,[4] despite the touted economic prosperity of the 1990s. And like many other cities, Milwaukee fell victim to the dislocation brought on in part by NAFTA and other global policies that encouraged companies to locate overseas where workers are cheaper and unions are nonexistent, including the paper and textile industries that have all but vanished.

In addition to these economic pressures, racial tensions and inequality also exerted a strong influence on the direction of Milwaukee's public schools. In the late 1970s, the federal courts ordered Milwaukee to desegregate its mostly white public schools, but the majority of white residents refused to endorse judicial, community, or local efforts at desegregating schools. Gradually white families fled to the outlying suburbs and many placed their children in private Catholic schools.

The shift in racial composition and the de-industrialization of the city reconfigured Milwaukee's neighborhoods, human services, and daily urban life. African Americans tended to settle on the north side of the city, while the second largest ethnic group, Hispanics, moved in, first to the city center, then made their way to the south side. Whites filled up the outer rings of suburbs. Currently, twenty-four suburban districts that are 95 percent white encircle the inner city, and Milwaukee remains one of the nation's most highly segregated cities, second only to Chicago.

The effect of this reconfiguration on the public schools was dramatic. From 1978 to 1999, the white student population in Milwaukee public schools shrank from 60 percent of the student body to an astounding 19 percent.[5] The percentage of minority children in Milwaukee schools increased from 28 percent in 1970 to over 80 percent in 1997. Initially, the increase in the minority population of schools was almost all African-American, but in more recent years almost 20 percent of the student body is neither black nor white.[6]

In short, Milwaukee, like many postindustrial cities, is caught up in the neoliberal policy of shifting industrial manufacturing to Third World countries. Countries such as Indonesia, China, Mexico, Malaysia and others in Central and South America are increasingly becoming export economies while the United States imports the goods and services once manufactured in cities like Milwaukee. The consequent economic and social problems associated with shifts in capital and the dislocation of labor have spilled over into the Milwaukee Public School system. The associated lack of funding and the increase in low-income minority students has compelled the system to reexamine its social, economic, racial, and educational practices.

ORIGINS OF THE MILWAUKEE
PARENTAL CHOICE PLAN

Although the media have consistently credited Rep. Annette "Polly" Williams, a Democrat, with the founding of the Milwaukee Parental Choice Plan (MPCP), it was in fact Governor Tommy Thompson, later Secretary of Health and Human Services under George W. Bush, who first introduced the Wisconsin school voucher bill in 1988. The governor's initial bill, Bill 816, would have included all private schools in the voucher program, not just nonsectarian schools. It also would have allowed current private school students (up to sixth grade) to receive vouchers without requiring the schools to implement a "random selection" admissions process or mandating any accountability to the public.[7] The governor's original bill represented a bold step toward "universal vouchers;" however, the bill failed when the democrats successfully removed it from the state budget.

In 1989, Thompson tried again, this time with a bill modified to exclude religious private schools. On October 11, Williams introduced an alternative bill (Assembly Bill 601) that modified the governor's proposal, limiting it to an experimental "targeted" voucher program—targeted specifically at families with incomes equal to 1.75 percent of the poverty line or lower. The number of students who could participate in the voucher experiment was legally limited as well to 1.5 percent of the 100,000 students eligible, students currently attending a private school were excluded, random selection of students was required, minimal school performance standards were imposed, and an annual audit of the program was mandated.[8] The bill passed by one vote in the state legislature. Beginning in the 1990–1991 school year, targeted vouchers, for the first time in modern American history, had become a reality.

The appeal of the MPCP was threefold: 1) public funds were funneled *only* to nonsectarian private schools inside the Milwaukee city limits; 2) it offered support to the children who needed it most—low-income minority children enrolled in inadequate programs in dilapidated facilities; The MPCP private voucher program continues to be targeted at low-income families at or below 1.75 percent of the poverty level. However, in a 1997 interview in the *Journal Sentinel,* Milwaukee mayor John Norquist revealed that he intended to either raise or phase out the income qualifications.[9] That adjustment would move the program away from William's limited, targeted voucher plan and closer to closer to Thompson's original bill, which called for broad, universal vouchers. With George W. Bush as president, Norquist would see support for his idea grow. 3) it promised to help all public schools by introducing competition, which MPCP proponents had for years argued was lacking in the public school system. In 1995, however, the Wisconsin legislature radically changed the MPCP. It voted to allow religious schools to enter the voucher program (a controversial decision that has been appealed all the way to the U.S. Supreme Court, but most recently upheld.[10]), lifted limits on the number of children eligible, and dropped requirements that at least 35 percent of those at voucher schools be students who pay tuition. It also cut off funding for data collection and yearly evaluations of the MPCP. According to the new law, the Legislative Audit Bureau of Wisconsin is required to file only a brief annual report. Accountability requirements were virtually removed,[11] and students from kindergarten to grades three who were already attending private schools became eligible to participate.

On June 10, 1998, the Wisconsin State Supreme Court declined to consider the legislation in *Jackson v. Benson.* The high court's decision had the immediate effect of upholding the Milwaukee voucher plan by allowing the state to provide direct support to sectarian schools. This decision was not only a tremendous victory for those seeking public funding for parochial school education in Wisconsin; it would also change the entire mission, scope, and reality of the MPCP, and it would have major implications for national public policy.

Initially, the program was modest, with just about 742 students participating in the 1993–1994 school year. However, with the Supreme Court in effect allowing for the state to subsidize religious schools, the number of participants in the program is rising.[12] In the 1998–1999 school year 87 schools participated in the voucher program with 6,200 students enrolled in private schools supported by public vouchers. Of this total, thirty secular schools enrolled about 2,200 students while 57 religious schools enrolled about 4,000 students.[13]

The voucher, which is given in the form of a check payable to the student's parents, must be signed over to the school on a quarterly basis. At the beginning of 1996, the program gave out vouchers worth approximately $3,600 (the cost of educating a child in the Milwaukee Public Schools) to about 1,100 students.[14] For the 1997–1998 year, the MPCP voucher was worth $4,696.[15]

Charitable choice policies, recently being considered by the legislature, and well-established private philanthropic scholarship efforts to award grants to targeted students, will have a tremendous impact on the future of the MPCP. In this scenario, many students would have both philanthropic funds or charitable funds *and* public monies in the form of a voucher to spend at the school of their choice. When the program was initially implemented, only 49 percent of a school's attendees could be choice students, but the cap was raised to 65 percent starting in 1994–1995. According to the Center for Education Reform, by the year 2000, 1,650 students were also using what are called "choice scholarships" to attend participating nonsectarian schools.[16] (See chapter six) Schools were allowed to charge costs above and beyond the voucher, but they could only be minimal. Also, in some cases, the program itself augmented transportation benefits that allowed many students to travel outside of their neighborhoods to schools of private choice.[17]

Some estimates have concluded that currently around $28.6 million dollars in state aid has been diverted from the Milwaukee Public School system and directed to private choice schools—the majority of them religious institutions, which currently account for close to one third of all students in the MPCP. Three schools, specifically Bruce Guadalupe, Harambee, and Urban Day, enroll a substantial majority of the MPCP participants and account for 80 percent of all voucher students.[18] According to the 1995 Wisconsin Legislative Audit Bureau report, 23.2 percent of participants in the Milwaukee voucher program in 1994–1995 were enrolled in kindergarten, 61.1 percent had enrolled in kindergarten through third grade, leaving 76 percent of participants in kindergarten through fifth grade.[19]

CHARTING THE MAJOR RESEARCH STUDIES

The following table, compiled by Alex Molnar, at the Center for Education Research, Analysis, and Innovation at the University of Wisconsin-Milwaukee, compares the three most important Milwaukee Parental Choice Program methodological studies, conducted by 1) Jay P. Greene, senior fellow at the Manhattan Institute for Policy Research, Paul Peterson, professor of government and director of the Program on Education Policy and Governance at Harvard University, Jiangtoa Du, professor of statistics at Harvard University,(hereafter referred to as the GPD study), 2) John Witte, professor of political science and public affairs at the University of Wisconsin, and 3) one by Cecilia Rouse of Princeton University.[20]

CONSIDERING THE CONTROL GROUP

Professor John Witte, in his five official evaluations of the MPCP, compared voucher students' average test scores and changes in these scores to the same figures of two other groups, a random sample of Milwaukee public school students and a random sample of low-income Milwaukee public school students. He also combined the choice and nonchoice students into a single sample or "set," and then used statistical controls to account for the impact of family and individual differences (i.e., prior test performance, family income, race, class, and gender) on test scores.

However, Greene, Peterson and Du argue that when Witte compared choice and MPS students, his controls for family and individual characteristics were inadequate.[21] As a result, they adopted a methodology different from Witte's in analyzing the MPCP. They compared students who attended choice schools with those who applied but were not admitted. Because the law mandates a random selection process for vouchers applicants, GPD can argue that their methodology is valid.[22]

In their study, "Methodological Issues in Evaluation Research: The Milwaukee Program,"[23] GPD defend what they term "randomized experimental data" and argue that their positivistic methodology provides reliable randomized data. But are the data subjects truly random? Molnar's critique of positivism suggests that several factors mar the natural experimental efforts and methodology of the GDP study. Most important, no school has actually selected voucher candidates randomly. For example, as Molnar points out, siblings of children already enrolled in choice schools did not have to go through a lottery process but were guaranteed

Table 5.1

Findings of Three Studies of the Milwaukee Parental Choice Program

	Witte	*Greene, Peterson, and Du*	*Rouse*
Main Comparison	Compares voucher students' achievement with that of a random sample of Milwaukee Public School (MPS) students, controlling for observed indi vidual and family characteristics.	Compares voucher students' achievement with that of unsuccessful applicants who returned to the Milwaukee Public Schools.	Compares achievement of successful applicants for vouchers with that of a random sample of Milwaukee Public School students, controlling for an estimate of innate ability and family influences.
Reading Findings	No significant difference between voucher students' achievement and that of the MPS comparison group.	In their 1997 "main analysis": 2–3 percentile rank advantage for voucher students in year four. Conventional levels of statistical significance approached only when 3rd and 4th years are jointly estimated. When background characteristics are controlled for, voucher students' advantage in 1st and 3rd years approaches significance.	Similar to Witte: no statistically significant difference between successful voucher applicants' achievement and that of the MPS comparison group.
Math Findings	No significant difference between Choice students and MPS sample.	5–11 percentile rank advantage for voucher students over unsuccessful Choice applicants in years 3 and 4. Conventional levels of statistical significance achieved in 4th year and in joint estimate of 3rd and 4th years.	Similar to GPD: statistically significant advantage in years 3 and 4 for students selected for Choice schools. Effect size of 0.08–0.12 per year.

	Witte	*Greene, Peterson, and Du*	*Rouse*
Main Statistical Limitations	Does not control for unobserved individual differences. Voucher students who remain in program may be a nonrandom high-scoring group. Does not include school variables (e.g., class size, curricula).	Control group of unsuccessful voucher applicants who return to MPS is a small and shrinking sample (26 in year 4). Control group may be a nonrandom, low-scoring group. Voucher students who remain in program may be a nonrandom, high-scoring group. Does not include school variables (e.g., class size, curricula) that may explain observed differences.	Successful voucher applicants have more educated parents with high expectations: improvement in math scores over time might take place without voucher program. Does not include school variables (e.g., class size, curricula) that may explain observed differences.

Source: Molnar, Alex. (October 1999) "Educational Vouchers: A Review of the Research. When are Significant Results Not So Significant?" Center for Education Research and Analysis, and Innovation. Milwaukee: Wisconsin. (Reprinted with permission)

seats. Furthermore, because lotteries took place at the school level, each school's group of Choice students had its own control group of rejected applicants. Finally, the GPD data did not indicate the particular choice school to which unsuccessful applicants sought admission.[24] To model the lottery process, GPD therefore assumed that Hispanic students applied to predominantly Hispanic schools and that African Americans applied to one of the two other schools with large numbers of African-American voucher recipients. Their rationale was simple: not enough data is available to identify the particular choice school to which a student applied. Given this lack of data they then used ethnicity as a proxy for the schools to which students applied.[25] According to Molnar, this technique of assuming facts not in evidence led GPD authors to leave white students out of their analysis.[26]

Is this methodology based on sound assumptions? Professor Cecilia Rouse of Princeton University has undertaken the most recent ex-

amination of the Milwaukee Parental Choice Program. Rouse's methodology looks at the performance of all students selected to attend Choice
schools (including those who never attended—a relatively small
group—and those who subsequently left the program). Rouse compares this group's performance to that of applicants not admitted to the
MPCP and to a random sample of Milwaukee public school students.
Rather than restricting the sample to those currently receiving vouchers, Rouse includes all those awarded vouchers in the Choice control
group as a better way of assessing the overall impact of the MPCP program. Rouse also does an analysis and comparison between students
who actually attended choice schools and her Milwaukee public school
sample.

In her analysis, Rouse acknowledges numerical and statistical inadequacy—specifically the fact that a large number of students in the
data sets she uses have no total math scores. For 1993, this forced Rouse
to impute the total math score (from scores on the components of the
test) for 40 percent of the unsuccessful Choice applicants and 34 percent for the students in her Milwaukee public schools sample. For 1994,
she had to impute 69 percent of the total math scores for the unsuccessful Choice applicants and 67 percent of the Milwaukee public
school sample.[27]

This lack of data was a problem for all three academic research
teams, as was the fact that the data groups in the MPCP accounted little
for social variables such as class size, school size, curriculum innovation, per-pupil spending, or the socioeconomic profiles of the students,
including their racial, gender, and cultural backgrounds.[28] As a result,
none of the three maintain that these variables have or do not have an
impact on student achievement claims.

ACCOUNTING FOR THE SUBJECTIVE ELEMENTS
OF TEACHING AND LEARNING

What about the subjective *and* objective aspects of teaching? Why are
these topics addressed only in generalities in the scholarly studies?
These important factors seem to have been omitted in all of the research
studies. This is a particularly bewildering omission, because these subjective aspects of teaching—defined here as curriculum design and implementation, teaching methodology, student-teacher interaction—all
constitute the daily life of both students and teachers. Consequently,
they have a tremendous effect on student achievement and educational
opportunities. The fact that they are missing from the research indicts

the positivistic research methodology that Kincheloe counsels against— the tendency, explicit or implicit, conscious or unconscious, to ignore the sum total of the human condition and students' multiple intelligences in favor of generating formula-driven, technocratic numerical data from state mandated testing The reductionist, positivistic paradigm coaxes researchers to view students as inanimate objects of study. Consequently, the major academic studies done on the MPCP do not effectively speak to these important subjective issues; nor do they address what actually goes on in day-to-day interactions between students and teachers.

Greene, Peterson, and Du would, of course, disagree. They would argue that when they analyzed student achievement levels in the MPCP, they took into consideration such elements as the students' mothers' education, educational expectations, parental time spent with the student, how many times the parent contacted the school, students' participation in school organizations, family income, and the grade applied. But Greene and Peterson acknowledge, in an earlier article on their study, that this was done through parental questionnaires, prepared by the MPCP, and that Greene, Peterson and Du had no opportunity to review the questions, let alone provide input into the manner in which they were framed.

Thus it is difficult to develop intellectual confidence in such methodological approaches or their findings. For example, when discussing their methodology for controlling for family backgrounds among MPCP students, Greene and Peterson readily admit that their first analysis revolved around parental questionnaires but that background information supplied was for only 47 percent of the selected students and 36 percent of the control group. The number of cases available for analysis is therefore considerably reduced and the estimates become less reliable.[29] However, in their second analysis they do report that they controlled for education and income differences.[30]

If one adds to the problems with their data Greene and Peterson's admission that all data was blocked for ethnicity—a way of saying that ethnicity was not taken into consideration—and gender difference was controlled only in the main analysis by numerics, we are left with severe methodological shortcomings. Why did Greene and Peterson employ this methodology? They argue that "blocking is designed specifically to adjust for the fact that random assignment did not occur between the entire choice and nonselect populations and instead occurred within 72 possible small lotteries." Therefore, they argue, they had to block to control the real world of randomized studies.[31] But does this strategy answer Witte's concern and is it acceptable research?

CONSIDERING CLAIMS TO OBJECTIVITY
IN RESEARCH

Theoretically, objectivity is the starting point for all scholarly inquiry; in reality, it is impossible to achieve. Though they might not like to admit it, all researchers have biases, intentional or unintentional, in both their approach and methodology. New York University political scientist Jay Rosen has pointed out that objectivity as a theory of how to arrive at the truth is intellectually bankrupt. Everything researchers have learned about the pursuit of truth tells us that in one way or another, the knower is incorporated into the known.[32] The popular notion of science, as Kincheloe points out, assumes that scientists' activities are shaped not by their values, but by their intellect and curiosity. This belief is misleading, because values—both the researcher's values and the predominant values of the surrounding culture—continually shape research. If educational researchers operate in a college of education dominated by positivist assumptions about the nature of research, for example, they may lose their tenure and career by conducting research that deviates from the rules of positivist methods. Furthermore, because grants from government and private foundations often determine the type of research that takes place, research typically reflects the values and interests of funding agencies.[33]

Even so, many progressive researchers maintain that educational research cannot be reduced to mere quantitative exploration, extrapolation, and bean-counting but must take into account, in both constructing and applying methodology, issues such as poverty, gender, culture, and race. Thought, they argue, cannot be meaningfully separated from human feelings and actions—or from one's subjective and objective place in history. They contend that all research is subjective and biased—that objectivity is a myth and that the researcher is always implicated in the object to be researched. Some go even further, arguing that if researchers incorporate this understanding into their research, the research itself would, of necessity, paradigmatically shift. By making his or her research findings public and reconciling them with disparate points of view, the researcher can become a self-conscious analyst, aware of how his or her particular methodology and assumptions are historically situated and implicated in research, methodologies, and findings.

If progressive educational researchers are correct, and if we can correctly assume that the studies by GPD, Witte, and Rouse are based on reductionist research methodologies, then we must ask, are they really measuring student achievement and teaching professionalism? Or are they simply measuring how well students perform on standardized tests and how efficaciously particular schools organize their learning and teaching to permit them to accomplish this feat?

The impact of reductionism on the study of educational methods is one of the most difficult subjects to bring to the public debate. Many reductionist research studies depend on observation within strictly controlled teaching situations that have little to do with everyday classrooms. What teachers perceive as the irrelevance of such research relates to what noted educational author Lee Shulman labeled "task validity," that is, the degree to which the environment in a laboratory is similar to the complex dynamics of the classroom.[34]

What happens when we choose to adjust specific portions of educational research to see how our students might be faring? Can we separate the question of how well a program is "working" from political issues such as the purpose of education, what students *should* be learning, and what techniques might be best employed by pedagogical professionals? Many researchers are quick to proudly proclaim their independence, impartiality, and neutrality. However, they fail to speak to the purpose(s) of education—other than how education might help students pass tests so they can enter a global economy that is becoming increasingly less competitive.

THE ISSUE OF DATA DEFICIENCY

It is important to remember that regardless of the methodology or techniques they used to measure student achievement, all researchers involved in the MPCP studies had to contend with a small—and shrinking—sample of students. Greene and Peterson noted that cases are missing from the analysis for several reasons—students were not in school on days tests were given, and students were not tested every year. Furthermore, because low-income, urban, minority families are highly mobile, many of these students left both Choice and public schools during the study period. [35]

This lack of data and evidence leads to a deficit of information. Consequently, the facts must be considered incomplete, and conclusions drawn from them must be regarded as more speculative than reliable. Peterson acknowledges this deficiency, noting that without data beyond the Milwaukee program's first four years, one can only speculate as to whether his conclusions are warranted.[36]

REPORTING THE RESULTS OF
THE MPCP STUDIES

Although researchers' conclusions vary as to the effectiveness and achievements of the MPCP, they do tell us something. Greene, Peterson, and Du conclude that participation in the MPCP confers academic achievement benefits to Choice students. They argue that if vouchers were universal, that is, provided to all parents and their children, the achievement gap between white and minority students in reading would be significantly narrowed, and in mathematics, completely eliminated. But Witte finds that Choice students in Milwaukee perform no differently than unsuccessful applicants,[37] and Rouse's conclusions are similar to Witte's.[38] Molnar's studies and other public policy institute research analyses indicate that the impact of vouchers and private choice has been less than favorable for schools, students, or society.[39]

Compounding the problems of accurately analyzing the efficacy of the MPCP through the data available is the fact that much of the research is rhetoric driven, often misquoted, and frequently and speciously miscommunicated by the media. The Heritage Foundation, in its July 14, 2000, publication, *School Choice 2000,* offers a case in point. It reports that Witte finds choice to be "a useful tool to aid low-income families."[40] But this claim is not correct. Witte is far more guarded in his assessment. In his book *The Market Approach to Education,* Witte asks us to consider the following question. Why do so many businesses and political proponents of educational choice have blind faith in competition as the salvation of education in our cities? Witte suggests that they may not really think about what they are saying, relying instead on slogans that become self-fulfilling prophecies. And, of course, they may not be supporting choice with the education of inner city youth in mind at all; instead, they may see private choice as a way to retaliate against educational bureaucracies and teachers' unions.[41]

Even though Witte does support "targeted vouchers" in the same book, his support is tied to a larger, more substantial and compassionate defense of public education in general. He notes that the problems of American education have been so exaggerated over the last decade that a targeted voucher program may not provide a wake up call to public schools but will serve instead as a constant reminder and even irritant for those public school systems.[42] But one thing is certain: contrary to the impression given by the Heritage Foundation, Witte does not believe private choice itself is either a panacea or a mechanism for reforming education and increasing achievement at all inner city schools. And unlike Greene, Peterson, and Du, he is suspicious of the objectives of "universal voucher" proponents and apprehensive about their implications for public educational policies.

HOW ACHIEVEMENT IS MEASURED

Many educators and progressive policy makers complain that much of the official research on the issue of student achievement, so central to the MPCP researchers' claims, is mired in old-fashioned, uncontested paradigms of intelligence. The research has been based on measurements conducted through calibrating mechanisms and high-stakes standardized testing appended to traditional notions of intellectual aptitude. Many modern scholars contend that achievement is a complex and a multi-definitional concept and that the contentious assumptions behind it beg for critical discourse not found in these studies.

To assume that all educational stakeholders have the same definition of student achievement creates a hollow public policy debate, because there is no general intellectual agreement or public accord about the meaning of the term or the implications of defining it one way or another. Most attempts to define student achievement are still wedded to traditional and technical notions of quantified, positivistic intelligence that are more interested in method and efficiency than in a larger sense of educational purpose. As a result, a concept of education as training for state tests based on the productive needs of the global workplace has replaced the idea of education as a means for the development of a productive, insightful individual life and a commitment to societal justice.

The public debate over high-stakes testing and student achievement has ignored some of the crucial questions. This oversight is significant, because researchers rely solely on the results of these tests to bolster their point of view or policy recommendations. However, questions such as these must be addressed.

> What should we be teaching our elementary students and what should they be learning?
> What are the roles of standards and assessment in the conception of education?
> How can we use evaluation and valid assessment to further authentic instruction?
> What should we be assessing and why?
> What does it mean to be intelligent, and how will our definition of intelligence impact how we teach and measure student performance?

What about emotional intelligence—should we be assessing it as well?

What about multiple intelligences and testing?

What is a problem-based curriculum? How can we test skills wedded to thinking?

Should we rely solely on one test, or should we develop new methods and instruments of assessment on a weekly or monthly basis?

Do the test scores really tell us much about how students are performing?

Take the skill of reading, for example. Reading critically and reading uncritically are simply not the same processes. To read critically implies thinking critically—a process whereby the reader actively engages in a silent dialogue with the author as an attentive, questioning participant in the process of interpretation. To read without comprehension represents little more than the act of decoding—what Donaldo Macedo has aptly called "barking at print."[43] Yet reading is usually broken up into its components and taught as phonics, comprehension, language, etc. When doing phonics the student is not concerned with comprehension. Understanding vocabulary is divorced from both as lists of vocabulary words are constructed for memorization purposes. Spelling is taught as a separate subject, again, usually relying on assembled lists to be memorized. By breaking reading down into separate component parts, teachers fail to teach students the interdisciplinary connections and processes necessary to comprehend what they read. Students do not learn how the parts make up the whole. Reading and its component skills become so many marbles in a bag.

A person can have specific skills but not know how to use them for a given task. For example, knowing how to use a hammer does not mean that one can build a house. This is especially true if the instruction in learning how to use a hammer was broken down into its component parts and practiced in isolation from the construction of the house. However, these insights seem to be lost on the educational researchers that studied Milwaukee students' achievement in reading. State mandated testing, which forms the basis for the researchers' claims, relies on inauthentic assessment of students' skills—inauthentic because it breaks subjects down into isolated fragments. This is especially true in the elementary school, where reading comprehension is tested by reading short passages rather than testing reading comprehension within the body of literature. By tying standardized tests in primary school to staged developmental readiness, specific skill acquisition, and rote memorization, we have designed tests that assess knowledge as information retention and competency as specific skill acquisition.

In her book, *Contradictions of School Reform: The Educational Cost of Standardized Testing,* Linda McNeil reports that teachers complained that after reading only short passages like the one above in preparation for the test, students were actually hampered in their ability to read critically. One sixth grade teacher found that when he gave his students a Newberry Award–winning book to read, they stopped after a few minutes. They were accustomed to reading brief, disjointed passages in preparation for the test and did not develop and sustain reading habits. Nor were they able to carry information from the first chapter to the next. As a result of the tests and the classroom preparation time devoted to passing them, students' ability to read critically was actually undermined.[44] In short, they were learning how *not* to read.

One of the problems with standardized testing lies in the assumptions behind it—assumptions that serve to define notions of intelligence. These assumptions reduce learning and knowing to preordained linear stages and thus argue that students in the younger grades simply cannot reason. This approach to testing achievement fosters low expectations of students and leads to the design of bankrupt educational opportunities for their learning. Yet it is precisely this approach that has been the foundation for the researcher's claims.

Take for example, the Stanford Achievement Test given in California, which mirrors the achievement tests given in all areas of the nation, including Milwaukee.[45] The test begins with reading vocabulary. Students are asked to choose a word or group of words that means the same, or about the same, as the underlined word given them. For example:

> Something that is *huge* is very
>   a. damp
>   b. big
>   c. pretty
>   d. bright

The test goes on to ask students to read a sentence, use the words in the sentence to help them figure out what the underlined word means:

> Because the child was very *cautious,* he looked both ways before crossing the street. *Cautious* means—
>   a. Happy
>   b. Silly

c. Playful
d. Careful

As the test proceeds, the students are asked to read a sentence in a box. They are then to choose an answer in which the underlined word is used in the same way:

He had a *ring* on his finger.
In which sentence does the word *ring* mean the same thing as the sentence above?
a. He lost his new key *ring*.
b. The teacher will *ring* the bell.
c. The children held hands to form a *ring*.
d. She was wearing a gold *ring*.

There is no doubt that students in the elementary grades need to know the meaning and definition of words. However, to test word comprehension with short, irrelevant sentences does little to foster a critical understanding of vocabulary as it pertains to the act of critically interpreting the written word. If we want students to develop effective communication skills, of which language usage is paramount, we need to instruct them to use language in multidimensional contexts so they can see the varied uses of language. Simply knowing the meaning of a word does not adequately assess whether a student can use or understand the word within interdisciplinary contexts. Furthermore, by reducing the test to simply vocabulary, teachers are encouraged to spend instructional time to teach word recognition within fragmented, as opposed to holistic, contexts.

The test never asks students to use the words themselves, thereby helping them seat vocabulary within their own subjectivity and context. And of course the reductionism within the test itself exacerbates the reductionism within teaching. Practice for this test would entail having students read small irrelevant passages similar to the ones in the test, as opposed to reading critically, in depth, within multidimensional contexts.

In the reading comprehension section of the test, students are asked to read each question about the passage, then decide which is the best answer to the question. The students are giving the following sample:

TALL TALES
Light from the candles bounced of the dark windows and made strange shadows on the walls. After hearing Uncle Sal's stories, we all sat nerv-

ously, listening for creaking footsteps and squeaking doors. Leo was the first to speak.

"You don't really believe all those stories about the old Potter place, do you, Uncle Sal?"

"I don't know," Uncle Sal said slowly. "No one has seen Mr. Potter in town for the last five years. Some say he hasn't set foot out of the house."

1) What time of day is it in the story?
   a. Morning
   b. Noon
   c. Afternoon
   d. Evening
2) What kind of stories did Uncle Sal tell?
   a. Peaceful
   b. Scary
   c. Sad
   d. Funny

Not only do the questions contained in the comprehension section of the reading examination fail to ask for any reasoning, relying on recall answers only, but the test itself relies on short, irrelevant passages that are not linked from story to story. The entire conception of reading is divorced from higher-order thinking and what it means to critically interpret a story. Instead, reading is reduced to remembering the facts of a brief story for sequencing or recall purposes. Students are asked to perform, not think.

The concept in the number section of the test is no better. Here, students are asked to read each question and then choose the best answer:

Which is the numeral for twenty-three?
   a. 23
   b. 203
   c. 230
   d. 2003

The test encourages students to *do* math, not to *think* mathematically. Once again, no reasoning is required—solely simple recognition divorced from critical thinking. Math is not seen as something that is necessary for real-life problem solving; instead, it is reduced to identifying numbers in rote isolation. Computation is divorced from meaningful life problems, and math is presented as if it existed in a vacuum.

The mathematics applications section in the test is similar. Students are given word problems and asked to pick the right answer after applying the correct mathematical formula and computation. Yet once again, students are not asked to think mathematically but instead are asked to manipulate numbers relative to trivial and irrelevant word problems. The test does not assess whether students understand the algorithms they are applying. They are never asked to explain their mathematical reasoning, reengineer and explain the thinking processes they used to arrive at the right answer, or even use the algorithm in varied, and multidimensional contexts. Understanding is equated to mathematical manipulation, not mathematical problem solving within real-life contexts. As a result, preparation for the examination also concentrates on doing math as opposed to thinking mathematically, and students spend inordinate amounts of preparation time ritually manipulating numbers—often without knowing or caring why.

The spelling section of the examination concentrates on finding the word that is not spelled correctly by having students read a list of words. Fragmented and divorced from any relevant contexts, spelling is assessed in rote isolation from reading or writing, where words and language are used. The result collapses into the use of spelling lists and memorization of words as vehicles for passing this portion of the test.

Grammar and language expression are also tested in rote isolation from reading comprehension. The test goes on to assess science by relying on short passages, as well. For example, one question asks students:

> If you have to ride a bicycle at night, you should—
> a. ride facing the traffic
> b. wear reflective clothing
> c. make noise so you can be heard
> d. carry an extra rider to help you

Students are never asked to construct or develop their own products or experimental designs, and thus we do not know what they really know about science—only what they have memorized. Further, they are never asked to explain their answers, to give reasons for why they believe what they believe. The tests fail to tell us whether students understand the scientific process, for they are never asked to observe, test, or otherwise expose scientific hypotheses and ideas to critical scrutiny.

For those who propose that schooling should be designed to help students learn *how to think* and not *what to think*, the standardized tests prevalent throughout the nation are not simply ineffective methods for assessing students; they are harmful instruments that promise to stupefy rather than edify. They fail to test active, critical thinking, and because they are mandated and tied to teacher and principal perform- ance and job security, they actually perpetuate poor teaching and inau- thentic learning. They create an educational environment of irrational necessity. This does not simply imposé a minor disservice to educators but culminates in a ruinous educational theory and practice—a cruel hoax perpetrated on students, teachers, and the public at large.

Critical thinking advocates argue that authentic testing would and must concentrate on helping students in the elementary grades learn to monitor their own thinking and performance—to engage in *metacognition*. The tests should focus on assessing whether a student has understood the logic of what they are studying. As the tests are cur- rently constructed, students have little interest in seeing if they have passed, where they might have erred and why, or what the test actually means. They do not look at these tests as a tool for supervising their own thinking, which is why many students simply fill in the blanks or bubble in the "answers" without thinking. Thus, not only are the tests inau- thentic, but they fail to motivate either the teacher or the student to monitor their own thinking for purposes of self-evaluation and correc- tion; in other words, neither teachers, parents, nor students profit from the test results. Authentic testing would engage students in metacogni- tion within a relevant, problem-posing curriculum. By testing reason- ing, authentic assessments would actually help students think critically rather than teaching them to mindlessly take tests.

For example, as we saw by looking at the Stanford Achievement Test, traditional science assessment still concentrates primarily on hav- ing students passively memorize science information, though what is needed is to help students develop a deeper connection between scien- tific understanding and relevant, real-life situations as they probe the inner logic of what they are studying.

A good example of authentic assessment in science can be found in the Massachusetts Department of Education response test questions posed to elementary students concerning *endangerment* and *extinction:*

When prairie dogs are near farms they eat farmers' crops. Be- cause of this, farmers have killed thousands of prairie dogs. Black- footed ferrets eat prairie dogs. Explain what problem this poses for the ferrets and why this is a problem.

The following was one student's response:

> If there aren't enough prairie dogs for the ferrets to eat, many of them
> will starve to death. That is because prairie dogs are their main food.
> If farmers kill most or all of the prairie dogs, this will be a big problem

because most of the ferrets might die. This would mean that their population would become very low. This would mean that they would become extinct. Then there would never be any other ferrets. And maybe this would not just be a problem for the ferrets. If other animals depended on the ferrets for their food, they would become extinct too.[46]

Clearly what is being tested here is scientific reasoning as it pertains to the concepts of extinction and endangerment. We can see that the student understands the logic of extinction because she

- can clearly understand the problem or question at issue
- can clearly use language to identify the problem with accuracy and clarity
- can use the concept *extinction* critically
- can make plausible inferences based on substantiated assumptions
- can recognize assumptions and marshal evidence for them
- can understand the implications and consequences of extinction
- can synthesize the subject matter insights and transfer these insights into new situations

Compare and contrast this assessment question with the Stanford Achievement Test of the same grade that asks students:

Which is characteristic of an animal?
    a. Needs oxygen to live
    b. Has roots
    c. Uses carbon dioxide
    d. Uses sunlight to make food.[47]

Compare and contrast this with the portion of the Stanford Achievement Test that provides a black and white picture of an ecosystem containing water and asks:

Which of these characteristics would best suit an animal living in this environment?
    a. Sharp hooves
    b. Fur
    c. Branched horns
    d. Webbed feet

In mathematics, authentic assessment would look similar to that discussed in science. In a third grade assessment adapted from the *New Standards Project* in Wisconsin in 1991, the following math problem was given to students.

The class is told they will be getting a thirty-gallon aquarium. The class will have twenty-five dollars to spend on fish. The students will plan which fish to buy using the *Choosing Fish for Your Aquarium* (available at any pet store) to help them choose the fish. The brochure explains the size of the fish, how much they cost, and their needs. Students choose as many different kinds of fish as they can, and then they write a letter to the principal of the school explaining the fish they have chosen.

In the letter they must:
   a. tell the principal how many of each kind of fish to buy
   b. give reasons why they chose the fish they did
   c. and exhibit how they are not overspending and that the fish will not be too crowded or non-compatible[48]

This is far different than the Stanford Achievement Test, which asks for no student reasoning and simply requires that students look at pictures and statements and circle correct answers. Here the student must write, compute mathematics, identify problems, make decisions, support their thinking with reasoning, and use the information they are given critically.

The Milwaukee Stanford Achievement Test is similar to the California Stanford Achievement Test. Both of them measure rote memorization and regurgitation. However, GDP, Witte, and Rouse use these tests to buttress their claims as to student achievement and the efficacy of private vouchers.

For David Hursh, director of teacher education at the Warner Graduate School of Education and Human Development at the University of Rochester, the pervasive use of high-stakes standardized tests and economic necessity–driven educational curricula suggest an intent to restrict educators to a particular kind of thinking and teaching—the kind that views education as a process of producing economically productive individuals.[49] Hursh argues that when the notion of schooling as preparation for testing and work replaces the idea of education as the path to citizenship, intelligence, and rational and emotional growth, then intellectual measurement is reduced to evaluating how well students acquire basic skills and memorize bits and pieces of discipline-oriented information. Kincheloe, Hursh, and others contend that assessment of student achievement based on how well students memorize information, acquire skills out of context, and perform on standardized tests is neither a positive nor a productive measurement of intellectual growth or moral and emotional development. It provides little if any reliable evidence for or against student achievement. Research based on such procedures incorporates a flawed methodology that results in biased, unreliable research.

For example, People for the American Way (PFAW) recently examined research by Paul Peterson that allegedly shows that African American students realize higher student achievement rates and actually operate more successfully in voucher schools than in public schools. The PFAW has characterized this assertion as an "exercise in deceptive mathematics," arguing that the mathematical manipulation behind Peterson's claims of voucher success, in at least one of three cities studied, involved averaging all African American scores (test results) together and including a subgroup of sixth graders whose scores were atypical of the rest of the student groups. PFAW claims that by reporting only the average and not the grade-by-grade scores, Peterson made it appear that all African American students performed better in private schools. In fact, according to PFAW, what Peterson's actual numbers demonstrate upon close scrutiny, is the contrary: that there is no difference between private and public school students in test score achievement for any group of students, except for that one atypical group.[50]

It is important to note that the financial supporters of Peterson's research are the same right-wing foundations that are the financiers of the provoucher movement —financiers whom we consider in more detail below. And this is precisely what Kincheloe, Hursch, and others implore us to consider when combing through controversial research findings—specifically, how the "knower" is implicated in that which is to "be known."

John Witte is conscious of the problems inherent in methodology and evaluation of the MPCP. The quick-fix approach to controversial and complex issues in education has frustrated even the most ardent defenders of academic research, such as Witte, and he makes no apologies for his thinking regarding hasty and uncritical educational reform efforts. In his most recent book regarding the MPCP, Witte points out that the pressure to produce quick and often premature evaluation results has skewed many studies. Meaningful educational change takes time. To expect students to react immediately to new environments is nonsensical. Yet for high-profile experiments, first-year or even more immediate results are eagerly awaited and zealously reported.[51]

Keeping some of these key methodological considerations and key criticisms in mind, let us now turn to specifically analyzing the Milwaukee Parental Choice Program (MPCP).

THE MILWAUKEE PAVE PROGRAM AND
THE GROWTH OF RELIGIOUS SCHOOLS

We spoke in the first chapter of some of the constitutional issues involved in public funding of religious schools, along with some of the claims made by those who support public funding of private, nonsecular schools and those who do not. In Milwaukee, the majority of recipients of public monies in the form of private vouchers are religious schools.

No discussion of religious schools or student admission practices in MPCP can be understood without considering the organization, Partners Advancing Values in Education (PAVE). Formerly the Milwaukee Archdiocesan Education Foundation, PAVE, founded in 1992, is a nonprofit organization privately funded through corporate, foundation, and individual donations. It is one of the largest nonpublic programs in the country that provides private educational scholarships. Although chapter six looks specifically at scholarships and their role in the privatization of education, it is important that we look at the PAVE program as part of our consideration of the MPCP.

The PAVE scholarship program was created in the summer of 1992 by a group of business, civic, and religious leaders. Their stated goal was to address the educational needs of Milwaukee's low-income children. How these needs were defined, and based on what reasoning, is not fully ascertainable. PAVE provides low-income families with educational scholarships worth half of the tuition charged by a private religious or private nonreligious school, up to a maximum of $1,000, for elementary and middle school students. It also provides $1,500 scholarships for high school students to attend private schools. PAVE may refuse any applicants it wishes and for basically any reason.[52] To enter the program, families must live within the city of Milwaukee and they must meet the same criteria established for participation in the MPCP. Applications are furnished to parents who apply through the school of their choice and the school administrators help parents fill out the PAVE application. Families who are eligible receive a grant for more than one child and grants are also available to students who do not qualify for a state voucher. If a scholarship is granted, parents or their proxies become responsible for paying the remaining portion of the school tuition.

During PAVE's first year, it received 4,094 student-scholarship applications and awarded 2,089 scholarships. In 1997–1998 PAVE awarded $4.1 million to 4,371 students who attended 112 private and religious schools in Milwaukee. Most of these scholarship students qualified for the MPCP private voucher to attend the school of their choice for the 1998–1999 school year. However, approximately 1,000 students enrolled in religious schools still needed PAVE scholarships to continue their education.[53]

Currently, half of PAVE's scholarships are awarded to students who already attend private schools. Approximately 95 percent of PAVE-supported students attend religious schools, and 60 percent of these students are enrolled in Catholic schools. PAVE enrolls a higher percentage of white students than Milwaukee Public Schools.[54] Although PAVE does award scholarships to secular schools, it is fair to question whether their aim is to help establish religious schools through private scholarships and whether their agenda is devoted to the further dismantling of public schools in favor of a private conglomerates of religious schools. One thing is certain: their goal is to help subsidize the transfer and relocation of children from public schools to private schools. As we shall see, such private scholarship organizations are flourishing state-by-state at an accelerating rate throughout the nation. Between the years of 1996 and 1997, PAVE raised millions of dollars in private funds for students in the 1996–1998 school years. From 1997 through 1998, the Heritage Foundation notes that in the MPCP, the number of low-income children benefiting from school choice increased to 6,000.[55]

However, PAVE does not like publicity surrounding its students' achievements nor do they appreciate any public scrutiny of their schools. They prefer to focus on parental satisfaction within PAVE-sponsored schools, and they seem to be accountable only to their immediate constituency. For example, the last evaluation of the PAVE program conducted in 1996 examined student discipline in participating schools, the mobility of families, and the reasons that many families did not participate in the PAVE program. However, the only evaluation of PAVE's student achievement was done in 1994 and this study depended entirely on the voluntary cooperation of parents. This is hardly an in depth analysis and thus no conclusions should be drawn from the mainly anecdotal evaluations that have been completed regarding the PAVE program's effect on student achievement.[56]

In 1999, ReThinking Schools (RTS) attempted to gather specific information about private schools and student achievement. According to RTS, when they began their examination, PAVE warned voucher schools against allowing ReThinking Schools to conduct research. Daniel McKinley, executive director of PAVE, agreed in a telephone interview that newspaper reporting generally helped increase understanding of the voucher program. But McKinley said he had recommended that voucher schools not speak with ReThinking Schools because of the publication's antagonism toward the voucher program.[57] Until more information regarding the PAVE program is released to the public, it will be difficult if not impossible to ascertain the efficacy of PAVE's claims regarding students' achievement.

ARGUMENT: VOUCHER SCHOOLS LEAD TO BETTER PUBLIC SCHOOLS AND HIGHER STUDENT ACHIEVEMENT

Elsewhere in this chapter, we noted the difficulty of defining exactly what is meant by *student achievement*. If our assessment of student achievement is based on high stakes testing, then the answer as to what constitutes student achievement will be born from this assumption. However, if the notion of student achievement is not wedded to strictly standardized tests but also incorporates assessment of multiple forms of intelligence, then the answer will be more difficult to surmise.

Greene, Peterson and Du use the results of standardized tests exclusively as a baseline for measuring student achievement. Based on results from these standardized tests, they conclude that attendance at voucher schools had a positive cumulative achievement effect that showed up only after three or four years. For those students in the program three or four years or more, Greene, Peterson and Du found that the choice students had significantly higher scores in mathematics and reading (see Table 5.1) than nonchoice students. The research compared students who applied to the program but were not admitted to those who were admitted and enrolled.

Paul Peterson, who has spent a decade studying private choice, claims that the Milwaukee Parental Choice Program has led to notable improvements in test scores. But in two contradictory findings Peterson, along with Greene, also acknowledge that the gains in student achievement resulting from privatization are in dispute because of disagreements over methodology and student assessment data. So even though researchers from two different traditions have attempted to measure the comparative efficiency of public and private schools, neither has succeeded in providing an answer.[58] The best that can accurately be said about the Milwaukee choice experiment on the basis of standardized test scores is that privatization in education *may* result in efficiency gains.[59]

Dr. Cecilia Rouse has conducted the most recent scholarly study of the MPCP. Using Witte's data, she found that a significant advantage in math achievement was apparent in voucher students who were in the program for three or four years, but her research found no improved achievement in reading scores for voucher school students. Her analysis and methodology has also been discussed in the prior section.

Nevertheless, on the basis of this incomplete and ill-defined research, the Center for Education Reform recently announced that competition from school choice not only improves public schools and boosts students' achievements levels, but it also seems to be the key to future graduation rates and wage gains. The center bases its conclusions on the Heritage Foundation's recent publication entitled *Policy Review.* Its author, Nina Shokraii Rees, claims that actual student achievement rises with competition.[60] But once again, we must define the concept of student achievement and the basis for measuring it. The Heritage Foundation is noticeably mute on both counts, preferring to silently assume that student achievement is best addressed and measured by standardized tests.

ARGUMENT: VOUCHER SCHOOLS DO NOT LEAD TO BETTER PUBLIC SCHOOLS AND HIGHER STUDENT ACHIEVEMENT

Professor John Witte was appointed to conduct the five annual investigations required by government legislation authorizing the MPCP. His findings, unlike Greene and Peterson, showed that attending voucher schools conferred no achievement advantage to students. However, since the Wisconsin legislature expanded the voucher program in 1995 to allow more students and religious schools to participate and at the same time cut off funding for evaluation of the MPCP, the debate remains unresolved.[61] Voucher schools currently are not required to participate in standardized testing programs; nor are they required to administer the same tests as public schools or to share testing data they have on their students or their performances with any state, private, or local body. As a result, it is doubtful that the annual Wisconsin Legislative Audit Report will have much to say about student achievement, no matter what definition is used, and more to say about the particulars of whether a school is accredited, what type of curriculum it employs, its level of financing, and other budgetary concerns.[62]

The controversy over voucher accountability exploded in 1998, when Wisconsin Legislators passed a bill that would allow private schools to spend taxpayer dollars without any oversight by federal and state laws. According to William Lynch, an attorney who has represented the Milwaukee branch of the NAACP, there simply is not sufficient accountability built into the requirements for voucher schools. "There's certainly nowhere near the level of accountability that is expected from other publicly funded, tax-supported schools," Lynch says. This lack of accountability, he maintains, "interferes with the public's ability to evaluate whether or not continuing this new recent entitlement program for religious and other private schools is good public policy. It also means consumers of education have a hard time evaluating schools in order to determine what choices to make. And there's no democratic process through which citizens can complain about lack of information or about the operation of the voucher schools. It's a program that is state funded by state mandate without any locally elected citizens who are responsive to parents."[63]

The refusal of the Wisconsin legislature to authorize additional yearly evaluations of student achievement, even in light of the arguments that the tests are skewed to favor voucher schools, is troubling both to voucher critics and voucher supporters. In Wisconsin, all public school students are tested in the fourth, eighth, and tenth grades; the results are sent both to the Department of Public Instruction (DPI) and to individual schools. In fact, even charter schools are forced to adhere to accountability requirements and the same testing standards as public schools; yet private schools in the MPCP have no accountability requirements for student achievement.

Professor Alex Molnar agrees. Although voucher supporters claim private schools do a better job of educating students. It would be helpful to know how Catholic and other private schools participating in the Milwaukee voucher program are performing. The problem is that since 1991, the Milwaukee Archdiocese has refused to release its test results. In 1991, results suggested that Catholic schools were doing no better and perhaps a bit worse at educating minority children than the Milwaukee public schools.[64]

The Wisconsin Legislative Audit Bureau, which recently completed its year 2000 report of the ten-year-old voucher program in Milwaukee, Wisconsin, found that

•➤ There is no uniform testing policy, so taxpayers have no way of knowing if the voucher programs they support are actually academically viable.

•➤ Only 10 percent of the participating schools in the MPCP offered special education services, thus abandoning Milwaukee's neediest kids.

•➤ Upkeep of the MPCP necessitated a property tax increase, indicating that the voucher program saved no money.[65]

These facts coupled with other accountability deficits led Witte to raise important questions that people should ask about the voucher system. Will anyone be asked or able to adequately evaluate the results of the program? Who will benefit? How much will it cost? What will be the short-term and long-term results and for which students? What will be the impact on schools? And perhaps, most important, what will be the impact on communities and their willingness to support education and a high standard of educational success for all students? Witte is pessimistic that such studies will be done, and if they are, they will fail to have much impact on the expanding politics of educational choice.[66]

The Wisconsin Legislative Audit Bureau Report of 2000 echoes Witte's concerns. In the cover letter to its year 2000 report, it flatly states that student achievement cannot be documented.[67] And in addition to the lack of student achievement accountability requirements, schools participating in the MPCP do not have to conduct open meetings and need not make their records available to any person or government body; nor do they have to release information on employee wages or benefits. They are, however, still theoretically subject to a random selection plan for admission to Choice schools.[68]

The Department of Public Instruction in Milwaukee has threatened to withhold voucher funds from a number of voucher schools that have failed to show that they even have occupancy permits for the schools they claim to open. One such school, the Sensas-Utcha Institute of Holistic Learning, told the state it would be registering 130 students and applied for voucher funds. A newspaper reporter, who later conducted an analysis of the school, arrived at the address given for the school only to discover a single-family residence. When he inquired about the Sensas-Utcha Institute of Holistic Learning, neighbors informed him that they had never seen students coming or going from the home.[69] And according to RTS, of the eleven voucher schools they contacted requesting access to school buildings, only one visit was permitted.[70]

As to the claim that public schools are forced to improve with competition from private voucher schools, not one study has produced findings that would buttress this claim. In fact, it was not even one of the goals or stated objectives of any of the Milwaukee studies to come to any conclusions regarding claims of increased effectiveness and performance of the Milwaukee public school system. The studies simply concentrated on "student achievement" in private schools compared to public school students' achievement—all based on controversial standardized test results. The claim that competition forces public schools to improve their services and enhance educational opportunities for all students remains unsubstantiated.

ARGUMENT: PRIVATE CHOICE SCHOOLS DO NOT DISCRIMINATE IN THEIR ADMISSION PRACTICES, NOR DO THEY CREAM OR SKIM THE BEST STUDENTS

Creaming is the not-so-blatant practice of admitting the "best" students to private choice schools and excluding others based on student characteristics such as race, class, special needs, physical and mental disability, religion, or gender. Creaming, though illegal, can be accomplished in myriad ways, yet no extensive study of the MPCP has been undertaken to see if creaming or discrimination is occurring. Part of the problem comes from the lack of accountability requirements built into the legislation governing the Wisconsin Legislative Audit Bureau and the lack of information regarding the MPCP as a whole.

However, Jay P. Greene and Nicole Mellow presented a paper at a 1998 meeting of the American Political Science Association where they argue that voucher schools do not discriminate in the admission of students. From their point of view, private schools are more successful at integration than public schools, partly because private schools do not require that their students live in particular neighborhoods, so they can more easily triumph over segregation in housing to provide integration in school. The strong religious mission and higher social class found in most private schools are also causes that contribute to better racial integration.[71]

The Heritage Foundation goes one step further, extolling the virtues of publicly financed religious schools not simply for reasons of moral virtue, but for what they maintain the inclusion of religious schools accomplishes for all students. They cite a report by the state's Legislative Audit Bureau that finds, despite fears of creaming and segregation, that school choice is serving a student population indistinguish-able from that of the Milwaukee public school system. The report finds that most of the schools participating in the Milwaukee Parental Choice Program offer high-quality academic programs and tests, the founda-tion claims. They also report that racial integration has increased since a 1998 Wisconsin Supreme Court decision adding religious schools to the Milwaukee Parental Choice Program, according to a recently re-leased study by Marquette University's Institute for the Transformation of Learning. The new study analyzes public and private school enroll-ment in 1999–2000, the second year religious schools participated in the program.[72]

But how do low-income students travel outside their neighbor-hoods to choice schools? What about public transit and costs associated with student mobility? Greene and Mellow are quiet on these issues, even though ReThinking Schools has found that only about 38 percent of the voucher schools provided transportation for students in an at-tempt to ensure equal access to choice schools for all students.[73] With transportation a real and documented problem, will public schools be-come dumping grounds for immobile and less economically fortunate students citizens? Will they become schools of last resort with no one to 'vouch' for them?

ARGUMENT: PRIVATE CHOICE DOES LEAD TO DISCRIMINATION AND THE CREAMING AND SKIMMING OF STUDENTS

According to People for the American Way (PFAW), even the poor ac-countability requirements regarding creaming do not obfuscate the fact that private choice leads to discrimination and the creaming of students in admission practices. To begin with, PFAW is critical of the MPCP's random, lottery selection process. They claim that as many as 40 per-cent of the religious schools in the program failed to prove that they met random-selection requirements. Some religious schools overtly ex-empted their parishioners from random selection, and a number of re-ligious schools recoiled at having to comply with the state's Pupil Nondiscrimination Act, which prohibits public schools from discrimi-nating against students on the basis of sex, race, religion, sexual orien-tation, or physical, mental, emotional or learning disability. Facing po-litical pressure, the Department of Public Instruction (DPI) removed the requirement that religious schools pledge to follow the rule.[74]

In a legal complaint filed against the DPI in 1999, PFAW and the NAACP charged that more than a third of the 88 private voucher schools in Milwaukee are, or may be, violating state law concerning how voucher students must be selected for admission.[75]

According to Rethinking Schools, the Wisconsin DPI requires that the participating MPCP schools sign an agreement stating they will adhere to:

- → The state pupil non-discrimination law, which bars discrimination in any public school activity or services because of sex, race, religion, national origin, ancestry, creed, pregnancy, marital or parental status, sexual orientation or physical, mental, emotional, or learning disability
- → Title IX of the federal Civil Rights law prohibiting discrimination on the basis of sex in education programs.
- → The Federal Age Discrimination Act of 1975 and the Rehabilitation Act of 1973, which bars discrimination on the basis of handicap
- → The Americans with Disabilities Act
- → The Federal Family Education Rights and Privacy Act, which requires access to and release of student's education records
- → The Federal Drug Free School and communities Act, which requires schools to certify they are drug free
- → State and federal guarantees of freedom of religion, expression, association, unreasonable search and seizure, equal protection and due process[76]

Secular schools had no problem complying with these laws, but religious schools, admitted into the MPCP as a result of a 1998 court ruling, balked. (Initially, the DPI considered the half-dozen single-gender religious schools ineligible for the voucher program. Eventually, though, the DPI bowed to pressure from the legislature's Joint Committee for Review of Administrative Rules and admitted them to the program.[77]) The religious schools declared that they would respect the spirit of these laws but insisted that they would not be legally bound by them. Their argument: Observing these laws would remove resources from their "educational mission." The Wisconsin DPI once again relented and withdrew any requirement that religious schools sign a pledge agreeing to obey civil rights laws. [78]

The MPCP requires that participating schools, both secular and nonsecular, select students randomly, by lottery. Are nonsecular schools complying with the law or simply voicing acquiescence? The answer can be found in a far-reaching review of the Wisconsin random selection requirements filed with the DPI by voucher schools themselves. According to the review, seventeen voucher schools are in clear violation of the requirement to institute a "random selection process." An additional eighteen schools were named for investigation by the DPI for probable violations. A number of choice schools have adopted admission plans that give preference to their own parishioners, and many other MPCP schools simply ignored the requirement for a random selection process.[79]

In March of 1999 two dozen private schools participating in the MPCP received an admonition from the Wisconsin DPI that their final voucher payments would be cut unless they complied with state regulations requiring them to submit plans for random selection of voucher students. The PFAW and the NAACP had filed a complaint demanding that the DPI end tax payments to these schools until their admissions process complied with the law, citing several examples of schools violating the random selection requirement. Saint Alexander School openly states in its "random selection" plan the following order of preference: siblings, Catholic students from Saint Alexander's Parish, Catholic students from other parishes, and then non-Catholic students. At Blessed Sacrament School, the "random selection" plan states that parishioners are not subject to the random selection process. St. Marcus Lutheran School, another nonsecular choice school, failed to tender a random selection plan at all—in violation of state regulations. Instead, they simply notified the DPI that their congregation had voted to partake in the voucher program and the very next day the school "accepted" choice applications during its regularly scheduled enrollment day. All students who applied were accepted. But by publicizing the voucher openings to its worshippers before tendering them to the general public, the school simply filled its openings with its own students.[80] This is not random selection.

In a nonpartisan effort, trained civil rights examiners from the Metropolitan Milwaukee Fair Housing Council conducted a PFAW investigation concerning discrimination in student enrollment.[81] The results of the investigation were disappointing for those concerned with acceptable legal compliance. A number of the schools examined were found to be violating voucher laws by establishing admission hurdles and requirements. These same schools also collected illegal fees and dissuaded parents from exercising their statutory right to opt out of religious activities. In addition, in examining the 1999–2000 random selection plans of a number of voucher schools in Milwaukee, the study found that the schools' so-called open enrollment periods for voucher students were so early in the calendar year or so limited in length, they suggested the schools were not engaging in random selection but were instead targeting an elite group of preferred students, such as parishioners, who are more likely to be well-informed about the timing of these initial or restricted enrollments.[82]

The National Education Association (NEA) agrees with the findings of PFAW and researchers who argue that parental choice is really misleading. The real "choice," claims the NEA, lies with the schools, not the students. By definition, private schools are discriminatory and use a wide range of criteria to reject or cream students. For example, because the voucher only pays for partial tuition, many low-income students cannot take advantage of the program, since they simply do not have the funds to supplement the cost of tuition. Furthermore, they argue that in the voucher system, individual choice is little more than a figment of the imagination, because often no openings are accessible for the many students who wish to take part in the voucher program.[83]

Are theses concerns valid, or are they exaggerated?

Barbara Miner, executive director of ReThinking Schools, recently found that parents do not necessarily wish to dump the public schools but instead want them to work more efficiently. Despite ten years of vouchers in Milwaukee, Miner notes, African Americans and Latinos have not flocked to the private schools as promised. In Milwaukee there were only 1,359 more blacks in private schools than in the year 2000; during the same period, the number of African Americans in the public schools increased by 4,419. The voucher schools did not enroll as many students as the public schools according to the Legislative Audit Bureau.[84]

According to a new study published by the Applied Research Center (ARC) in Berkeley, California, almost half of all private schools nationally have entrance examinations. For many parents, this is a Catch–22. Many low-income families desire to take their children out of schools where they are falling behind academically. Yet when they apply to some voucher schools, they find that because their children are academically behind they cannot pass the admission tests and are therefore barred from participating in the voucher program. For instance, when one Milwaukee parent attempted to take advantage of the MPCP, she was told that her child could not attend the school because he had poor grades in the Milwaukee public school system. Yet that is specifically the reason she wanted to send him to a choice school in the first place.[85]

The ARC also reports that 72 percent of private schools participating in MPCP either failed or declined to respond to the 1998 survey requesting information about their racial and gender makeup. Only 17 percent gave comprehensive information. According to ARC, research indicates that private schools in Milwaukee are disproportionately white. Although Milwaukee public schools are 33 percent white, over 84 percent of the private schools students in MPCP are white, and at two of the most well-known private high schools in the city, only 3 percent of the students are African-American. This discrepancy is even higher than the national average for private schools, which is currently 78 percent white.[86]

Witte expresses similar concerns regarding racial discrimination in admissions. He concludes that the pure market model has obvious racial implications and that the MPCP almost certainly worsened segregation in the schools. The undeniable social result of the school-integration movement was white flight from our major cities, and the enticements favoring elite schools will hardly be reduced under the pure market model. Witte argues that a market model of choice can only hasten the racial balkanization of our schools and country.[87] Private schools will be a magnet for better students who are less difficult to educate, from families with higher incomes, and thus more likely to be white. That will mean enhanced working environments, smaller class sizes, more funds, and a more inspiring intellectual environment for students, staff, and parents.[88] Why would anyone want to open a school in an urban ghetto? Perhaps out of altruism, a desire to provide religious instruction, or because one is a part of the community, Witte suggests, but no one will if the intention is purely profit, or custom, or to produce the best school.[89]

Even though the MPCP has an income cap, claimants argue that parents who have participated in the voucher program have a higher level of educational achievement and parental involvement than the average parents involved in the Milwaukee public school system. According to Molnar, MPCP parents are so-called high-voice parents—they are generally better educated and more involved in their children's education. Since only a small number of students apply to choice schools relative to the number of eligible students (about 60,000) each year, one can infer that many less advantaged parents are not flocking to choice schools.[90] Even Terry Moe, prominent voucher supporter and author of the seminal work on private school vouchers, acknowledges that unrestricted choice may well lead to selection effects with class bias.[91]

Finally, in an interesting epigraph, Annette "Polly" Williams, in a statement to the *Boston Globe*, forthrightly alleged a perfidious relationship between voucher advocates and the African-American community. She knew from the outset, she says, that the white, rich Republicans and right-wing foundations that used her to validate their agenda would do so only as long as it suited their needs. She also knew that once they no longer needed her as a Black spokesperson, they would try to take control of vouchers and use them for their own selfish interests.[92] From William's point of view, "universal choice" means white choice. She is clear in her belief that the wealthy and racially privileged would use their rights to snatch the first available spots in private voucher schools, leaving little for those "targeted parents" for which "targeted vouchers" were designed to help.

Currently, Cambridge, Massachusetts, has universal, controlled choice. Even so, privileged white families are clustered in the most desirable choice schools. This is why, says Williams, most Black groups like the NAACP oppose vouchers. Without the income cap, private choice becomes just another free-market program that keeps richer families subsidized and religious schools financially in the black with state money, with no commitment to improve public schools. Williams now believes that voucher supporters exploit low-income Black children, stating they are creating vouchers for them when what they really have in mind is bringing in "a White Trojan horse."[93]

The issue of discrimination is not confined to race or gender; "special needs" students may also be in danger under private choice programs. According to the Legislative Audit Bureau in Wisconsin, in 1998–1999 only 3 percent of the voucher students had been previously recognized as requiring special services, compared with about 15 percent of public school students.[94] The report also notes that voucher students are more likely to receive services that are cost-effective as opposed to special services such as those needed by children with speech and language disabilities or those students with learning disabilities.[95]

For this reason, Williams, Witte, and others actively oppose the movement toward universal vouchers in Milwaukee—or anywhere else for that matter. They may back "targeted voucher plans," but misrepresenting their support for targeted vouchers as support for universal approaches to privatizing education, as both the media and political commentators have done, is deceitful.

ARGUEMENT: VOUCHERS DO NOT DIVEST PUBLIC SCHOOLS OF NEEDED FUNDS NOR DO THEY THWART EFFECTIVE EDUCATIONAL REFORMS

According to the Heritage Foundation, private choice does not lead to disinvestment in public schools. Instead, the foundation concluded that privatized schooling through school vouchers is cheaper and more cost effective than public schools. They based this conclusion not on a study of the Milwaukee MPCP program, but on a 1999 study by the Children's Educational Opportunities Foundation (Children First CEO America) of San Antonio's Horizon program, the country's first fully funded private voucher program offered to all parents in the whole district. Pro-choice advocates cited evidence that private choice is an economical way to educate students, arguing that the cost of the Horizon Program is half the cost of the district's public school system.

The CEO study, conducted by Harvard's Paul Peterson, also came to the conclusion that the program did not lead to a mass departure from the public school: Only 800 students left the public schools, thereby reducing the district's budget by only 3.5 percent. However, after the commencement of the Horizon Program, the Edgewood Independent School District put in place an interdistrict choice program that permitted 200 students from other districts to transfer to Edgewood Schools, bringing with them $775,000 that would otherwise have gone to other districts.[96]

Are markets and the private sector better at achieving lower costs than public schools? This is one point on which all stakeholders can agree: private schools are able to keep costs down. The disagreement arises when the discussion turns to the reasons for the savings and the price the public pays in the long term.

The basic neoliberal argument claims that the cost savings arises because market pressures eliminate the unnecessary bureaucratic costs associated with managing public institutions.

Opponents see the cost savings differently. They point out that private schools are notorious for paying their staff, including teachers, below public school levels. They do not have unionized employees and are therefore not obliged to bargain collectively with classified and certified staff. Teacher salaries in MPCP were much lower than those paid by the Milwaukee public schools. As one principal observed, the teachers who stay in choice schools for a long time are either very dedicated or can afford to stay on what the school can pay.[97] Not only has low teacher salary been shown to lead to high turnover rates at private choice schools in Milwaukee, but low salaries also have allowed private schools to escape the pressure to use general funds to increase salary and benefit packages for private school workers.

These cost estimates, using beginning voucher levels and a highly restricted set of schools to project savings, are of little use in understanding the long-term dynamic costs of an open-ended voucher program, opponents argue.[98] Why? Because, theoretically, as more and more schools materialize under private voucher programs, pressures to unionize these school workers, both certified and classified, will grow. This would make all the current data and statistics worthless as wage and benefits rise significantly due to collective bargaining agreements—and nowhere is this fact figured into the cost studies or even considered.

ARGUMENT: VOUCHERS DO DIVEST PUBLIC SCHOOLS OF NEEDED FUNDS AND IMPEDE EFFECTIVE EDUCATIONAL REFORMS

According to People for the American Way, vouchers drain resources from public schools. The amount of money redirected from the public schools in Milwaukee since 2000 has been considerable—$22 million in Milwaukee for the 6,000 voucher students, a sum that could triple if the program reaches its maximum size of 15,000 students.[99] According to a recent study conducted by PFAW, a defect in the formula for voucher funding in Wisconsin cost taxpayers an extra $11 million in a single year—at a time when the public school system was cutting programs and reducing staff in order to make up for a $32 million district budget deficit. The PFAW found that payments made to voucher schools in the city of Milwaukee amounted, on an average, to a 40-percent markup above the real tuition costs the schools charged to their self-paying private students. And because the substantial majority of schools participating in the publicly funded Milwaukee voucher program are religious, about 78 percent of the overpayments went to religious schools.[100] The PFAW study contends that as a result of the MPCP, public school districts will now be forced to reduce school expenditures. Estimating a price tag of about $4,900 per private voucher, PFAW computes that this will cause a loss to the public schools of $29.4 million, which they equate with the cost of approximately 500 experienced teachers, or more than 850 new teachers.[101]

Few would argue that the city's public schools are faced with ominous financial problems. According to Rev. Dr. Rolen Womack, pastor of Progressive Baptist Church in Milwaukee, this crisis could deliver a financial knockout blow to 100,000 Milwaukee children who depend on public schools for their education. The numbers seem to predict a future for public schools that is likely to include fewer teachers, fewer computers, fewer textbooks and research resources, and an overall deterioration in the quality of education for the vast majority of our children.[102]

PFAW and concerned individuals like Reverend Womack, worry that the problem of public school disinvestment will persist unabated if more and more parents choose to take their children out of public schools by use of private tuition scholarships, private school vouchers, and/or tax credits. PFAW estimates that the loss of public funds for Milwaukee public schools could reach $73.5 million in the near future. This sum represents nearly 10 percent of the schools' district operating budget for the 1998 school year. And according to PFAW, it could call into jeopardy such programs as special-focus high school curricula, Montessori programs, all-day kindergarten, and the Milwaukee Early Childhood Center. It could also affect continuing summer school remedial programs in core academic subjects as well as special proposals to improve reading at the twenty lowest-performing schools.[103] In short, they argue, the disinvestment of funds would be devastating for students forced to remain in public schools.

If vouchers take money from public schools, as PFAW and others claim, then how can public schools be forced to compete with private schools? How do private vouchers help public schools become more proficient if public schools have less funding for resources and professional development than their private school counterparts? How will bleeding public schools of financial resources put them in position to compete for academic excellence with private schools? According to Elliot Incberg, legal director for PFAW, the injury we can predict in Milwaukee should give nightmares to every state legislature that is being enticed down the voucher path.[104]

It is not easy to imagine how impoverished school districts, forced to cut important programs, would be in a position to offer excellent educational services to students, their parents, and the community at large. If private school choice, through vouchers and various private scholarship programs and tax schemes, actually drains monies from public schools, what does this signify for the future of public schooling and the claims that competition increases public school performance? Perhaps by analyzing and examining the twenty-year-old private choice program that has existed, and continues to subsist in the country of Chile, we might uncover some of the answers to these crucial questions.

THE CHILEAN SCHOOL CHOICE PROGRAM

Opponents of school privatization of schools would caution the public to be very careful before adopting private school vouchers, because disinvestment in public education is not simply a national trend, but an international inclination and neoliberal economic movement as well. They point to international experiments with vouchers and argue that in many countries these school privatization measures are part and parcel of the structural readjustment measures imposed through institutions such as the International Monetary Fund and the World Bank. Where vouchers have been tried internationally, they argue, they have caused inequities and class division. To buttress their claims, they point to Chile where Milton Friedman's neoliberal proposals were instituted by the Pinochet military dictatorship in the early 1980s.

In a notable yet rarely referenced analysis of the Chilean voucher reform movement, Stanford professor Martin Carnoy maintains that the experience with vouchers has been a disaster for Chilean children from low-income families. He invites us to critically examine the Chilean private choice program and learn from the failed Chilean experiment before we go blindly forward. Carnoy's findings have not, to my knowledge, been refuted by contradictory claims.

A BRIEF HISTORY OF
THE CHILEAN VOUCHER PROGRAM

The Chilean school voucher plan began in 1980 under the dictator Augusto Pinochet as part of a general project to reduce the role of government in education in favor of market-based reforms. It was the first conscious attempt to implement the modern, neoliberal policies in education that for years had been advanced by Milton Friedman. It is based on fully subsidized, universal, voucher-driven, deregulated private schools that compete directly for students with deregulated municipality-run public schools situated in metropolitan areas—from middle class suburbs to low-income barrios.[105]

The Chilean voucher plan called for immediately privatizing teacher contracts and eradicating the teacher's union as a national collective bargaining unit. Teachers were quickly removed from the public employee system to the private sector, and by 1983, even public schools (those schools run by municipalities) could employ and fire teachers at will. At the same time, schools no longer had to abide by a defined national curriculum or set of standards but were free to create their own curriculums, assessments, and calibrating systems. There were no legally mandated accountability systems in place. Nor were there open meeting laws or public sunshine laws.[106]

Chile offers a universal voucher to all its students. Fees can be charged at private schools that are above and beyond the value of a voucher, and private schools are allowed to arbitrarily screen students in their admission practices. Elite private schools serve upper-income parents and families, but because these schools are not sheltered under the voucher program, parents must pay the full cost of education. Clearly, Chile has a class system when it comes to educational access and opportunities, and the country consciously and publicly supports it.

MARTIN CARNOY'S FINDINGS

The results of the privatization experiment in education in Chile, according to Carnoy, ran contrary to what neoliberal proponents claimed would happen if schools were unleashed from government controls. Total spending on education fell dramatically, after at first increasing in the early 1980s when the central government was paying teachers' severance pay as part of privatizing their agreements. In 1985 the federal contribution to education was 80 percent of the full amount of educational spending, and total spending for education was 5.3 percent of the nation's Gross National Product (GNP). Five years later, the federal portion was 68 percent of the total, and the full amount had fallen to 3.7 percent of the GNP. Although private spending had increased, it was not enough to counterbalance the loss of federal funds. The real decreases occurred at the secondary and university levels. Carnoy also found that those who enjoyed the benefits of the subsidized private schools were mainly middle and higher income families. Vouchers seemed to be functioning—but for a privileged minority.[107]

Carnoy observed an enormous transfer of students into private schools, in particular middle-class and upper middle-class children. By 1990, of families whose income was in the lower 40 percent nationally, 72 percent had children enrolled in municipal public schools. In the next highest 40 percent income bracket, only 51 percent of the families sent their children to public schools, with 43 percent in subsidized private schools and 6 percent in select private schools where parents shelled out full tuition. In the top 20 percent income level, Carnoy found that only 25 percent had their children in public schools, with 32 percent attending subsidized private schools and 43 percent in the top private schools.[108]

Carnoy also discovered that the increase in student achievement predicted by voucher proponents never occurred. In fact, on the basis of standardized test scores, he found the opposite was true. Scores in language arts and mathematics, as measured by two nationally standardized cognitive achievement tests implemented in 1982 and again in 1988 for fourth graders, went down by 14 percent and 6 percent respectively. Surprisingly, declining test scores were found not solely among low-income students in public schools, but also noted for low-income students in private schools supported by vouchers. Among middle-income students, test scores rose slightly, whether they were in public or private schools. And although succeeding tests in 1990 showed increases of 9 percent in language arts and 11 percent in math, they still were at 1982 levels. The claims for heightened competition as the road to higher achievement appeared to Carnoy to be more fiction than reality.

Paradoxically, Carnoy found that middle-income students in private schools averaged higher scores than those found in public schools, while low-income students averaged higher scores in the public schools. This fact was independently verified by University of Georgia political scientist Taryn Rounds, who found that using the 1990 test results, students in lower socioeconomic classes actually performed better in public schools on both the language arts and mathematics examinations while middle class students scored higher in subsidized schools. Once again, the research seemed disprove neoliberal claims about low student achievement levels in public schools and the assurance of improvement through the introduction of private vouchers. Carnoy found that market competition had and continues to have, a negative effect on student success; that the Chilean voucher plan, in its 20-year existence, increased inequality in student achievement without enhancing the overall quality of education; and that private voucher plans in general actually increase inequality in education without elevating student achievement or making public schools more effectual.[109]

Carnoy's study also reported that not only were "difficult to manage" students usually consigned to public last-resort schools, but once private voucher plans were put in place, middle class parents derived pleasure from the idea of segregating their children from these problematic and usually low-income students. This situation created further social and class stratification throughout the country's educational system, which in turn advanced increasing segregation and inequalities in the social order. Teachers in the last-resort schools—those educational institutions that remained public but underfunded—discovered that along with the deterioration in these schools resulting from the loss of public money, their ability to be innovative and imaginative in their teaching was diminished or eliminated. These teachers voiced serious complaints that their efforts at educational improvement were thwarted, their energy diminished, and their morale reduced by an underfunded, failing educational system. This finding is in opposition to the neoliberal contention that competition increases school efficiency in the public sector by developing innovation, experimentation, imagination, and meaningful reforms.

Readers might also wish to consider the following account by

Eduardo Galeano, a Latin American author. At the end of 1993 Galeano attended the closing of a Chilean trade school that had existed in Santiago, Chile, since 1990. The school had provided vocational education opportunities to some of the most disadvantaged students from some of the worst slums in Santiago. Rather than being consigned to a life of delinquency, begging, or whoring on the city streets of Santiago, these children were provided an opportunity to become ironworkers, carpenters, gardeners, and, most of all—to learn to love themselves and what they were doing to improve the quality of their lives.

The school was a government trade school, part of the class-based Chilean privatization system of education. As a result of disinvestments in public education, it was required to depend on overseas financing. When the money was no longer there, the committed teachers at the school turned to the Chilean government for assistance. They went to the educational ministry but were unable to garner financial support. When they turned to the city government in Santiago to plead for financial help, the mayor told them, "Turn it into a business." The school closed in 1993, and the children, who for the first time had heard people say that they were of value, now found themselves consigned to the streets of Santiago.[110]

SUMMARY

Currently there are three significant voucher programs operating in the United States—Milwaukee, Cleveland, and Florida. These programs all rely on public dollars to pay for tuition at private schools, including religious schools. But even though voucher initiatives were defeated in Michigan and California in November of 2000, they are on the legislative dockets in at least twenty states and are expected to appear on state agendas in all fifty states

Progressive policy makers find themselves in a difficult position. As advocates of learning and student achievement they must continue to criticize and expose the impoverished offerings of many public schools and demand that they provide a quality education for all children. At the same time, they must be aware that such critiques invite the nostrum of private choice and vouchers, which ultimately provides an opening for political groups that argue for the elimination of public education such as the Libertarian Party and the Religious Right groups Focus on the Family, Citizens for Excellence in Education, and Coral Ridge Ministries.

Vouchers and private choice are a policy direction that Milwaukee Democrat Gwen Moore, one of two African-American state senators, says feels good and resonates well in a climate of increasing faith in the market and decreasing investment in and commitment to public schools. Nevertheless, Moore concludes that privatization is feeding on our public institutions. Public schools, she maintains, are the only assurance that all children will receive some fundamental level of education.[111] Is Moore right or is educational privatization the thoroughfare to school improvement and student achievement?

Before we can decide the best course for our educational policy, we as citizens must address the difficult questions raised in this chapter and the implications of our answers. Are vouchers at best a temporary solution for a select few or are they an answer for the many? If choice schools are not accountable to the public or the state they serve, how can parents effectively find and select choice schools? And what about the poorest of the poor, like the children in Santiago, Chile, who lost their chance for an education because they were not involved in a "business"?

We must also address even more fundamental questions. Is the role of government in education collecting and utilizing taxpayer dollars to fund for-profit ventures aimed at privatizing schools? Are we as a public comfortable with providing public funds for parochial school education? If so, are vouchers the best means for the transfer of public funds to private schools? And if vouchers encourage an unconstitutional relationship between church and state, how do we accommodate religious and constitutional concerns regarding public education?

The voucher experiment has been tried, in Milwaukee, Cleveland, Florida, Chile, and in a number of other locations. We now have the benefit of that experience to help us evaluate the success of voucher programs and understand its implications. Before adopt an educational policy that could radically change or even replace our public education system and alter the educational opportunities for all of our children, we must make sure that an in-depth public discussion takes place and that we understand the implications of the changes we make.

NOTES

1. Molnar, Alex. (October 1999). "Educational Vouchers: A Review of the Research." Milwaukee: The Center for Education Research, Analysis, and Innovation.

2. Kincheloe, Joe. (2001). "From Positivism to an Epistemology of Complexity: Grounding Rigorous Teaching." Pp. 8. In: *Standards and Schooling in the United States*. Edited by Danny Weil, Joe Kincheloe, and Shirley Steinberg. Santa Barbara: ABC-CLIO.

3. Alterman, Eric. (December 25, 2000). "C'est n'est pas un president." *The Nation.* Pp. 12. New York, NY. Volume 271. No.: 21.

4. Ibid. 40.

5. Peterson, Bob, and Larry Miller. (Fall 2000) "Forward to the Past?" In *ReThinking Schools.* Pp. 18. Fall 2000. Vol. 15. No. 1.

6. Witte, John. (2000). *The Market Approach to Education: An Analysis of America's First Voucher Program.* Pp. 37. Princeton: Princeton University Press.

7. Ibid. 43.

8. Ibid. 44.

9. Williams, J. (Novermber 22, 1997). "Norquist: MPS Needs to Satisfy Parents." *Milwaukee Journal Sentinel.* http://www.jsonline.com.

10. *MTEA v. Benson.* Case heard March 4, 1998, in Wisconsin Supreme Court and upheld June 10, 1998.

11. La Follette Public Affairs at the University of Wisconsin–Madison. Fifth Report on the Milwaukee Parental Choice Program. Pp. 2. Madison: University of Wisconsin–Madison.

12. Ibid. 5.

13. Ibid. 5.

14. Miner, B. (1996). "What Can We Learn from Milwaukee's Voucher Program?" http://www.rethinkingschools.org.

15. Molnar, A. (October 1999). "Educational Vouchers: A Review of the Research. Sorting through the Conflicting Voucher Results." Pp. 4. Milwaukee: The Center for Education Research and Analysis, and Innovation.

16. Center for Education Reform (August 30, 2000). "School Choice in the States." Pp. 3. http://edreform.com.

17. Ibid.

18. Ibid.

19. Wisconsin Legislative Audit Bureau (1995). Audit Summary Report 95-3. In: Molnar, A. (October 1999). "Educational Vouchers: A Review of the Research." Center for Education, Research, Analysis and Innovation at the University of Wisconsin–Milwaukee.

20. Molnar, A. (October 1999). "Educational Vouchers: A Review of the Research. When Are Significant Results Not So Significant?" Milwaukee: The Center for Education Research and Analysis, and Innovation.

21. Greene, J., P. Peterson, and J. Du (March 1997). "The Effectiveness of School Choice in Milwaukee: A Secondary Analysis of Data from the Program's Evaluation." Pp. 15. Cambridge: The Kennedy School of Government, Harvard University.

22. Molnar, A. (2001) "School Vouchers: The Law, the Research, and Public Policy Implications." Paper presented at the Hechinger Institute on Education and the Media. Online at the Center for Education Research, Analysis, and Innovation. http://www.asu.edu.

23. Greene, J., and Peterson, P. (August 29, 1996). "Methodological Issues in Evaluation Research: The Milwaukee Program." Pp. 3. Cambridge: Department of Government and Kennedy School of Government, Harvard University. http://www.worldbank.org.

24. Molnar, A. (2001) "School Vouchers: The Law, the Research, and Public Policy Implications."

25. Greene, J., and P. Peterson (August 29, 1996). "Methodological issues in evaluation research: The Milwaukee school choice plan." Pp. 3. Paper prepared for the Program in Education Policy and Governance, Department of Government and Kennedy School of Government, Harvard University.

26. Molnar, A. (October 1999). "Educational Vouchers: A Review of the Research. Sorting through the Conflicting Voucher Results." Pp. 3. The Center for Education Research and Analysis, and Innovation.

27. Ibid. 4.

28. Molnar, A. (2001) "School Vouchers: The Law, the Research, and Public Policy Implications."

29. Greene, J., P. Peterson, and J. Du (March 1997). "Effectiveness of School Choice: The Milwaukee Experiment." Pp. 9. Occasional paper 97-1 March, 1997. Program in Education Policy Governance Center for American Political Studies. Department of Government. Harvard University.

30. Greene, J. and P. Peterson. (August 29, 1996). "Methodological Issues in Evaluation Research: The Milwaukee School Choice Plan." Pp. 10. Paper prepared for the Program in Education Policy and Governance, Department of Government and Kennedy School of Government, Harvard University.

31. Ibid. 3.

32. Eric Alterman (December 25, 2000). "Ce n'est pas un president." Pp. 12. *The Nation*. Volume 271. No. 21.

33. Kincheloe, J. (2001). "The Nature of Reductionism: The Irrationality of Technical Standards." *Standards and Schooling in the United States*. Santa Barbara, CA: ABC-CLIO.

34. Ibid. 30.

35. Greene, J., and P. Peterson. (August 29, 1996). "Methodological Issues in Evaluation Research: The Milwaukee School Choice Plan."

36. Peterson, P. (1997). "The Case for School Choice." Pp. 2. *Harvard Educational Review*. http://www.harvard-magazine.com.

37. Witte, J. (2000). *The Market Approach to Education: An Analysis of America's First Voucher Program*. Princeton: Princeton University Press.

38. Rouse, C. (1997) "Schools and Student Achievement: More Evidence from the Milwaukee Parental Choice Program." Princeton and NBER. *The Economic Policy Review*.

39. Molnar, A. (November 17, 1999). "Unfinished Business in Milwaukee." *Education Week on the Web*. http://www.edweek.org.

40. The Heritage Foundation (2000). "Wisconsin." Pp. 2. The Heritage Foundation. http://www.heritage.org.

41. Witte, J. (2000). *The Market Approach to Education.* Pp. 5. Princeton: Princeton University Press.

42. Ibid. 208.

43. Macedo, D. (1994) *Literacies of Power. What Americans Are Not Allowed to Know.* Boulder, CO: Westview Press.

44. McNeill, L. "The Educational Cost of Standardization." Pp. 9. In: *Re-Thinking Schools.* Summer 2000. http://www.rethinkingschools.org.

45. Stanford Achievement Test: Intermediate 2 (1989). Harcourt Brace Jovanovich, Inc.

46. The Massachusetts Department of Education (1989). Science Assessment. Boston: Massachusetts Department of Education.

47. Stanford Achievement Test: Intermediate 2 (1989). Harcourt Brace Jovanovich, Inc.

48. Wisconsin Department of Public Instruction (1991). *The New Standards Project.* Milwaukee: Wisconsin Department of Public Instruction.

49. Hursch, D. (2001). "Standards and the Curriculum: The Commodification of Knowledge and the End of Imagination." Pp. 6. In: *Standards and Schooling in the United States.* Santa Barbara, CA: ABC-CLIO.

50. People for the American Way (September 26, 2000). "Pro-Voucher Research Unmasked as Deception by Numbers: Ten Reasons to Doubt the Latest Claims by Vouchers." People for the American Way, Washington, D.C.

51. Witte, J. (2000). *The Market Approach to Education.* Pp. 194. Princeton: Princeton University Press.

52. Molnar, A. (October 1999). "Milwaukee's Private Voucher Program: PAVE." Pp. 2. The Center for Education, Research, Analysis and Innovation. The University in Wisconsin–Milwaukee. http://www.uwm.edu.

53. PAVE. Welcome to PAVE. http://www.pave.org.

54. Ibid.

55. The Heritage Foundation (July 14, 2000). "School Choice. State profile: Wisconsin." The Heritage Foundation. http://www.heritage.org.

56. Ibid.

57. ReThinking Schools. (Winter 1999). "Legislation Calls for Access and Accountability." In *ReThinking Schools.* Volume 14. No. 2. Winter 1999. http://www.rethinkingschools.org.

58. Greene, J., P. Peterson, and J. Du (March 1997). "Effectiveness of School Choice: The Milwaukee Experiment." Pp. 3. Occasional paper 97-1 March, 1997. Program in Education Policy Governance Center for American Political Studies. Department of Government, Harvard University.

59. Ibid. 11.

60. Rees, N. S. (January-February 1999). "Public School Benefits of Pri-

vate School Vouchers." Quoted from The Center for Education Reform. http://www.edreform.com.

61. Gunn, E. (1999). "Vouchers and Public Accountability." In *ReThinking Schools*. Pp. 4. Volume 14. No. 1. Fall 1999. http://www.rethinkingschools.org.

62. Molnar, A. (November 17, 1999). "Unfinished Business in Milwaukee." *Education Week on the Web.* http://www.edweek.org.

63. Gunn, E. (1999). "Vouchers and Public Accountability." In *ReThinking Schools.* Volume 14. No. 1. Fall 1999. http://www.rethinkingschools.org.

64. Molnar, A. (November 17, 1999). "Unfinished Business in Milwaukee." In *Education Week on the Web.* http://www.edweek.org.

65. People for the American Way (2000). "Wisconsin—Did You Know?" People for the American Way. Washington, D.C. http://www.pfaw.org.

66. Witte, J. (2000). *The Market Approach to Education.* Pp. 209. Princeton: Princeton University Press.

67. The Legislative Audit Bureau Report of the State of Wisconsin (2000). http://www.legis.state.wi.us.

68. People for the American Way (September 15, 2000). "Milwaukee Voucher Experiment. Rolling the Dice for Children's Future." People for the American Way. http://www.pfaw.org.

69. Miner, B., "Voucher Schools Overpaid," p. 13.

70. Ibid. 2.

71. Greene, J. P., and N. Mellow (August 20, 1998). "Integration Where It Counts: A Study of Racial Integration in Public and Private School Lunchrooms." Pp. 1. University of Texas at Austin. Presented at the Meeting of the American Political Science Association. Boston, September, 1998. http://www.schoolchoices.org.

72. The Heritage Foundation (2000). "Wisconsin." The Heritage Foundation. http://www.heritage.org.

73. Miner, B. (June 5, 2000). "Who's Vouching for Vouchers?" Pp. 23. *The Nation.* June 5, 2000. Volume 270. No. 22.

74. People for the American Way (April 20, 1999). "Grand Illusions: A Look at Who Backs School Vouchers and Who Profits, and the Dismal Performance of Vouchers to Date." Pp. 3. People for the American Way.

75. People for the American Way (February 2, 1999). "Voucher Schools Violating Wisconsin Law on Student Admissions." Pp. 1. People for the American Way. http://www.pfaw.org.

76. Gunn, E. (Fall 1999). Vouchers and Public Accountability. Pp. 6. *ReThinking Schools.* Volume 14. No. 1. http://www.rethinkingschools.org.

77. Ibid.

78. Ibid.

79. Ibid. 1.

80. Ibid. 2.

81. People for the American Way (2000). "In the Courts." Pp. 4. People for the Amererican Way. http://www.pfaw.org.

82. Ibid. 4.

83. The National Education Association (January 1999). "Legislative: Private School Vouchers." NEA. http://www.nea.org.

84. Miner, B. (June 5, 2000). "Who's Vouching for Vouchers?" *The Nation.* June 5, 2000. Volume 270. No. 22.

85. Johnson, T. ERASE Reports and Studies. (October 10, 2000). "Report Charges School Vouchers Are Racist." Oakland, CA: Applied Research Center. http://www.arc.org.

86. Johnson, T., L. Piana, and P. Burlingame (October 2000). "Vouchers: A Trap Not a Choice." Pp. 13. Oakland, CA: Applied Research Center.

87. Witte, *The Market Approach to Education,* 203.

88. Ibid. 206.

89. Ibid. 206.

90. Molnar, A. (October 1999). "Educational Vouchers: A Review of the Research." Pp. 5. Center for Education Research, Analysis, and Innovation. University of Wisconsin–Milwaukee.

91. Moe, T., ed. (1995). *Private Vouchers.* Stanford: Hoover Institution Press.

92. Jackson, D. (October 28, 1998). "The corruption of school choice." *The Boston Globe.* Pp. A23. Boston: MA.

93. Ibid. A23.

94. The Legislative Audit Bureau Report of the State of Wisconsin (2000). http://www.legis.state.wi.

95. Ibid. 28.

96. Peterson, P. (1997). "The Case for School Choice." *Harvard Magazine.* May-June. http://www.harvard-magazine.com.

97. Witte, J. (November, 1991). "First Year Report: Milwaukee Parental Choice Program." Pp. 12. Department of Political Science and the Robert M. La Follette Institute of Public Affairs, University of Wisconsin–Madison.

98. Ibid. 106.

99. People for the American Way (April 20, 1999). "Grand Illusions."

100. People for the American Way (2000). "The 40 Percent Surcharge: How Taxpayers Overpay for Milwaukee's Private School Voucher Program." http:// www. pfaw.org.

101. People for the American Way (August 26, 1998). "Milwaukee's Vouchers Leave Public Schools More Than $29 Million Short." Pp. 1. People for the American Way. http://www.pfaw.org.

102. Ibid. 1.

103. Ibid. 2.

104. Ibid. 1.

105. Carnoy, M. (1996). "Lessons of Chile's Voucher Reform Movement." *ReThinking Schools.* http://www.rethinkingschools.org.

106. Ibid.

107. Ibid.

108. Ibid.

109. Ibid. 27.

110. Galeano, E. (December 11, 2000). "By the Grace of God." Pp. 61. *The Nation.* December 11, 2000. Volume 271. Number 19.

111. Miner, B. (June 5, 2000). "Who's Vouching for Vouchers?" Pp. 24. *The Nation.* Volume 270. No. 22.

Chapter Six
❧ Private Scholarships and Faith-Based Charitable Contributions

The private voucher movement is one piece of the larger effort to provide universal, market-based solutions to educational problems. In its most familiar form, the private voucher movement simply seeks to provide vouchers for students to attend private schools. But the movement's platform is much more comprehensive. It includes initiatives designed to provide private tuition scholarships to low-income students to entice them from public schools; it seeks to establish educational tax credits within the Internal Revenue Code; it backs legislation to allow for educational tax shelters; it supports an increase in niche contracting (the process of contracting out vital school services); and it supports "voucher zones," where residents would automatically be eligible for private school vouchers based on their geographical location.

The first part of this chapter looks at the growth nationwide of private, philanthropic student scholarship funds. The second section examines what is known as "charitable choice." Both of these recent public policy strategies are at the forefront in the development of creative, neo-liberal approaches to ending, or at the very least, reconfiguring public education. The decision to employ these strategies may have an enormous effect on how we educate our children for democratic citizenship.

Will privatization result in a loose consortium of religion-based, entrepreneurial private schools that will incrementally replace public, common educational opportunity? To fully understand the agenda of privatization proponents, it is important to look behind the stated goals of organizations and individuals and delve more critically into their public policy positions.

A BRIEF HISTORY OF PRIVATE PHILANTHROPY: PRIVATIZATION OF EDUCATION

The idea of channeling public money into private schools was first inspired by J. Patrick Rooney. As a member of the State Policy Network, an affiliation of state-based conservative think tanks that provides arguments and model legislation to citizens seeking to change the law, Rooney serves on the boards of many conservative think tanks, including the National Center for Policy Analysis in Texas and CEO America. Rooney is also the chairman of the American Education Reform Foundation, which has advocated voucher proposals in several key locations. Rooney began his work with private vouchers in 1991, when he sought to convince the Indiana state legislature to channel public money to private schools.[1] At that time he was also the largest financial donor to House Speaker Newt Gingrich and a leading financial backer of the Gingrich GOPAC and Progress Freedom Foundation. His associates include Phyllis Schaffley of the Eagle Forum, a right-wing think tank, Steve Forbes, former presidential candidate and CEO of Forbes Magazine; and Pete Wilson, former mayor of Los Angeles and currently a talk show host on KGO radio station in San Francisco.[2]

Rooney is the originator of the idea that private scholarship money could be used to leverage public money—a stratagem adopted by CEO America, the Children's Scholarship Fund (CSF), and a host of like-minded organizations.(Leveraging public funds through private money means that if more private money is made available to students in the form of partial private tuition grants, then students will be more willing and able to opt out of existing public schools, taking with them public funds made available through private voucher programs.)

Although Rooney originated this approach, the program really got off the ground in 1989, when James Leininger, a wealthy Texas physician teamed up with Rooney to reengineer the Texas educational landscape. During the 1990s, Leininger spent $5.6 million of his own money on donations to politically organized nonprofit organizations, both in Texas and nationally. The San Antonio Current, a Texas newspaper, has labeled him "God's sugar daddy."[3] He also established the Texas Public Policy Foundation, modeled after the Heritage Foundation, a right-wing think tank that publishes views on politics and public policy. With the help of a $2 million bequest from the Walton Foundation and CEO America, the national private scholarship organization was created in 1995. (Former Wal-Mart employee Fritz Steiger, whom Leininger had hired to run the Texas Public Policy Foundation, transferred to CEO America and now serves as the group's president.) Leininger also convinced the Walton Foundation to give him $100,000 for the A+ PAC for Parental School Choice, another provoucher advocacy group.[4]

Leininger's influence does not stop with private school vouchers. He also helped elect three of the six religious-right-supported members of the Texas State Board of Education. He also secured loans of $1.1 mil-

lion and $950,000 for two provoucher candidates: Rick Perry for lieu-
tenant governor and Carole Rylander for state comptroller.[5] In many
ways, Leininger put Rooney's ideas into practice and, through Walton's
generous grant monies, started the privatized education program in
Texas. That program has served as a neoliberal model for educational
privatization efforts throughout the nation.

CEO America: The Birth of the
Private National Scholarship Movement

CEO America was the first national organization to directly award private vouchers to low-income students. The organization began with a
fanfare. It created a public policy network composed of a mixture of
wealthy individuals, conservative pundits, corporate executives, and
representatives from the religious right. Its purpose is to build public
support for educational privatization by demonstrating the efficacy of
private vouchers and to soften legislative and public resistance to the
idea of using public monies to fund private schools.

According to CEO America's original mission statement, the organization would work to expand privately funded voucher programs
throughout the nation.[6] And by developing private scholarship funds
through entrepreneurial venture capital, CEO America hoped to do
more than simply provide legitimacy to voucher programs. Not unlike
its counterpart, the Children's Scholarship Fund, CEO America's unstated mission is to open up an enormous new venture capital market
with the potential of producing sizable returns for investors.

CEO America uses a two-pronged strategy: First, it designs and
endorses educational public policy changes through legislation. To this
end, it helps finance citizen initiatives to legalize and legitimize public
funding for private school education through organizations such as the
State Policy Network, an umbrella group active in 35 states. Among its
associate members are the Heritage Foundation, Grover Norquist's
Americans for Tax Reform, J. Patrick Rooney's Golden Rule Insurance
Company, and CEO America.[7] The impact of the activities of these
groups and affiliates cannot be underestimated. Second, CEO America
solicits large donations from wealthy benefactors in an effort designed
to convince the public of the legitimacy of educational privatization.

CEO America has identified areas of concern that it feels must be
addressed immediately for its mission to be successful. Foremost is
reaching out to disenfranchised parents and students, especially students of color in inner cities. The organization's leaders want to give
these constituencies the strong ideological impression as well as the ma-

terial hope that private schooling is not only possible, but also the best of all educational designs and structures—that private schools mean higher student achievement for disenfranchised students and thus assure equitable entry into the new global economy. Promoting this idea as an educational reform package to disenfranchised constituencies, such as low-income school districts, is high on CEO America's agenda.

In attempting to convince the public of the importance of private school choice and the superiority of privatized education, CEO America seeks to create successful model voucher programs to galvanize public support for private school choice. Through these carefully orchestrated efforts CEO America wages a public relations campaign to convince the public to embrace the role of the marketplace in providing educational opportunity, with the government footing the bill.[8]

Yet those who are concerned about the development of a profit-driven educational system point out two fundamental falsehoods inherent in the privatization claims. First, the notion of "choice" is a misnomer. Most of the scholarships from both CEO America and the CSF do not provide sufficient funds to enable poor urban residents to escape faltering public schools. Supplementing the vouchers to come up with the private school tuition is frequently impossible for low-income families. Add to this the problems associated with the lack of transportation for low-income students, and the promise of "escaping failing public schools" seems unattainable. Opponents contend that the privatization of education through private choice is a cruel hoax. These opponents, such as People for the American Way and the NEA, say the agenda of CSF and CEO America is opening the door to profit, not improving education for the poor.

The second falsehood, according to privatization's critics, is the claim that competition creates incentives for public schools to improve. The assumption is that when students have a choice of school to go to, all schools will have to offer a quality education in order to keep their "customers" happy—including public schools. And CEO America believes that it is up to the "consumers" of education—that is, the parents and their children—to determine educational "quality," not the government. In other words, CEO America reasons, accountability for student achievement should be the province of parents and their children who attend voucher schools, not the public at large.

The Children's Scholarship Fund

When two wealthy benefactors, Ted Forstmann and multibillionaire John Walton, aided by technology venture capitalist John Doerr, decided in 1997 to offer partial scholarships to 1,000 low-income families in

Washington, D.C., they were inundated with nearly 8,000 applications. Impressed by this response, they founded the Children's Scholarship Fund on 9 June 1998. The new organization's leaders—which included Forstmann, Walton, Senate Majority Leader Trent Lott, House Speaker Newt Gingrich, former Education Secretary William Bennett—described the CSF as a means for creating educational opportunities for poor people and giving parents a private choice, rather than continuing to force them to send their children to failing public schools.

According to its Web site, CSF claims to work with "investors, entrepreneurs, educators, and public policy experts to rethink the way education is funded, organized, and delivered." It does this by touting the merits of a market-oriented system of education that reflects what the organization considers to be the American dream: freedom, opportunity, and the entrepreneurial spirit.[9]

The goal of CSF, like many similar-minded organizations, is to bring together leaders from business, religion, and education to explore how our free enterprise system can improve education. Forstmann and Walton approach their task with religious zeal. But they are also savvy political organizers with an astute understanding of the economic and ideological work involved in convincing the public of the virtues of privatized education. In some cases, the interests of these new "educators" clearly lie in profits and politics as much as in education. Doerr, for example, invests heavily in for-profit educational ventures through the New Schools Venture Fund and was a campaign adviser to Vice President Al Gore in his 2000 bid for the presidency. Walton is active in conservative politics. According to Forstmann, "Some people in this effort are actually going to make money." He adds, "They are, like everybody else who does a good job."[10]

A $100-million contribution from Wal-Mart heir John Walton gave CSF its initial start. To acquire the capital necessary to offer the private scholarships, Forstmann and Walton used their own funds but also solicited some of the largest entrepreneurial and philanthropic donors in the United States interested in privatizing education. And while CSF attempts to present a beneficent image of public nonpartisanship—arguing that what works for children is what is best for America—both of its founders are zealously ideological. Together Forstmann and Walton were the major financial backers of the Washington Scholarship Fund, a private voucher program in Washington, D.C.

Private Philanthropy as a Social Movement

When there is an obvious pay-off for those advocating public policy changes, it behooves citizens to critically examine those advocates, their agendas, and the implications of their claims. So let us begin with Ted Forstmann.

Forstmann is not an unfamiliar face. Besides being a multimillionaire venture capitalist, Forstmann considers himself "a pioneer of the leveraged buyout."[11] He has served on the boards of, or as a spokesperson for, many similar conservative organizations. His interest in school privatization and commercialization was born long before he founded the Children's Scholarship Fund.

According to Forstmann, his interest is governed by what he has learned about schools. He suggests that before the American Revolution and for 100 years of our country's history, education was widely available and diverse. He argues that competition kept quality high and education was voluntary. Further, he claims that literacy was very high—in fact, he maintains it was higher then than in some states today. For Forstmann, a combination of competition, charity, and private and semipublic institutions "worked" in the past. The problem, he argues, is that starting in the 1850s with Massachusetts, America began a dramatic shift from free-market and charitable education to "government-run schools."[12] And even though America today cannot be compared to the America of the pre–Civil War era, his position is clear—we need to replace public schools with charitable choice and privatization.

Perhaps Forstmann's educational vision is heartfelt. But many argue that Ted Forstmann is an entrepreneurial capitalist with a marketplace agenda for education that seems more commercial than altruistic. Forstmann claims that his interest in privatizing education through the use of private school scholarships is driven by beneficence, not profit. As recently as 1998 he commented in a speech to the Washington Press Club: "This is a real moral issue. I hate talking about the economics of it."[13] But is it just his value system and sense of morality that fuels the scholarship fund idea, or does Forstmann have another agenda?

Forstmann is senior partner of Forstmann, Little & Company, a private investment firm. Pioneering the leveraged buyout, Forstmann, Little has compiled an unprecedented record of performance over the past twenty years, investing nearly $15 billion in twenty-three acquisitions including Gulfstream, a jet manufacturer; Community Health Systems; Ziff-Davis Publishing; Dr. Pepper; and Yankee Candle. In the past, the firm attempted to acquire major investments in Whittle Communications, a company already beginning to profit from public school financing and once the home of the Channel One television programming utilized in thousands of public schools today. At the time of the attempted Forstmann deal, Chris Whittle was in the research and development stage of what he then called the Edison Project, the development of a national chain of private schools, which we will discuss in some length in a subsequent chapter. Suffice it to say, Forstmann, like many other prescient educational entrepreneurs, saw a tremendous investment opportunity in private schooling and the private management of public schools. Thus his scholarship efforts must be understood as a for-profit educational venture.

Forstmann not only serves with John Walton on the board of the Children's Scholarship Fund, but he also assists as an honorary chairman of the Washington Scholarship Fund. Described by the New Republic magazine as "one of the Republican party's leading moneymen," when former House Speaker Newt Gingrich resigned his post in 1998, Forstmann was adroit enough to persuade the former politician to join him as one of the directors of his New York buyout firm.[14]

Apparently the ambition of both entrepreneurs is to realize the construction of private educational enterprises subsidized by public funds and controlled by a few large, multinational corporations—much like the health maintenance organization (HMO) structure for health care today. Their efforts have been enormously successful. And Ted Forstmann's efforts to disassemble public schools go beyond mere advocacy speeches.

For example, after a Florida judge rejected the nation's first statewide school choice program in a decision rendered in 2000, Forstmann immediately stepped to the forefront and offered to fund private tuition scholarships for fifty-three children in Pensacola, Florida, whom he felt would be adversely affected by the court's ruling. Under the Florida Supreme Court ruling, children who were currently receiving "Opportunity Scholarships" to attend private schools would be allowed to finish the school year, but the state would not pay their tuition beginning in the fall of 2000. Currently, Forstmann is doing everything he can to work around the Florida Supreme Court's decision. He is using private school scholarships to help low-income families cover tuition costs at private schools of their choice in an attempt to give them economic incentives to abandon public schools. In a statement made directly after the court's decision, Forstmann voiced his support for the privatization efforts in Florida and despite the judge's ruling continues in his drive to separate schools from the government.[15]

However, Forstmann's attempts may not be necessary. House Republican leaders are looking at another way to save Governor Jeb Bush's centerpiece legislation in Florida: a proposed amendment to the state constitution that would allow state money to be used for vouchers. One suggestion is an amendment that, not withstanding any other provision of the constitution, would allow the legislature to create and pay for a program to help children attend private schools.

What started as an idea in the minds of two entrepreneurial billionaires quickly burgeoned into an educational and political strategy designed to divert public funds to private schools through a form of a leveraged buyout of public schools. In the private sector leveraged buyouts occur when investors purchase the stock of a corporation and retire most of it. The corporation then has less equity than it did before the purchase. The investors then replace the retired stock with bonds creating more debt for the corporation. A leveraged buy-out of public schools means that public funds are transferred to the private sector.

How could CSF accomplish this mission? With two simple steps: First, persuade parents to abandon public schools in favor of private schools by using private scholarship funds donated by wealthy benefactors to help them pay tuition. Second, unceasingly promote the ideology of educational privatization as sound economic, social, individual, and educational policy. Private philanthropy furthers the CSF mission by reducing public assistance in favor of private assistance.

As their privatization efforts succeeded in various states, CSF's founders quickly moved their agenda to the national level.[16] Besides wielding vast political and economic power, as well as bequeathing hefty donations to California's campaign for the passage of that state's antiaffirmative-action legislation, Proposition 209, Forstmann, along with former Education Secretary William Bennett and former HUD Secretary Jack Kemp, founded Empower America in 1993. Empower America was conceived as an advocacy group that would steer the Republican Party back to power along a new conservative road after its loss to Bill Clinton in the 1992 presidential race.

Probably contributors to CSF donate money simply in an effort to help children. Yet the record of the organization's founders raises disturbing questions about their motives. A look at the leaders of CSF shows that:

> Walton is not only the founder of School Futures Research Foundation, a nonprofit organization that manages a number of California's charter schools; he also directs a for-profit company, the TesseracT Group (formerly Education Alternatives Inc.), that manages charter and public schools.
>
> Walton, a regular speaker on the provoucher circuit, spent a quarter of a million dollars on voucher initiatives in California.

Seeing teachers' unions as an obstacle to vouchers, Walton personally contributed $360,000 toward passage of California's antiunion Proposition 226, supplemented by $50,000 from his American Education Reform Foundation. This initiative would allow teachers to opt out of the teacher unions that represent them. Other prominent voucher proponents, including James Leininger, J. Patrick Rooney, David Brennan, Howard Ahmanson, and Richard DeVos (via his Amway Corporation) also contributed substantial amounts to the initiative.

Forstmann donated $10,000 to help secure passage of California's antiaffirmative-action Proposition 209. Proposition 209 now prohibits the use of race when assessing qualifications for government positions, government contracts, and admissions to four-year universities and state colleges.

Forstmann's leveraged buyout firm attempted to acquire one-third ownership in Whittle Communications, the creator of the controversial Channel One television program that has injected commercials into the classroom, and of the Edison Project, a national chain of private schools.

James Leininger, cofounder of CEO San Antonio and director of CEO America, has also founded several religious-right organizations, including the American Family Association, Family Research Council, and Focus on the Family. His A+ PAC for Parental School Choice supports the campaigns of state and local provoucher candidates in Texas.

The Walton Family Foundation and the Foundation of Ohio voucher proponent David Brennan contributed half a million dollars for Brennan to set up two private, for-profit voucher schools in Cleveland immediately after the state legislature enacted voucher programs.

California venture capitalist Tim Draper, who pushed for a voucher initiative on the March 2000 ballot that was resoundingly defeated, continues to invest heavily in education-related companies.

Michael Milken has turned from junk bonds and jail to schools, with investments of $500 million in education-related companies.[17]

Following the private scholarship fund's conception, 1.25 million low-income parents from 20,000 communities applied for private foundation scholarships through CSF. Winners of the random drawing were awarded scholarships to the private schools of their choice—secular or otherwise. Families had to qualify by demonstrating financial need, measured by standards similar to those adopted by the federal school lunch program, which takes into account family size and income. Eligibility was restricted to students in grades K–8, because the CSF specifically maintains that the earlier a child receives "sensible schooling," the more likely he or she will become a successful learner.

In 1999 nearly 40,000 children in over 7,000 private schools nationwide benefited from four-year scholarships as part of CSF's mission to unlock the doors to what supporters like to refer to as "innovative educational opportunities."[18] The demand for these private scholarships was even higher than the Children's Scholarship Fund had dreamed. Since its inception in 1998, CSF has received 1.25 million applications from students nationwide. That is an almost mind-boggling response— even more so when one bears in mind that these applicants are low-income families who must pay $1,000 a year, on average, to supplement the tuition costs only partially paid by the scholarship fund.

But with many children not fortunate enough to win a private scholarship through the lottery process, CSF realized that its scholarship program was barely adequate to address what it viewed as a severe educational problem. So, CSF reasoned, the program was in need of expansion, and the organization's leaders also saw a political window of opportunity to expand their privatization initiatives nationwide. CSF has now targeted private scholarship markets in twenty-five other major cities, and the list is growing.[19] Throughout the 1990s CSF exerted a formidable degree of influence in the struggle to privatize public schools.

The goal of the Children's Scholarship Fund is to encourage the development and growth of diverse varieties of private schools, secular and nonsecular, so that all families might have a private choice of the kind of education they believe is best for their children. But once CSF had awarded 40,000 students scholarships in April 1999, it became nearly impossible, in most cities, for parents to find available seats for their children in private schools. So Forstmann and Walton decided that they could not reach their goal through philanthropy alone; there were simply not enough private schools to accommodate those who wished to attend.[20] This shortage, they argue, is the result of the public monopoly on schooling, which tends to discourage fewer charitable contributions to schools as well as the private venture capital that could be used to build the private schools that people want and need. Government by its very nature, they claim, discourages private innovation and erodes the market incentives that would satisfy the demand for good, affordable schools.

The CSF, as well as other school privatization supporters, accepts the unquestioned assumption that today's "new economy" opens doors for more people than ever to participate in the market. But they also warn that while the knowledge economy is dissolving traditional impediments to production, the one notable barrier to growth and equal access to the free market remains inadequate schooling. Their position postulates that if there is no learning and knowledge then there will be no entry into the new global economy for masses of people. Thus it is imperative, in the judgment of the CSF, to maximize the chance to participate in the economy by maximizing each child's chance to learn. We can do this, they claim, by privatizing education through private vouchers, philanthropic scholarships that enhance private choice, high-stakes testing that boosts student achievement, zero-tolerance policies that end student violence, school policies that end social promotion, and by dismantling cumbersome government regulations and bureaucratically inefficient public schools that smother the development of private and imaginative educational alternatives.

Certainly it is a compassionate deed to donate money to help a child in need obtain a decent education. And certainly there is little doubt that public schools need revitalization. Deteriorating physical plants, anachronistic text materials, poor teacher training, lack of professionalism, overcrowded classrooms, inadequate salaries, and a shortage of teachers are just some of the issues that public school students and teachers confront. As a result, many public charities and private philanthropists are targeting their donations to public schools.

Private tuition scholarships are not simply altruistic endeavors aimed at subsidizing private tuition for the economically and socially disadvantaged. Instead, these private scholarship funds, like CSF, are implicated in a larger strategy to disassemble the school-state relationship in its entirety.

The long-term effects of private philanthropy on education are uncertain, but the questions it raises must be addressed now, before the course of national educational policy is permanently altered by it. Will private philanthropic measures improve public school performance and bolster student achievement? Or are they merely another example of entrepreneurial scheming? Can anyone simply turn his or her advocacy of a personal ideology into a "school" and then ask the public to fund it through private vouchers? What will be the standards for quality schools and who will set them? Will privatization decimate the public schools? And perhaps the most important question, will privatization create charitable-based schools funded with philanthropic donations and public funds? For many, this possibility is not only unsettling, but also antithetical to national and constitutional principles.

CHARITABLE CHOICE, FAITH-BASED CHARITY, AND EDUCATIONAL RELIGIOUS ACCOMMODATION

John Ashcroft, U.S. attorney general under George W. Bush, introduced a proposal when he was a senator from Missouri that he termed "charitable choice." It promises to become one of the most controversial suggestions in the history of church-state relations in the United States, because it seems to address the claims of denial of equal protection under the law that many religious organizations make.

Many progressive religious institutions and leaders accept this concept of government subsidization of religious services through charitable choice as a matter of principle. They argue that the government currently denies eligibility for government grant monies to sectarian organizations on unconstitutional grounds: thus it in effect denies nonsecular organizations equal protection under the law. It also discriminates against those who are religious and seek to provide private schooling, social services, and other religious activities that benefit society. They also claim that allowing for what they term "charitable choice" will strike a balance between pure private choice advocates, those who wish to separate schools from the government, and those religious sectors that do charitable work that helps society. Therefore, they contend, the idea of charitable choice serves as a pragmatic strategy to avoid political crisis and accommodate diversity in a pluralistic society.

Opponents of subsidizing charitable, faith-based organizations advocate a secular state—one that does not fund or otherwise sponsor religious institutions and activities. They believe a democratic polity should not sponsor the display of religious symbols and should not allow for policies that discriminate based on religious belief. They argue that the government should guarantee not just freedom of religion, but freedom from religion. They maintain that government subsidy of religious activity of any kind equates morality with religion, stigmatizes those who are nonreligious, and defers to religious claims in fashioning public policy. Many also point out that history disproves the claim that morality is safe only in the hands of religion. Arthur Hertzberg, a professor at New York University, claims that no society where the church was dominant emancipated the Jews. He points to the Balkans, where Roman Catholics and Orthodox Christians have slaughtered Muslims in the name of religion.[21] Former Senator Tom Hayden of California is concerned that this move toward "faith-based charities" creates a theocratic private sphere to replace what public institutions remain. He also points out that with entitlements for religious charities, the notion of resistance to privatization policies will be smothered as the charities seek to remain in the good graces of government bureaucrats doling out the federal funds.[22]

Even though the religious right is one of the most vocal architects of the movement toward educational privatization through charitable choice, many of their organizations argue that they will not take federal funds if it means bifurcating their mission and separating conversion from their charitable services. Despite these concerns, they have significantly forwarded the neoliberal ideological agenda concerning educational privatization—with the support of multimillionaire philanthropists and friendly political and judicial decisions.

As a senator, Ashcroft inserted the idea into proposed legislation every time he could. It turned up in the Welfare Reform Bill, the Substance Abuse and Mental Health Reauthorization Act, the Older Americans Act, the Juvenile Justice Act, and a community renewal bill. Before accepting the nomination as attorney general, Ashcroft pledged to include the charitable choice proposal in every public health and social service bill proposed in Congress.[23]

Charitable Choice in Public Policy

In July 1996 when President Clinton signed the Personal Responsibility Act into law as part of the Welfare Reform Act, it included a section known as Section 104, commonly referred to as "charitable choice." Representative Mark Souder, a Republican from Indiana, summarized the legislation in clear terms: "The U.S. House of Representatives passed a bill that would strengthen the partnership between government and religious institutions in providing housing for the nation's low-income, elderly, and disabled citizens and administer and provide services to beneficiaries under any program that permits contracts with organizations or permits certificates, vouchers, or other forms of disbursement to be provided to beneficiaries as a means of providing assistance."[24]

Religious leaders and activists were delighted when the bill passed. The bill promises that faith-based charities will not have to sacrifice their religious purpose in order to partner with the government—and partnering with the government means receiving government subsidies. The bill provides federal block grants to states to decide how, when, and what funds will be dispersed, through which charitable agencies, and for what purposes. This legislation played nicely into the hands of states' rights advocates who had long sought to eliminate all federal public policy in education in favor of decentralized local control. It also married the idea of federal block grants to states with government subsidization of nonsecular institutions. Under the charitable choice plan, those who seek nonsecular social services, such as low-cost housing, or drug rehabilitation, would receive services at taxpayer expense. However, the bill also provided that those clients availing themselves of any service must be afforded the choice to opt out of any explicit religious activities. And furthermore, these nonsecular social programs would be legally held to strict financial accountability standards.

Supporters of the idea argue that these features have been available for some time in analogous federal subsidy programs. They point to the GI Bill as just one example. In the 1960s, they point out, government funding of faith-based organizations in health and human services grew enormously. Not only did time-honored established groups like the Salvation Army and Catholic Charities become major recipients of federal funds in the Great Society's War on Poverty, launched by President Lyndon Johnson, but the trend continues with the funneling of economic development, housing, education, and other funds to multieducational congregations and to nonsecular corporations.

Shifting the Public Policy Terrain

Critics of government involvement in religion argue that promoting the power of a specific religion is very different than coordinating organizing efforts with nonsecular institutions; supporters maintain that nonsecular institutions have partnered with government not to promote the power of a particular religion, but as a matter of public concern and coalition building around social change efforts that they support.

Currently, both centrist liberals and conservatives are working to dilute the separation of church and state and increase the power and control of religion in everyday life. This bipartisan government-religion relationship is something quite new, very different from historical efforts within the secular left to partner with the Catholic Church or black evangelical churches on labor, class, and cultural or racial issues. Critics of public aid to religious institutions point out that their concept of the role of religion in moral and political life is radically shifting the terrain of public policy and the definition of democracy and government. Religious organizations are now posing as victims of the government, claiming that government policy in awarding of contracts and public funding for public services discriminates against them, denying them their freedom of religion.

Peter Dobkin Hall, writing for *Religion in the News*, a publication of Trinity College, pointed out that over the past quarter century, radical changes in religious life and public policy have converged in ways that have transformed both. However, aside from some attention given to the increasing significance of spirituality and the growing political activism of religious conservatives, the news media have generally failed to understand the scope of what may be the most important and fundamental adjustment in the character of American public life since the disestablishment of religion in the first quarter of the nineteenth century.[25]

Two prominent Christian intellectuals have been key players in developing a the language that makes this new argument more broadly palatable. Richard John Neuhaus, now editor of the journal *First Things,* wrote one of the most important contemporary religious advocacy books, entitled *The Naked Public Sphere,* first published in 1984 during the height of the Reagan administration. Yale law professor Stephen Carter published his famous book, *The Culture of Disbelief,* in 1993. Though the two authors differ on many points, they are in adamant agreement that religion is essential to democracy, morality, and everyday life. They argue for an institutional check-and-balance on secular state power and maintain that the main purpose of the Establishment Clause in the Constitution is to protect the church from the state—not the other way around.[26]

From Neuhaus's perspective, the secular state is itself its own religion. It works consistently to discriminate against those who hold religious convictions, denying them equal protection and personal liberty. Secularism is antidemocratic, in the minds of Neuhaus and his supporters. He argues that secular democracy borders on totalitarianism. What is reprehensible, in the eyes of Neuhaus, is the intervention of the state on behalf of individuals such as homosexuals and others who do not toe the religious line. Carter, on the other hand, equates religion in daily life with the causes of the oppressed. He links the civil rights movement with Martin Luther King, Jr. and the black church in an attempt to argue for the inclusion of nonsecular institutions in government partnerships and publicly funded activities.

To critics of the idea of the government–nonsecular partnerships, religion is not the problem nor are conflicts between citizens of different faiths. The problem arises when organized religion pursues its interests, beliefs, and purposes by developing public policies and social and political institutions—and when it attempts to conflate morality with religion. As long as the boundaries between public and private beliefs remained intact, the conflict between secular and nonsecular groups was kept to a minimum, they contend. But now, the situation is considerably different. After twenty years of intensive political organizing by the religious right, the (bitterly contested)election of a member of the religious right, George W. Bush, to the presidency, and Bush's appointment of religious right activist John Ashcroft as attorney general of the

United States, the religious right has accomplished a coup d'état, at least in reformulating the public policy debate over charitable choice and faith-based subsidies.

Charitable Choice: The Argument

Charitable choice is basically a mechanism to allow religious groups that provide social services to receive government grants and contracts to continue to provide that assistance. The reasoning behind it is simple: These institutions provide needed social services that are not themselves religious in nature. Therefore, giving them public funds does not violate the separation of church and state and does provide for efficient delivery of services that otherwise the government would have to take on itself.

Barry Lynn of Americans United for the Separation of Church and State is acutely aware of these dramatic changes in religious life and controversies over public policy that have arisen in the last two decades. In an interview with Jim Lehrer on PBS, Lynn argued that it was impossible to separate the evangelical nature of the church from the social services it provides. His concern, shared by many even in the religious community, is that to get the "soup" one must accept God.[27] According to Lynn, a nonsecular institution faces a bifurcation of its purpose in the charitable choice scenario. It exists primarily to bring people to God, but it is expected to "turn the message off" when federal funds for social programs arrive. Separating conversion to religious faith from the social services it provides is not only impossible, claims Lynn, but it sets up a situation whereby one must accept God to receive aid.

Dennis Hoover, a liberal supporter of charitable choice, disagrees. Hoover argues that charitable choice is really quintessentially American. In a pluralistic society such as ours, he argues, charitable choice levels the playing field by not forcing nonsecular institutions to abandon their mission of social service and become sectarian to receive public funds.[28] Hoover argues that the current judicial test to determine which organizations are "pervasively sectarian" is wrong; the issue the courts should focus on is whether these services provide for people in need and whether they are responsible and accountable for their use of the public funds.

What Hoover and others advocate is a charitable choice law that allows for the legal use of public funds to support nonsecular programs and services. They argue that states have long contracted with religious groups to provide programs like job training, foster care, child-rearing classes, adult education, day care, and drug rehabilitation. Furthermore, nonsecular organizations can provide these necessary services without the notoriously bloated bureaucracies of government agencies. They claim that charitable choice reduces administrative costs by concentrating on the use of lower-paid volunteers and employees who often work for the satisfaction they receive rather than solely for the income.

Thus charitable choice not only codifies into law the right of faith-based agencies to contract with the federal and state governments, but the aim of the charitable choice project, according to many supporters and opponents, is to free the government of its responsibility to address social problems and instead make churches administrative arms of government. What are we to make of this project? Is it some kind of plot bent on coalescing government and religion and moving away from the period of the Enlightenment toward a theocracy?

No, it is not, say defenders of legal charitable choice. They contend that the concept is consistent with American ideals and principles. They point out that progressives and liberals have long railed against the censorship of privately funded speech, yet they are seemingly indifferent to the stifling of the voices of religious organizations. Religious accommodation with government, they maintain, is long overdue, and private religious charitable organizations should not be denied their equal protection under the law or right of free speech due to their religious beliefs. Furthermore, allowing faith-based charitable organizations to compete for federal funds, according to advocates, is constitutional and compassionate—because in this form, it is not direct aid to religion but to the programs that provide secular services under religious auspices.

But does it undermine the purposes and concept of a secular democracy?

Frances Kissling of Catholics for a Free Choice certainly thinks so. She pointed out in March of 2001 that even before charitable choice and faith-based charities emerged as an issue, the Catholic Church had not only demanded from government but has received exemption after exemption from taxation and other federal policies for providing what she believes is the most unacceptable form of reproductive health care: No emergency contraception for women who have been raped, no voluntary postpartum sterilization for women who are having what they hope to be their last child, and no fertility treatments for women who wish to have children. In fact, many secular hospitals that have recently merged with Catholic Charities of California are now witnessing a lawsuit by the group against the state. It seeks an exemption from state law that requires employers—other than religious institutions engaged in narrowly defined religious activities—to provide contraceptive coverage to their employees.[29]

Of course there are many who are displeased with the concept of charitable choice, both within the church and outside it, for a variety of reasons. Rev. Peter Laarman of the Judson Memorial Church and the Rev. Paul Chapman of the Employment Project argue that the idea is founded on an individualistic ideology that views people as economically and socially impoverished because of bad individual choices and irresponsible behavior. Laarman, as well as others, points out that the systemic causes of poverty in the face of unprecedented wealth for a few privileged individuals are never implicated in the debate over public policy. To Laarman and Chapman, the idea of charitable choice is part and parcel of a neoliberal agenda to privatize education and to temper the severity of material conditions under capitalism with a measure of good old-fashioned religion. This agenda, they note, accepts basic systemic injustice and does little to eradicate poverty and racism.[30]

Laarman and Chapman also point out that many charitable choice advocates favor the destruction of the Horace Mann conception of a public, common school. What charitable choice really provides, they argue, is a slippery slope to educational theology: the beginning of a new conception of privatized schooling based on a hodgepodge of faith-based or religious schools. In this scenario, they contend, churches would be transformed into administrative arms of the state that would eventually become fully subsidized moral institutions. For them, the boundary between state and religion is clear: there shall be no government financial aid to religious organizations, directly or indirectly, even if their activities serve to benefit society at large.

Laarman and Chapman are not alone. Many religious organizations, ranging from conservative to liberal, perceive the charitable choice concept as a threat to a secular democracy. Among them are the Baptist Joint Committee, the Presbyterian Church USA, the American Jewish Committee, the Church of the Brethren, the Conference of Seventh-Day Adventists, various Catholic organizations, the Friends, and the Unitarian Universalist Association. These organizations maintain a high commitment to religious freedom and the preservation of the secular state, and they warn that proselytizing will become rampant—at taxpayer expense.[31]

Phil Strickland, director of the Texas Baptist Christian Life Commission, worries that big government will monitor the activities of nonsecular institutions because they receive federal or state funds. He argues that religion should find its own resources in church, not through government.[32] According to the Leonard Greenberg Center for the Study of Religion in Public Life, charitable choice also permits the hiring of staff based on religious tests.[33] But perhaps the strongest argument is that charitable choice violates the separation of church and state by allowing "pervasively sectarian" institutions, including houses of worship, to receive federal funding to administer social services and public health benefits on behalf of the government.[34]

So far the issue of charitable choice has been a topic of controversy primarily in the arena of social services. Lately, however, it has become one of many contemporary vehicles for the promotion of educational privatization efforts. This idea, in its infancy, promises to be a controversial issue for years to come and will no doubt produce contentious court decisions, heated public policy debates, and perhaps, eventual legal implementation.

DEVELOPING A FEDERAL OFFICE OF FAITH-BASED CHARITIES

The 1996 Welfare Reform Act, Section 104, allowed for federal funding of nonsecular welfare services, drug rehabilitation treatment, and community development projects. But bolstered by Clarence Thomas's argument in the *Mitchell v. Helms* case, which redefined the notion of direct versus indirect aid to faith-based institutions, President George W. Bush has proposed a faith-based initiative and accompanying federal agency. (This initiative represents a significant expansion of the promises John Ashcroft made while a senator from Missouri.)

In January 2001 President Bush created the Office of Faith-Based and Community Initiatives. This office reports directly to the president. The office provides resources for groups seeking federal funds, including information about more than 100 federal programs and guidelines for the legal requirements associated with federal funding.

This administrative government agency utilizes a taxpayer-funded federal office and an accompanying government bureaucracy to coordinate federal funding from multiple federal government agencies, including the departments of Justice, Housing and Urban Development, Health and Human Services, Labor, and Education. Its objective is to encourage states, through federal block grants, to directly subsidize the pervasively nonsecular, faith-based, charitable groups that they, as government officials, feel provide important social services.

The office opened in February 2001, with a staff of ten federally paid employees and was headed by University of Pennsylvania professor John Dilulio. Dilulio, who served six months in the position, is a self-described Democrat with close ties to religious conservatives, who worked to expand AmeriCorps, a federally funded community-service organization, so it could serve as a more effective link between religious and secular organizations.

With the advisory board of the Office of Faith-Based Charities funding religious charities and AmeriCorps boosting the capacity of charities and charitable services with manpower, Bush may avoid delicate constitutional problems. Providing volunteers may be interpreted as indirect assistance to religion and thus seen as constitutional under Clarence Thomas's new judicial test.

Bush's proposal also includes a $5,000 per person charity credit and a charitable deduction for those who do not itemize their taxes.[35] It will eventually provide "compassionate joint venture funds" through tax subsidies, making public capital available to support private faith-based organizations. It would permit public funding of nonsecular mentoring for child prisoners as well as public funding of nonsecular organizations attempting to aid broken families and neighborhoods. Furthermore, his plan would create a national agency, funded by taxpayer money, to mobilize forces for his army of "compassionate conservatism."

The Bush agenda raises many important questions. Will charitable choice conducted by faith-based organizations mean that private nonsecular agencies and organizations are legally considered social service providers eligible for federal funds? Will private vouchers then become moot as a state political issue? After all, if the federal government acquiesces in faith-based charitable choice and provides direct block grants to states, allowing them to decide which faith-based organizations qualify, will eligible faith-based organizations be interpreted to include schools? The National Center for Policy Analysis thinks so. It observes that those who are intent on disengaging government from private sectors of the economy see a link between charitable choice and school privatization. After all, if private entities can administer welfare, they ask, why should they not be allowed to administer education through private school vouchers or charter schools?[36]

The answers to these and other important questions are difficult to discern. The Bush agenda may ultimately find support across a wide band of constituencies, but it will certainly face resistance from broad-based coalitions of both secular and nonsecular groups adamantly opposed to the idea. Many religious leaders believe that contributions to religious, faith-based charitable groups must be voluntary rather than forced by the state or federal government. The director of health and welfare studies for the conservative Cato Institute, Michael Tanner, counsels, "No one would deny that private charities, especially faith-based initiatives, can transform individual lives and help raise people out of poverty and despair; but the essence of private charity is voluntariness." To Tanner, receiving tax money is tantamount to state coercion.[37]

What about reducing the role of government? Traditionally, that principle has been the centerpiece of the conservative agenda. But the Bush agenda flies in the face of this principle and that of downsizing the federal government when it creates a new federal program and cabinet-level agency that siphons public funds from government coffers and transfers them directly to private, nonsecular caregivers. Is this the neoliberal agenda for reducing "big government"—or simply an attempt at redefining government's role and tying it to the functions of business and religion?

THE OUTLOOK FOR PRIVATE PHILANTHROPY AND CHARITABLE CHOICE

Presently, the development of private tuition scholarships by multimillionaires, the emergence of faith-based, federally funded charities, and the explosion of charitable choice scholarships are limited projects. However, some of these same charitable choice supporters and private philanthropists also work assiduously to elect religious right representatives to school boards; they support antiunion and antiaffirmative-action efforts; they labor to outlaw bilingual education; they work to deny schooling to undocumented workers; and they toil to control the content and delivery of curriculums in schools.

Many neoliberal economists and politicians, along with such groups as the Family Research Council, the Christian Coalition, the Eagle Forum, and others are regular, if not comfortable, bedfellows in the movement to privatize education. Rooney, Forstmann, Walton, and Leininger promote an image of business support for the private voucher idea, the acceptance of charitable choice, and support for private tuition scholarships. They cast themselves not as zealots looking to dismantle public education, but as concerned public policy makers looking out for the best interest of our nation's children. With the election of George W. Bush and his plans for a national educational voucher system along with the expected Supreme Court replacements in the future, they may find themselves with the judicial, legislative, and executive support they need to promote and legitimize their agenda.

The Supreme Court will also be another important battle front for neoliberal proponents and their religious allies. On 10 July 2000 the U.S. Supreme Court rendered a six-to-three decision to allow private schools to use federal funds for nonreligious purposes. This ruling may provide the precedent necessary to allow the Court eventually to find that private vouchers are constitutional. But the more compelling ruling deserving critical attention occurred in June 2000: the Supreme Court decision in *Mitchell v. Helms* that has encouraged and enlivened private voucher advocates and private scholarship proponents.

The *Helms* case involved the Federal Education Consolidation and Improvement Act of 1981. The Court's decision allowed for the allocation of federal funds for "secular, neutral, and non-ideological" programs that provided computers and other instructional materials to public and private schools, including religious schools. The majority opinion, written by Clarence Thomas, struck down the age-old doctrine that any government aid to private schools is automatically unconstitutional. This radical shift in the Court's thinking may signify that private vouchers will turn out to be legally acceptable as long as the parents of the voucher-receiving children and not the government decide which schools students will attend. The Court's decision has prompted CEO America to claim that school vouchers will become the law of the land, and soon.[38] This prescient prediction seems to be correct.

For defenders of a secular democracy, the issue is simple—it is crucial to protect secular culture and democratic principles, as it is imperative to protect secular law. When religion defines morality, the firewall between church and state is corroded and the secular state itself begins to be seen by the public as intrinsically immoral. Many critics of state-church accommodation go even further, arguing that secular liberalism and the American democracy have been shaped by the Enlightenment. Organized religious beliefs, on the other hand, find their expression and origin in a patriarchal religious ideology and a particular sexual morality unacceptable to many Americans.

How this controversy ultimately plays out in public policies and community debates, especially as they affect the public subsidy of nonsecular schools, will be of utmost concern to all Americans. The stakes are high.

NOTES

1. "Conservative Spotlight: J. Patrick Rooney." *Human Events* (31 March 1995). Volume 16. Washington, D.C.

2. FECInfo Data Base. Search for contributions from James Leininger. http://www.tray.com.

3. Falwell, J. (1979). *America Can Be Saved.* Wheaton, ILL: Scripture Press Publishing.

4. Dubose, L. (27 March 1998). "Deschooling Society." *The Texas Observer.*

5. Bryce, R. (1 February 1999). "Million Dollar Man." p. 4. *Austin Chronicle.*

6. CEO America's Mission Statement. (5 June 1998). http://www.ceoamerica.org.

7. People for the American Way. (20 April 1999). "Privatization of Public Education: A Joint Venture of Charity and Power." p. 9. http://www.pfaw.org.

8. CEO America's History. (5 June 1998). http://www.ceoamerica.org.

9. http://www.scholarshipfund.org.

10. Forstmann, T. (19 November 1999). "Ted Forstmann Calls for a Competitive System That Rewards Educators for Excellence and Penalizes Failure." The Children Scholarship Fund. Washington, D.C.

11. People for the American Way. "Privatization of Public Education."

12. Forstmann, "Ted Forstmann Calls."

13. Forstmann, T. (15 March 2000). "Ted Forstmann to Fund Scholarships for Florida School Children Abandoned in Court Ruling." http://www.scholarshipfund.org.

14. Bloomberg News. (6 January 1999). "Gingrich Set to Return Home, Will Serve on Advisory Board of New York Buyout Firm." pp. 14. *Washington Times.*

15. Forstmann, "Ted Forstmann to Fund Scholarships."

16. People for the American Way. "Privatization of Public Education."

17. Coleman, N. (20 April 1999). "New Report Details Links between Charity and Vested Interests in Campaign against Public Schools. Children's Scholarship Fund Head Urged to Target Aid to Public Schools." People for the American Way. http://www.pfaw.org.

18. Forstmann, T. (27 April 2000). "Utopia: Competition vs. Monopoly in Education." Speech given at the Commercial Club of Chicago. Chicago, IL.

19. People for the American Way. "Privatization of Public Education."

20. Ibid.

21. Hertzberg, A. (12 March 2001). "Bully in the Pulpit!" p. 20. *The Nation* 272, no. 10.

22. Ibid.

23. Americans United for Separation of Church and State. (12 December 2000). "Talking Points on Charitable Choice." http://www.au.org.

24. Section 104 of the Welfare Reform Bill of 1996. Available through the Texas Department of Human Services. http://www.dhs.state.tx.us.

25. Hall, P. (Summer 1998) "Religion and the Post-welfare State: An Untold Story." p. 3. *Religion in the News.* Vol. 1. No. 1. The Leonard Greenberg Center for the Study of Religion in Public Life, Trinity College. Hartford, CT.

26. Willis, E. (19 February 2001). "Freedom from Religion." p. 14. *The Nation* 272, no 7.

27. Hall, P. "Religion and the Post-welfare State: An Untold Story."

28. Hoover, D. (6 November 2000). "Hoover Replies." p. 24. *The Nation* 271, no. 14.

29. Kissling, F. (12 March 2001). "Bully in the Pulpit!" p. 2. *The Nation* 272, no. 10.

30. Ibid. 2.

31. Matsui, E., and J. Chuman. (10 February 2000). "Charitable Choice: Two Views." p. 2. *The Record Online.* http://www.bergen.com.

32. Baptist Press. (29 August 1996). "Charitable Choice Entangles Church and State, Say Ethicists." pp. 1, 2. UMR Communications. Dallas, TX. http://www.umr.org.

33. Weiner, D. (Summer 1998). "Missing the Boat on Charitable Choice." p. 1. *Religion in the News.* Volume 1. No. 1. The Leonard Greenberg Center for the Study of Religion in Public Life. Trinity College. Hartford, CT.

34. Americans United for Separation of Church and State. (12 December 2000). "Talking Points on Charitable Choice." http://www.au.org.

35. Milbank, D. (30 January 2001). "Bush Unveils Faith-based Initiative: Effort Will Team Agencies, Nonprofits on Social Issues." p. A01. *Washington Post.*

36. The National Center for Policy Analysis. (28 December 2000). "The Charitable Choice." http://www.public-policy.org.

37. The Cato Institute. (30 January 2001). "Government-funded Faith-based Charities May Hurt Real Charity." http://www.cato.org.

38. Children First, CEO America. (1 January 2001). "Legislative Efforts around the Country." p. 1. http://www.childrenfirstamerica.org.

Chapter Seven

●◆ From Learning Centers to Earning Centers?

The business community has responded enthusiastically to calls for the privatization of the nation's public schools. Many multinational corporations have long been eager to publicly tie schooling to production and mass consumption, and many are already involved in the education of American children through unsolicited "educational kits" and "programs" sent to public school teachers throughout the country. These sponsored educational materials (SEMs) can come in printed or electronic form; they can be overt or covert in content design.

One online SEM curriculum organization, the Chalkboard, operates as a sharing center for SEMs by providing educators with lesson plans for science, language, math, special education, school-to-work programs, and much more. Classroom resources, including curriculum units for teachers and students are provided free by corporations. Chalkboard provides direct connections to corporations such as the Clorox Corporation, which has a "Keep America Beautiful Campaign" that teachers can use in their classes with their students.[1] General Motors has a curriculum to teach children about the environment; Pizza Hut offers incentives to help boys and girls learn to read; Fidelity Investment Brokers promises to teach students how to save and budget their money; Mobil Oil gets them to think critically about the environment; Miller Brewing Company provides materials about the contributions of African Americans to our culture; *USA Today* offers children an insider perspective on the newspaper publishing business; Chef Boyardee teaches students about nutrition while they discover holistic health from sing-along handouts provided by the NutraSweet Corporation.

Yet before we celebrate the involvement of corporate America in the development of so-called educational kits, programs, and other projects aimed at students, we need to examine the motives of these educational entrepreneurs. Should this seemingly benign preoccupation with our children's education be construed as simple benevolence on the part of corporate America?

According to Kathleen Tyner of the San Francisco-based Strategies for Media Literacy, education for American students has become

"McEducation." School is now an extension of the marketplace, where students are surrounded by advertisements—in classrooms, hallways, and school cafeterias.[2] Furthermore, the so-called student market is a rapidly increasing multibillion dollar opportunity—fertile ground for wholesale commercial penetration and profit harvesting.

As advertisers on children's television understand, advertising to create product awareness and consumer consciousness is crucial to increasing sales revenues. In 1998, for example, U.S. advertising expenditures topped $200 billion, indicating a 24 percent increase from the $161.5 billion spent in 1990 and an 89 percent increase from the $105.97 billion spent in 1980 (these figures are adjusted to 1998 dollars).[3] The average total spent by the advertising industry in 1998 to reach *one* household was estimated at $1,987.00.[4]

From the advertiser's perspective, children between the ages of four and twelve play a significant role in the marketplace: they influence the purchase of goods worth an estimated $500 billion annually. It's not difficult to imagine why advertising purposely directed at children has increased twenty-fold in the past decade, to a stunning $2 billion.[5] Older students are targets of even more advertising dollars. David Siegel, general manager of Small Talk, notes that Channel One's twelve-minute in-classroom broadcast, which we will shortly examine, has a daily teenage audience as big as that of Super Bowl—the most extensively watched TV event of the year. In 1997, the teenage audience that watched Channel One was fifty times larger than the teenage audience of MTV, and 42 percent of Channel One programming comprises ads and fillers.[6]

Corporate efforts to reach children are not confined to promoting products on in-school television programs like Channel One or sponsoring educational materials. Corporations also solicit personal information from students in an effort to develop consumer profiles that can then be used to target children for commercial messages. Of the 212 Web sites aimed at children that were examined in a 1998 survey by the Federal Trade Commission, 89 percent solicited personal information such as name, postal address, and social security number, but only 23 percent advised children to ask their parents' permission before providing personal information.[7]

Why are corporations so keen to gather personal information on children? The answer is simple, observes Paul Robertson, of Youth Unlimited (the Toronto affiliate of Youth for Christ): Children's spending has roughly doubled every ten years for the past three decades and has tripled in the 1990's. Children aged four through twelve spent $2.2 billion in 1968 and $4.2 billion in 1984. By 1994 this figure had climbed to $17.1 billion and by 2002, children's spending exceeded $40 billion.[8]

Adolescents and young adults aged twelve through nineteen spent approximately $94 billion of their own money in 1998. This represented an increase from $63 billion just four years earlier.[9] In the 1960s, children influenced about $5 billion of their parents' purchases. By 1984 that amount increased tenfold to $50 billion, and by 1997 it had tripled to $188 billion.[10] Children's marketing expert James McNeal estimated in 1999 that family purchases directly influenced by children would increase to almost $500 billion in 2000.[11]

Given the amount of money at stake, we can begin to discern why companies are concentrating on establishing a presence in schools. Schools have become an attractive new profit-making venture for marketers pitching their merchandise under the rubric of "educational reform" and "educational concern." In the educational arena corporate marketers find an attentive audience of young consumers. "Kids spend money," says Tyner, and "schools are an untapped market segment."[12]

When the most notorious bank robber of the twentieth century, Willie Sutton, was asked why he robbed banks, he answered, "Because that's where the money is." So why are marketers targeting schools? Because that's where the kids are, explains James McNeal, professor of marketing at Texas A&M University. Underfunded schools, financially desperate for resources, are increasingly trading access to their students for corporate giveaways. The companies benefit from the opportunity to build brand name recognition and customer loyalty in younger and younger consumers. According to Peggy Charren, president of Action for Children's Television, citizens are paying for public educational deficits by virtually selling kids to advertisers.[13]

CHRONICLING COMMERCIALISM IN EDUCATION

The Center for the Analysis of Commercialism in Education (CACE), formerly located at the University of Wisconsin in Milwaukee and now at Arizona State University, chronicles commercial advertising efforts aimed at schools and describes the various forms this advertising can take. Here are three typical examples:

In Service Marketing Group's Apples for Students project, which operated during the nineties, students converted cash register receipts from particular businesses into computer equipment. Stores attracted customers, particularly students and parents, through their participation in a "worthy cause."

In the Viewing Can Reward program, launched by Blockbuster video stores in Hawaii in 1996, school districts received videocassette recorders when their students or family members turned in punch cards showing that a combined total of 5,000 movies or video games had been rented.

In 1997, General Mills converted thousands of "Special K" cereal eaters to "Lucky Charms" by paying 15 cents per box to students at participating schools, according to the *Boston Globe.* Apparently students at Thomas Ditson School collected 27,000 box tops (117 per student) in this General Mills promotion. The *Globe* reported that parents had stopped buying Post or Kellogg's brand cereals.[14]

A 1999 report claims in many schools, children are now given the "opportunity" to participate in taste tests on cereals and to become marketing "focus groups" *in their own classrooms.* Robert Reynolds, president of Education Market Resources, the company in charge of the studies, argues that participation in the educational marketplace "empowers" the children.[15] An associate editor of *Youth Markets Alert,* Gene Newman, maintains that although commercial promotion in schools was once seen as insidious, this attitude is changing in this era of public school deprivation. Now the public, as well as parents and the schools themselves, favor business involvement in education.[16]

HOW DOES CORPORATE ADVERTISING ENTER OUR SCHOOLS?

If the corporate penetration of the educational arena is driven by profits parading as pedagogy, as many would argue, then why do educators and their communities acquiesce? The answer is simple: economics and an antiquated system for funding schools. Since schools are funded through property taxes, the quality of education and teaching is tied to the amount of money collected locally. Thus students living in affluent districts receive a top-quality education while students living in poor areas receive a less-than-satisfactory education.

This system of financing public schools is the problem, argues Alex Molnar, and changing it is the best way to restore a balance between schools and corporations. He advocates funding schools through a sharply progressive income tax. Such a funding system, administered evenhandedly, would eliminate the need for "adopt-a-school" programs, because no school would be left behind.[17]

Corporate-sponsored educational materials (SEMs) reach the classrooms of America through education conferences, unsolicited mass mailings put into teachers' boxes or placed on staff cafeteria tables, recommendations in education journals, advertising on product packaging, in supermarkets, or in other commercial sites. If textbooks are old and supplemental resources scarce, the prepackaged SEMs offer teachers a way to "jazz up" a lesson. However, many schools have no appraisal process to help teachers assess the pedagogical value of these resources. Careful assessment is important, as a study by the Commercialism in Education Research Unit at the College of Education at Arizona State University revealed. The study found that 80 percent contained biased or incomplete information and encouraged a viewpoint that favored consumption of the sponsors' product or service. Over half the materials studied were found to be "extremely commercial."[18]

Corporate messages are also deliberately inserted into the classroom curriculum by companies who specialize in doing just that. For example, Lifetime Learning Systems (LLS), a marketing service based in Fairfield, Connecticut, creates corporate-sponsored "educational programs" designed to promote a particular sponsor's products. According to company vice president and editor-in-chief Dr. Dominic Kinley, LLS's materials have reached over 2 million teachers since the company's founding in 1987.[19] Some LLS materials are simply product promotions thinly disguised as educational materials. For example, *Corporate Watch* describes a "Grow Up!" teaching kit on nutrition for preschoolers: "Each kit contained certificates and growth charts for the students, pamphlets for their parents, and up to 96 product samples of the company's 'Fruit Roll-Ups.' According to an LLS promotional brochure, over 1 million samples were distributed in the nation's kindergartens." For Lederle Laboratories, manufacturers of Centrum Jr. Multivitamins, LLS designed a teaching kit that "introduced fourth, fifth, and sixth graders in middle- and upper-income areas countrywide to the significance of vitamins and minerals."[20]

The strong presence of corporate America in the classroom leads many educators to raise a critical issue: When corporate interests are allowed to design curricula, they manipulate the ideas and culture disseminated within the classroom, installing in young minds a worldview defined by mass consumption, corporate allegiance, and advertising. Materials designed to sell products or worldviews gain trustworthiness when they are presented by teachers in a classroom setting, critics argue. Jill Savitt of the Center for the Study of Commercialism worries that "some kids will feel that information they are receiving is completely correct, unbiased, and valid because it is given to them in the classroom." Corporate messages are legitimized, Savitt points out, "by the social setting where learning is supposed to take place."[21]

For example, Exxon produced an environmental unit about the healthy ecology of Prince William Sound in Alaska. The lesson plan, which displayed stunning eagles flying in blue skies, cavorting sea otters, and sea birds in their natural environment, was simply a public relations campaign designed to clean up the company's image after the Exxon Valdez oil spill in 1989,[22] one of the biggest environmental disasters in the last two decades. To make matters worse, the Exxon's propagandistic public "educational" enterprise was paid for by public funds through school districts and local tax dollars.

Often corporate advertising enters the classroom through textbooks, which are viewed as an opportunity for product placement—much like Hollywood movies. For example, some textbooks show Michael Jordan eating Whoppers and Leonardo DiCaprio taking it easy at the Viper Room. This corporate advertising is actually unwittingly subsidized by taxpayers, who provide the money for textbooks to local school boards.

One example of textbook ad placement and corporate sponsorship is *Applications and Connections*, a McGraw-Hill mathematics text published in 1995 and currently used by sixth-, seventh-, and eighth-grade students in at least sixteen states. The book includes products such as Barbie dolls, Big Macs, and Oreo Cookies in its math problems. Students learn that "William is saving his allowance to buy a pair of Nike shoes that cost $68.25. If William earns $3.25 per week, for how many weeks will William need to save?" Thus teaching and learning become intertwined with the placement of products.[23] But this explicit product promotion does not seem to bother local and state politicians. The California state education department gave the book an energetic thumbs-up and spent millions of taxpayer's dollars to purchase these textbooks. Executives at Mattel, Nike, Sony, Spalding, Disney, Burger King, and other multinationals given exposure in the textbooks must have been delighted—they had managed to get their products deliberately placed in front of young consumers through publicly purchased textbooks without having to lobby, explain their intentions, or spend money.[24]

Corporations also enter schools with other, less overtly invasive programs, ranging from "adopt-a-school" mentoring programs to corporate-owned "academies" where students are tutored by company employees. Although many corporations, including American Express, Apple, IBM, and PepsiCo, have polished their images as good corporate citizens through their education projects, their motives are seldom purely altruistic. Often they earn exemptions from property taxes or other advantages for these benevolent give-aways, which drains the public financial resources that could have been used to fund our nation's public schools.[25]

SPONSORED EDUCATIONAL MATERIALS (SEMS): A PEDAGOGICAL PROMISE OR A PREDATORY PRACTICE?

In 2001 corporations advertised to over 3 million students on billboards placed in high school locker rooms through GymBoards, a program created by the American Passage Media Corporation. On these billboards, advertisements for Neet hair remover and Tampax tampons are displayed alongside information on health or social issues. Some students receive product samples in GymBags. Sampling Corporation of America, of Glenview, Illinois, has been disseminating Halloween safety kits containing product samples and coupons to elementary students for over ten years. Pizza Hut's Book It program, which rewards young students with free pan pizzas for reaching reading goals set by teachers, looks to entice parents into the restaurants as paying customers.[26]

Sponsored educational materials (SEMs)—that is, public relations materials in the form of learning kits—provide companies the means to build brand name recognition and consumer loyalty in the guise of helping schools to achieve educational distinction. For example, Little Willie Munchright, the diminutive cartoon character host of the McDonald's "What's On Your Plate" and "Healthy Growing Up" nutritional programs, tells students all about saturated fats and eating right. For a nominal cost of $7.32 and $11.30 respectively (plus shipping and handling), the program includes a video of "Willie's Public Service Announcements," as frequently seen on Saturday morning CBS children's television. And Campbell's soup wants to help, too. For 5,125 Campbell's soup labels the Campbell Company provides a school with the filmstrip "The Boyhood of Abraham Lincoln." For 20,000 more labels a school can get a remote projector to show it, and for another 6,750 labels a screen to show it on.[27] National Semiconductor, the computer chip maker, wants to ensure that teachers and students have the skills to benefit from Internet technology. In fall 1997 the company launched a three-year, $2.5 million program to provide free teacher access to Internet training and to encourage Internet use in the classroom.[28]

In 1981, when studying the development of school curricula by corporations, Sheila Harty, a noted educational researcher and author, examined the "Adopt-a-School" program in several big cities. She found that 29 percent of Fortune 500 companies, 47 percent of trade associations, and 53 percent of utilities designed materials for classroom use in grades K-12, along with teacher guides and mimeo stencils, and that 64 percent of Fortune 500 companies and 90 percent of the major trade associations and electric utilities provide free SEMs. A quarter of a century ago, "teaching aids" on the energy crisis were disseminated by local utilities, notes Harty, providing misinformation promoting nuclear power.[29] Add to this early effort more than two decades of corporate "educational" advertising efforts—from newspapers to discount stores, from muffler shops to restaurants and hotels—and we find an ocean of logo-encrusted paraphernalia flooding into public school classrooms in the form of SEMs. Couple the SEMs with direct corporate advertising appearing on school walls, on school supplies such as notebooks or pencils, on the sides of buses, and on athletic scoreboards, and direct infiltration has led to schools becoming commercial terrain. One of the fastest growing areas of corporate advertising in schools is the electronic media—SEMs that invade classrooms through broadcast networks, cable networks, and the Internet.

CHANNEL ONE TELEVISION: THE TECHNOLOGICAL SEM OF THE FUTURE

The front-runner in corporations' electronic sprint into the classroom is Channel One, a twelve-to-thirteen-minute news and advertising program broadcast daily to 12,000 middle and high schools across the nation. Students in schools where Channel One is employed are required, by school policy and by contract, to watch the program. Channel One sells four thirty-second advertising spots per show at $200,000 each to companies such as Nike, Nintendo, Pepsi, and Burger King.[30]

Channel One is appealing to underfunded schools. It loans school boards a television network for each sixth-through-twelfth grade school, provided that the board agrees to show the twelve- or thirteen-minute program called *Channel One News* in its entirety on 90 percent of school days and in 80 percent of all classrooms. This usually amounts to thirty-one hours of school time—the equivalent of one instructional week of school each year.

School boards must sign a three-year contract that renews itself automatically, but schools are allowed to end the contract at any time without any additional penalty or charge. Each school is advanced a satellite dish that can only pick up Channel One's signals, two VCRs, and a 19-inch television set for each classroom. The school receives the daily "news" show via satellite and can also receive the Classroom Channel, which provides a number of hours of documentaries that contain no commercials.[31] The content of Channel One is not controlled or monitored by the local community; nor is Channel One accountable to the students and teachers forced to view it. The corporate executives of Channel One and their employees decide on the program's content. Indeed, the community that contracts with Channel One through their school board must agree to regulate the number of times they may *not* show the program.

Whittle Communications created Channel One in 1989. Currently, Channel One is the name of both the marketing company in New York City and the TV show they produce in Hollywood. The company's main goal is to communicate commercial messages into classrooms— although the company would deny that this is their main goal. Instead, they would claim that they are offering sound pedagogical material to children, and if school districts cannot afford the apparatus the company loans it to them.

A Typical Channel One Program

A typical Channel One show begins with a piece of art submitted by a student that must contain the Channel One logo, followed by several headlines and the "quote of the day," which is usually related to one of the news stories featured on the show. Then news anchors introduce themselves MTV-style. The anchors then read the main story of the day, which may be either national or local. Other stories are read if time permits, and then the first cluster of two or three commercials, each one minute in length, begins. Generally they advertise junk food, including Snickers, Fruit Loops, Twix bars, M&Ms of all varieties, Snapple, Pepsi, Mountain Dew, Skittles, Mug Root Beer, and the Three Musketeers candy bar. From here, the scene changes and students immediately view another news story—not generally hard news, but stories designed more as "teen features," such as features on the world of sports or entertainment shown more to entertain than to edify. Immediately after the teen feature, one minute of commercials is shown, followed by a Pop Quiz that may have nothing to do with the news stories. Students are obliged to take the quiz in the class. The anchors then say goodbye and the program appears. Usually, however, one or two more commercials are displayed to students after the show ends. The total time for the whole broadcast averages thirteen minutes—even though the company advertises and contracts the programming as a twelve-minute show.[32]

Who Pays for Channel One?

The public pays for Channel One by subsidizing its use in schools through public-private contracts that use taxpayer funds to pay immense contractual fees to acquire it; Channel One is far from "free." But this fact is conspicuously not revealed to parents, students, and the community at large. A 1998 study by Alex Molnar, director of the University of Wisconsin's Center for the Analysis of Commercialism in Education, and Max Sawicky, an economist with the Economic Policy Institute, found that taxpayers in the United States pay $1.8 billion dollars per year for the class time lost to Channel One. Channel One's commercials alone cost taxpayers $300 million per year through straight public subsidies. The average secondary school spends $158,000 per year on the show using taxpayer funds, with $26,333 of this amount going to the creation of the commercials alone. Reaching 12 million middle school and high school students each day, Channel One is by far the single largest form of publicly subsidized commercialism in schools.[33]

Nationally, Channel One has run up against increasingly powerful citizen opposition. Opponents accuse the company of "selling children" to corporate advertisers. The news Channel One offers, they contend, is largely vacuous and serves only to package the advertising—to make it educationally palatable. For these reasons, critics argue that Channel One is detrimental to learning and teaching. And even if Channel One were of educational value, they contend, no community should want it in their schools because it costs an exorbitant amount of time and money. As Molnar and others have demonstrated, the time given over to Channel One is far from free.

The Channel One Web Site: On-line Learning or On-line Mall?

Channel One is not limited to television broadcasting within schools. It also runs a powerful Web site, access to which is sold to public schools. The Channel One Web site was the focus of intense controversy and public protest and was finally changed after Republican Richard Shelby, a senator from Alabama, called for Senate hearings on Channel One in April 1998.

Yet some claim that Channel One's Web site, Channelone.com, continues to place children in danger by virtue of the promotional materials they choose to present to the youthful users. Once they get to the Web site, which is promoted in classrooms, students can find reviews of R-rated movies and sexually explicit CDs, opportunities to post their picture on the Internet for anyone interested in "meeting them," a "Personal Ads" section that permits children to exchange personal information with nameless Internet users, and a chat room that is inadequately monitored and allows for almost any form of communication. And, according to Obligation Incorporated, a group highly critical of Channel One, Channel One has actively shown students how to cheat on a book report. At their web site from January 1998, Channel One helps kids cheat on book reports by directing them to the movie version of books they might be required to read. From *To Kill a Mockingbird* to George Orwell's *1984,* Channel One actually points to the movie versions students might watch to avoid reading the books.[34] The Web site can be accessed at home or in school and students can buy products on-line.

Learning and Assessment, Channel One Style

The following Channel One Web site advertisement, posted in January 2001 in the form of an "exam," shows Channel One's blatantly commercial function: providing advertising information to corporate sponsors who can ultimately tailor their sales pitch to specific students.[35]

The ad in question begins with a bright pink computer poster asking girls if they want to know what their personal beauty secrets are. Girls are then asked to click on an icon to rate beauty products, department stores, and their services.[36] The banner states that the survey is for girls only and that they will be answering a questionnaire about the types of stores where they might buy products for their hair, face, and skin. The questionnaire asks the girls to give their age. They are then asked to disclose what type of store they go to most often to buy personal cosmetic products and why. In checklist style, the questionnaire asks them to mark whether it might be a drugstore like Walgreens, or a department store like Sears, or perhaps a grocery store or discount shopping center. From here, girls are asked if they shop with brand names in mind and exactly when they develop their conception and decision about what to buy. As an example, they are asked if they make their consumer decisions at the store when they browse through the aisles, or ahead of time, before they arrive. The questions continue in a running checklist format asking girls to rank, on a chart, why they shop where they shop. They are asked on a scale to agree strongly or not to agree with specific statements which include the reasons why they shop at a specific drugstore or retailer—Expediency? Price? Because it is a enjoyable place to shop? Because it has the latest "in" items? Good consumer service? The girls are then asked about particular stores, such as Rite Aid, Walgreens, or Eckerd, and asked specifically where they usually shop for their cosmetic beauty needs. Finally, they are asked to rank the particular corporations mentioned from one to four, with one being the first choice and four the least desirable preference. This could all be taking place on publicly subsidized school time directly in the classroom and is promoted as part of teaching and learning.

Currently Channel One is burgeoning throughout the nation as one of the premier SEMs. Is it education or marketing? Is this the kind of partnership that business and communities should forge in helping meet the educational needs of our nation's children?

Many individuals and organizations would say no. Resistance to Channel One, both to its programming and its Web site, is increasing. Many individuals and educational organizations have expressed powerful opposition to the presence of publicly subsidized television commercials in our children's classroom. Diverse constituencies are calling loudly for the removal of Channel One from schools. Many educators understand that when commercials are shown to students under the influence of a public-private contract, without their consent, the school itself becomes a promoter of the products being advertised. Government's role in education is also altered. Instead of subsidizing educational organizations, it now subsidizes an educational marketplace, run for profit and tacitly endorses certain products and services.[37] And what about corporations spying on students' habits and preferences through students' Web site visits? Is this education for children or education for marketers?

Progressive educators are not alone in their opposition to Channel One. The American Association of School Administrators, the Association for Supervision and Curriculum Development, the National PTA, the National Council of Teachers of English, and the National Association of State Boards of Education are just a few of the organizations that oppose classroom advertising and Channel One. The National Council of Teachers of English recently passed a resolution condemning Channel One for imposing commercial advertising in classrooms.[38] The Southern Baptist Convention has also released a resolution condemning the use of Channel One. And according to Phyllis Schlafly of the Eagle Forum, it is time to call a halt to Channel One's exploitation of our children's minds. She is adamant that school time should not be for sale.[39]

OTHER EXPERIMENTS IN EXPLOITING
THE EDUCATIONAL MARKETPLACE

The Center for Analysis of Commercialism in Education (CACE) found that the number of articles published on commercial activities in schools increased 154 percent between 1990 and 1997, which suggests that the 1990s was the decade of sponsored schools and commercialized classrooms.[40] CACE, in a more recent and thorough analysis, discovered that the largest area of schoolhouse commercialism appeared to be sponsorship of programs and activities. They found that between 1990 and 1997 the number of citations describing this category of commercial activity increased by 199 percent. In 1997, they found almost 1,400 citations documenting sponsorship activities, suggesting that events such as the now notorious "Coke in Education Day" at Greenbrier High School in Evans, Georgia, have become commonplace and institutionalized in American schools.

The study also noted that the fastest growing area of commercialism in the schoolhouse appears to be what are known as exclusive or executive agreements. The number of citations reporting on exclusive agreements between schools and bottlers, sports apparel manufacturers, and other firms increased by a hefty 495 percent between 1990 and 1997.[41]

CONTESTS, SAMPLE PRODUCTS, AND INCENTIVE PROGRAMS: WHO IS GETTING EDUCATED?

In a quest to acquire demographic information on both students and their parents, many companies openly sponsor incentive programs and contests in public schools. Seemingly fun and innocuous in some cases, these contests require students and their parents to provide personal information to the sponsor. Students are encouraged to collect cash register receipts, used printer cartridges (as in the Santa Maria-Bonita School District in California) or read a certain number of books in order to win prizes for themselves or their school. Sometimes the prizes as well as the promotions are blatantly commercial, as in the promotion by General Mills that asked students to collect cereal box tops to win a visit to their school by the Trix Bunny. Sometimes the prizes are important to both the school and the students, as in the case of contests that award computers to the schools, and present a strong motivation.

To underfunded schools, these contests seem to be a good deal they can't refuse. The problem stems from the companies' commercial motivation. The unstated purpose of these programs is to collect information that can be used to target children as consumers and to build brand name loyalty into the psychological fabric of early childhood experience and identity.[42]

Resistance or Acquiescence?

Nationwide, more and more students, parents, and schools are display-ing irritation at advertising targeted at students in classrooms.

Although corporate offers may sound financially advantageous, schools often find that the advantages are minuscule considering the trade-off: the selling of students and instructional time for a very small return. Many of these schools still find themselves without the text-books they need and saddled with antiquated instructional materials, and lacking well-educated and qualified teachers.[43] Corporations have little if anything to say about the growing teacher shortage, low teacher salaries, and the consequent erosion of professional pride that under-cuts our public education system, and they are quick to avoid con-troversies regarding the influence of social class, gender, culture, or linguistic background and how they might play a role in students' achievement.

COMMERCIALISM IN THE CLASSROOMS—
THE BOTTOM LINE

The issue of commercialism in our classrooms raises both legal and moral questions.

Who owns a school when a particular company sponsors it? Who controls the curriculum? What are the long-term effects of commercial-ism on teaching, identity formation, citizenship, individuality, and free-dom of speech in the classroom? Who is receiving the publicly financed education, students or corporate sponsors? Where do we draw the line—or do we?

To be fair, socially minded corporations truly interested in edu-cation can and do provide noncommercial support for the kinds of pro-grams that really make a difference—sometimes millions of dollars for scholarships, science and math programs, mentoring, job and intern-ship placement, and funding for parent involvement programs.[44]

Corporate efforts to commercialize and privatize schools create an ethos and associated image of benign consumerism. Students learn quickly that the articulation of ideas, the expression of values, and the charting of experiences are all mediated by advertising, commodity ex-change, and corporations. They learn what is commercially "cool" in a world constructed by unbridled consumerism. Some argue that, as a re-sult, today's students choose their symbols of freedom, liberation, and self-actualization from corporate logos and product identification mascots. Education becomes reduced, or at the very least affixed, to the commercialization of everyday life.

SPONSORSHIPS AND EXCLUSIVE AGREEMENTS: THE RISE OF THE SCHOOL-BUSINESS PARTNERSHIP OR THE SELLING OF AMERICAN CHILDREN?

Imagine yourself a student at Greenbrier High School in Evans, Georgia, in March 1998. The principal of the school, Gloria Hamilton, has required that 1,200 of the school's students line up in the school parking lot to spell out the word "Coke" as part of a corporate high school competition sponsored by the Coca Cola Company. Each class is assigned to stand on one of the letters of the word, which have been marked off by the band director; the event is captured on film from a crane, and Coke executives flew in to attend the special "Coke in Education Day."

But not all students are eager to fulfill their assigned roles. One student, Michael Cameron, displays a Pepsi T-shirt. Principal Hamilton removes him and rebukes him for "disrespectful" behavior. He is later suspended for nearly having cost the school a considerable amount of money.[45]

The contest between competing high schools was initiated when the company challenged students to come up with the best strategy for marketing Coke-sponsored business discount cards. On the day of the photo shoot, about twenty Coca Cola executives were present to lecture Greenbrier students on economics, provide technical aid to home economic students who were baking a Coke cake, and help chemistry students analyze the sugar content of Coke.

"Coke in Education Day" at Greenbrier High was portrayed by Principal Hamilton as a "fun, instructional event," and the school did not receive any compensation for organizing it."[46] Hamilton's actions toward Cameron were provoked by her concern that Greenbrier's chances of winning the $10,000 prize in the national contest sponsored by Coca Cola, she says, as well as the opportunity to collect $500 from a local coke bottler, had been spoiled by Cameron's impertinent act.

"Coke in Education Day" illustrates one of the most insidious consequences of corporate "support" of schools: anticorporate attitudes on the part of public school students become intolerable and even punishable. It is alarming, to say the least, that a student can be suspended from school for refusing to toe the line for the Coca Cola Company.

EXCLUSIVE AGREEMENTS BETWEEN SCHOOLS AND CORPORATE SPONSORS: EDUCATIONAL PARTNERSHIPS OR CONTRACTUAL RELATIONS?

Greenbrier School and Principal Hamilton were involved in an exclusive agreement between the school and the Coca Cola Company. An exclusive contractual agreement gives corporations the right to sell and promote their goods and/or services in a school or school district without the threat of competition. In exchange, the district or particular school involved receives a percentage of the profits from the arrangement—in the Greenbrier's case, the school received a $10,000 prize. Exclusive agreements may also concede to the supplier of a product or service "solo" rights to market their wares, as in the advertisements found in high school basketball programs.[47] And many schools believe that such agreements are a more palatable funding alternative than tax bond initiatives or property increases. Yet John Sheehan, the vice president of the Douglas County, Colorado, school board, disagrees. He was the only person in a seventeen-member school board association to vote against a $27.7 million executive agreement between three Colorado school districts and corporations.

Why was Sheehan opposed? The answer, he says, is simple:

- Educating and marketing are like oil and water.
- We are opening the floodgates of consumerism to children with a daily, constant barrage of product ideas, logos, and mascots.
- Business is purposefully targeting a captive audience.
- We are letting our legislatures and the public off the hook, as it is the responsibility of the public, not corporate advertising, to finance schools.[48]

From Colorado to Texas, from Wisconsin to Ohio—contracts between soft drink companies and school districts for exclusive "pouring rights" afford a good picture of how schools are attempting to turn access to their students into money. An exclusive pouring rights contract grants to a specific corporation the legal right to be the only soft drink advertised or served at a contracted school. PepsiCo spokesman Larry Jabbonsky described the arrangement to the *New York Times:* Schools need to produce funds for programs and at the same time businesses are continuously looking for new ways to widen their contact with young people.[49] The arrangement has proven to have wide appeal. In 1998 the Center for Commercial Free Education in Oakland, California, identified twenty-four exclusive contracts between bottlers and school districts, with another twenty-five under deliberation.[50] In Pueblo, Colorado, for example, a marketing company negotiates these exclusive agreements for 240 high schools.[51]

SUMMARY

The 1990s was a volatile decade in the controversy over commercialism in schools. Direct marketing to students and personal data-digging became the pedagogical norm. But despite growing opposition over the concept of commercialism in the classroom, the educational press has reported practically nothing about the subject. The failure of educational media, unions, and think tanks to question the motives and practices of commercialism in the schoolhouse is disconcerting. Commercialism directly influences the quality of schools; the school curricula, activities, and programs; the teachers and instructional methods schools employ; the daily interactions between teachers and students; and the multifaceted daily workings of a public school district or school.

The lack of a larger understanding of neoliberal attempts to penetrate the educational marketplace deserves critical questioning and critical news reporting. After all, privatization is not just simply a matter of school choice and vouchers. As this chapter shows, products are being imposed on students, and teachers are pressurized into accepting them as part of their pedagogical experience; meanwhile corporations educate themselves about students' consumer habits. And all of this is financed at taxpayers' expense through direct public subsidies. This neoliberal economic arrangement is exactly what Noam Chomsky warned us of (see chapter one)—a public-private partnership whereby taxpayers subsidize the costs of large corporations while these same corporations privatize any and all profits.

We must ask ourselves as citizens, not merely as consumers, if this is the educational solution we want: the subsidization of private companies through public taxation. Do we want "learning centers" where our children acquire the knowledge and critical thinking ability to become conscious citizens? Or do we prefer "earning centers" tailored to the needs of large companies seeking to take advantage of need for educational financing? Is this the productive partnership between schools and business that we have been promised? Or is it simply an attempt to harvest profits from the burgeoning market of young children? Has MTV-style entertainment replaced education as students clamor to identify with corporate logos, brand names, and company mascots at an earlier and earlier age? Is this learning for personal and societal success, or is it a form of commercial propaganda aimed at managing young people's imaginations?

These questions are important in ascertaining the role businesses should play in the educational arena. Furthermore, before we can understand commercialism in schools as a form of neoliberal public policy, we must realize that the questions and problems associated with educational privatization pervade not just public education, but all public entities. Our understanding of the structural components of the privatization of education and their relationship to the neoliberal corporate agenda is crucial today, more than any time in our nation's history, whether or not we find ourselves in agreement with the concept of privatization.

NOTES

1. The Chalkboard: A Classroom Corporate Connection. http://www.thechalkboard.com.

2. Knaus, H. (1992). "The Commercialized Classroom." http://www.corpwatch.org.

3. McCann Erickson WorldGroup (US). http://www.mind-advertising.com.

4. Juliet Schor. (1998). *The Overspent American*. New York: Basic Books.

5. Molnar, A. (1998). "Sponsored Schools and Commercialized Classrooms." http://www.asu.edu.

6. Ibid.

7. Federal Trade Commission. (March 1998) "Survey of Commercial Web Sites." http://www.ftc.gov.

8. Robertson, Paul. (2000). "Marketing Madness Makes for Materialistic Kids." http://www.youthunlimitedgta.com.

9. Zolo, P. (November 1995). "Talking to Teens." *American Demographics* 17.

10. McNeal, J. (April 1998). "Tapping the Three Kids' Markets," *American Demographics* 20, pp. 37–41.

11. McNeal, J. (1999). *The Kids' Market: Myths and Realities*. Ithaca: Paramount Market Publishing; and "The U. S. Kids Market", a 2002 report from Packaged Facts. http://www.marketresearch.com

12. Ibid. 1.

13. Knaus, H. (1992). "The Commercialized Classroom."

14. Molnar, A. (August 1998). "Sponsored Schools and Commercialized

Classrooms: Schoolhouse Commercializing Trends in the 1990s." Center for Analysis of Commercialism in Education (CACE). School of Education. University of Wisconsin. http://www.asu.edu.

15. *Z Magazine* (July/August 1999). Editorial, p. 14.

16. Stead, D. (5 January 1997). "Cash Poor Schools Open Doors to Commercialism." *Commercial Appeal* News Section. P. 6A. Final Edition. Memphis, TN.

17. Knaus, H. (1992). "The Commercialized Classroom."

18. Center for Commercial-Free Public Education. http://www.commercialfree.org

19. Knaus, H. (1992). "The Commercialized Classroom."

20. Ibid.

21. Ibid.

22. Center for Commercial-Free Public Education. "What Is Commercialism?" http://www.commercialfree.org.

23. Grierson, B. (Summer 1999). "Brand Names in Textbooks." http://www.adbusters.org.

24. Ibid.

25. Knaus, H. (2001). "The Commercialized Classroom."

26. Ibid.

27. ReThinking Schools (1992). http://www.rethinkingschools.org.

28. National Semiconductor (2001). Internet Training Initiative Web site. http://www.national.com/training.

29. Harty, S. (1981). "Hucksters in the Classroom." *Social Policy* 12:2, 38–39.

30. Adbusters online magazine (Autumn 1998). http://www.adbusters.org.

31. Ibid.

32. Obligation, Inc. "Channel One in a Nutshell" http://www.obligation.org.

33. Sawicky, Max B., and Molnar, Alex. (1998). "The Hidden Costs of Channel One: Estimates for All Fifty States." http://www.asu.edu

34. Channel One (January 1998). "How to Cheat on a Book Report." Reproduced on Obligation, Inc. Web site (2001). http://www.obligation.org

35. Channel One. http://www.channelone.com.

36. Ibid.

37. Obligation, Inc. "Channel One in a Nutshell."

38. National Council of Teachers of English (1992). "On Advertising in the Classroom." http://www.ncte.org.

39. Schlafly, P. (May 20, 1999). Testimony to the Senate Committee on

Health, Education, Labor, and Pensions re: Channel One. http://www. eagleforum.org.

40. Stafford, B. "New Center Tracks Commercialism in the Classroom." University of Wisconsin, Milwaukee. http://www.uwm.edu.

41. Molnar, A. "Sponsored Schools and Commercialized Classrooms: Schoolhouse Commercializing Trends in the 1990s." http://www.asu.edu.

42. Commercialfree.org. "What Is Commercialism in Schools?" http:// www.commercialfree.org.

43. Ibid.

44. Ibid.

45. Friddell, G. (April 1998). "Student's Act of Cola Defiance Was Refreshing." *Virginian Pilot.* April 4, 1998. Section B. p. 1. Final Edition.

46. Choquette, K. (March 26, 1998). "Pepsi Shirt 'Joke' Lands Students in Hot Water." *USA Today.* Money section. Pp. 1B.

47. Molnar, A., and J. Morales. (August 1998). "Sponsored Schools and Commercialized Classrooms: Schoolhouse Commercializing Trends in the 1990s." Pp. 9. Center for the Analysis of Commercialism in Education. School of Education. University of Wisconsin, Milwaukee. Milwaukee, WI.

48. Sheehan, J. (October 1999). "Why I Said No to Coca-cola. Pp. 15. In *ReThinking Schools.* Winter 1999–2000. Volume 14. No.: 2. Wisconsin, MI.

49. Hays, C. (March 10, 1998). "Be True to Your Cola. Rah, Rah." In *The New York Times.* March 10, 1998. Section C, pp. 1, 4.

50. Center for Commercial Free Public Education (April 22, 1998). "School Contracts with Coke and Pepsi and Others." Oakland, CA.

51. Cristodero, D. (January 20, 1998). "Schools Find Aid in Ads, Sponsorships." *St. Petersburg Florida Times.* January 20, 1998. Sports sec. P1C. Pinellas Edition.

Chapter Eight

❧ Managing Public Schools for Profit: The Rise of the Educational Management Organization

As we have seen, the rise of what has been termed the "educational industry" occurred primarily during the 1990s, within the climate of neoliberalism and the concerted efforts to privatize education. One of the fastest-growing sectors in that industry—which includes private voucher proponents, private scholarship organizations, faith-based charitable contributions, tax credits, SEMs, exclusive executive agreements, and the like—is the business of managing public schools for profit. This completely new notion of allowing for-profit educational corporations to control and manage K–12 public education demands a drastic paradigmatic shift—from administration by the public to the wholesale for-profit control of curriculum, the private management of daily activities between students and educational stakeholders, the creation of formulized instructional materials, and the hiring of teachers and the actual running of the day-to-day operation of the school by private corporations; the practice of contracting out educational "niche" services to private companies is on the rise. These include landscape services, cafeteria services, transportation services, and the like. This chapter will look at both of these trends and their impact on schools.

FOR-PROFIT MANAGEMENT COMPANIES: PROS AND CONS

In the last two or three years, as for-profit companies began to run publicly funded schools, more than a dozen private management companies sprang up practically overnight. They offer widely different approaches to management and curriculum, but they share the same expectation of public funding: they want the public to subsidize their for-profit management of public schools with taxpayer funds based on local property taxes. They are not necessarily motivated by profit, they say; their goal is to radically alter education and quickly fix the problems that years of reform have failed to accomplish.[1]

Among these for-profit schools the National Education Association (NEA) lists Advantage Schools, Inc., out of Boston, Massachusetts; Beacon Education Management out of Nashville, Tennessee; Charter School Administration, which runs five schools in Michigan; the Edison Project, L.P., out of New York; the Tesseract Group, Inc. (formerly Education Alternatives Inc.) out of Minnesota; Educational Development Corporation, which runs eight schools in Michigan; Heritage Academy out of Arizona; Horizon Charter out of Arizona; the Leona Group, which runs charters in Michigan and Arizona; Mosaica Education, Inc., out of Minnesota; and SABIS Education Systems, another Minnesota-based firm.[2]

The questions at issue regarding privatization and for-profit management firms are multifaceted. Can for-profit companies solve the problems facing public education? Do a few Wall Street investors and entrepreneurs hold the key to student learning and educational organizational development? According to John McLaughlin, publisher of *The Education Industry Report,* the answer is yes. Privatization in education is making good on its promise to bring basic reform to education, McLaughlin writes. When we link business and education to free enterprise, we alter the status quo in the educational culture.[3] McLaughlin notes that 300 teachers, administrators, service providers, charter school advocates, venture capitalists, and educational entrepreneurs from every walk of life have attended "Edventures" conferences. Edventures is a think tank–type organization that assembles neoliberal champions of educational privatization policies—especially those companies that seek to manage public schools for profit.

CHARTER SCHOOLS AND THE EXPLOSION OF FOR-PROFIT OPPORTUNITIES

In search of for-profit management opportunities, these companies have been drawn to charter schools in particular. Here they have found an exceptional financial opening.[4] Because new charter schools usually receive only about 60 percent of their needed funding from public sources, the need for a private funding source is enormous.[5] In fact, in her study of privatization and charter schools, Amy Wells, educational analyst at the University of California, found that in California, charter schools have established partnerships with a variety of sources: universities, foundations, and educational reform groups. Wells reports that two schools were allied with the university, thereby gaining access to university personnel and facilities and increasing their public visibility. Others obtained grants from corporate sponsors, such as Wells Fargo, Apple Computers, and Hewlett Packard. [6]

In many states charter school laws have explicitly allowed for-profit companies to run publicly funded charter schools. The Center for Education Research, Analysis, and Innovation at the School of Education at the University of Wisconsin–Milwaukee found that as of March 6, 2000, thirty-seven states with charter school laws permitted the charter holder either to be a for-profit firm or to subcontract directly with for-profit firms for management assistance or total school management.[7] Because many charter school laws are either ambiguous or do not address the issue of for-profit management of charter schools, or actually embrace the idea, it seems that once a school has been granted a charter it can contract out educational management services to any company it wishes.

The NEA has identified Arizona, Massachusetts, and Michigan as the states that are leading the trend toward for-profit management of charter schools.[8] A study of Arizona charters reports that almost half of the state's charter schools and high schools are run by chains such as PPEP TEC High School, Excel Education Centers, Inc., and the Leona Group.[9]

In California, many new charter schools are operated on a for-profit basis. The Edison Project, another private, for-profit educational maintenance organization, runs six charters in California and is starting up twenty-five additional schools.[10] Their plans include the adoption and management of hundreds, if not thousands, more charter schools. However, because Edison and most of the other school management companies are privately held, their finances can remain off-limits to the public.

These possibilities may seem particularly attractive to grassroots charter schools in high-poverty communities of color. Parents and educators in these areas are furious about failing schools and often wish to declare their independence from public school bureaucracy. But we must critically examine the implications of these poorer schools and communities contributing to the profits of management firms.

According to the *New York Times,* both supporters and opponents of a plan to privatize five New York City schools and turn them over to the Edison Project have begun courting the Reverend Al Sharpton, a spokesperson for the black community. He was invited to visit one of the schools, Middle School 246 in Flatbush, Brooklyn. The invitation was

extended by the Reverend Floyd Flake, a former Democratic congress-
man from Queens, who now works for the Edison schools.

The New York City Board of Education agreed to allow Edison to
run seven charter schools starting in the fall of 2001 after 51 percent of
parents of children at these schools voted to convert them to charter
schools. Sharpton, who ran for mayor in 2001, involved himself in the
acrimonious battle over the plan in February of 2001 when he invited
Irving S. Hamer Jr., a member of the New York City Board of Education,
to voice his opposition to the plan to allow Edison to run public schools.

At a 2001 rally at the Harlem headquarters of the National Action
Network—the organization started by Sharpton—Hamer argued that
instead of handing public schools over to corporate interests, the board
should try harder to improve existing public schools for all students.
Sharpton is currently undecided on the issue of for-profit management
of schools, but unlike Flake, Sharpton is adamantly opposed to President Bush's voucher plans. Flake, on the other hand, supports vouchers
and was a contender for education secretary under George W. Bush.
Sharpton agreed to hear both sides of the issue but he maintains that he
is generally opposed to any form of privatization.[11]

PEDAGOGY OR PROFIT—
WHAT IS THE FOR-PROFIT MANAGEMENT AGENDA?

The concerns driving educational reform challenge public remedies, according to representatives of Mosaica Education, a privately sponsored
management organization. They point to the growing dissatisfaction
among voters and employers with the quality of public education. They
claim, as do all privatization proponents, that existing educational resources are simply insufficient to meet the future needs of a competitive
workforce. In fact, with student enrollment scheduled to reach 54.6 million students by 2005, U.S public schools are not equipped to meet the
challenge of providing a quality education.

Mosaica, like other for-profit management firms, claims that its
graduates are prepared to make immediate contributions to the workplace. They achieve this result, they claim, by investing private capital in
each school they manage. They also upgrade buildings, assure that
modern technology is available to both students and teachers, and take
pride in offering a safe and appealing learning environment. Mosaica
currently operates schools in six states and expects to open eleven
schools in 2001.

Much like Mosaica, other for-profit companies claim that a school's effectiveness is enhanced when it is operated by a for-profit company. They promise higher student scores on standardized tests, improved attendance, enhanced motivation, and increased morale for both students and teachers. But can they deliver on these promises? Do for-profit firms really enhance student achievement and reform education? Companies claim they can improve student learning *and* make a profit—that the two are not mutually exclusive. However, experience does not seem to support their claims. The best results reported by a school management company are those of the Edison Project, and they are mixed at best. The company claims that scores have risen considerably, but objective analysis of their data shows that student achievement in Edison schools ranges from quite good to very disappointing.[12]

If for-profit management has produced low or no gains in student achievement for more money, why is it still considered an option? Because there are profits to be made—if not in managing schools, then in taking the company public, trading its stock, and investing its assets. It is tempting for school boards and superintendents to see for-profit management firms as a quick, painless panacea for educational ills. But many educators argue that there is no panacea—that good schools have to be painstakingly built on the local level by staff and students with the support of parents and school administrators. In the end improvement of schools is the result of the hard work of school staff with administrative and parental support. Everything the for-profit companies say they can do has already been done in publicly run public schools. Every curriculum and program they use is available for every school in America to implement on its own—without adding corporate managers and without deducting corporate profits.

Edison Project's proposal to investors emphasizes the bottom line rather than the quality of its educational product. Chris Whittle, founder of the Edison Project, suggests that investors compare the company to Home Depot, McDonalds or Wal-Mart—companies that are not top-end companies but mass marketers that have become leaders in retail and profitable investments.[13]

In some cases, these for-profit companies have been a lucrative investment. Advantage Schools, a for-profit management corporation based in Boston, has gone from $4 million in revenues to $60 million in just a few years. The company opens and operates new urban charter public schools across the country. They begin with K–5 schools, then add a grade each year until they are K–12 programs. The Advantage Company opened its first two charter schools in 1997. Currently it has schools in nine states serving more than 9,000 students,[14] and it clearly intends to keep growing. On February 22, 2000, Advantage Schools Incorporated announced that it had secured $28 million in additional private equity capital. The earnings were to be used to open new urban charter schools in cities nationwide by the fall of 2000 and to develop the fourteen Advantage schools already in operation. Credit Suisse First Boston Equity and Partners, L.P., of New York secured the financing, and the affiliates that led the financing were a large conglomerate of private ventures.

From the point of view of Steven Wilson, executive officer of Boston-based Advantage, investors share the company's commitment to "offering urban families new choices in public education" and creating new environments where teachers can succeed. And Advantage claims that it has already achieved spectacular academic improvements in the schools it operates.[15]

What appears to be a grand opportunity for privatization efforts through for-profit management companies is catching the eyes of some mega-investors. J. P. Morgan and Fidelity Ventures are just two big names that have been watching the educational maintenance organization. Paul Allen's Vulcan Ventures is also poised to seize the opportunity that EMOs offer to make money off public funds. "We're on the brink of fundamental change," says Lamar Alexander, the former U.S. education secretary and Republican presidential candidate who now sits on the board of Leeds Equity Partners III, an investment firm specializing in the up-and-coming educational industrial complex.[16]

In 1999 Chase Capital Partners of New York led the initial financing of Advantage Schools, joined by Nassau Capital of Princeton, New Jersey. Nassau Capital invests in private equity and real estate exclusively on behalf of Princeton University. Salomon Smith Barney acted as a placement agent for the financing. Steven F. Wilson, president and chief executive officer of Boston-based Advantage, was ecstatic. Charter schools were an enormous horizon for the profit-driven company.

The Edison Project was one of the main players in the for-profit management of schools. After it opened its first four schools in 1995, its revenues rose from $12 million to $227 million.[17] At that time, Edison projected it would manage 423 schools in the future with 260,000 students, giving it revenues of $1.8 million. By 2009, they predicted that they would have taken over as much as ten percent of the $360 billion the United States currently pays annually for K–12 schools.* If true, this would signify a tremendous shift of public funds to for-profit companies and would successfully serve to accomplish the neoliberal agenda of furthering the privatization of education. According to Chris Whittle, "In twenty years 20 percent to 30 percent of U.S. public schools will be run by for-profit."[18]

Profits, however, continue to remain illusory. The answer to improving profits, according to Whittle, is to cut administrative costs. He figures that 27 cents of every dollar is spent on the central office of most public schools. Whittle promises to bring this amount down by a massive 19 percent, to just 8 cents. The savings, he claims, would be put right back into the classroom, with a slight 7 percent profit for the company.[19] In light of the cost-cutting measures, the companies' claim that they can improve student learning and simultaneously make a profit seems unsubstantiated; the evidence seems to point to the contrary. Little formal research has been done on the effectiveness of these for-profits that operate charter schools, but a 1998 report by the NEA finds that these companies fall through on their promises.[20]

THE ANTI-FOR-PROFIT MOVEMENT

Education Alternatives Incorporated (EAI) was the pioneer in for-profit management companies. Its record is a cautionary tale.

According to the National Education Association, EAI managed 10 schools in Miami and Baltimore and the entire Hartford, Connecticut, school district in 1995. Three years later, it no longer had any contracts. Miami chose not to renew its contract when the EAI students showed no improvement compared to students at public schools. In Baltimore, the EAI contract was cancelled after student learning failed to improve even though the company was paid $20 million more than the district would normally have spent on these schools.[21]

In Wilkinsburg, Pennsylvania, the experiment with for-profit management also ended badly. At Turner Elementary, run by Beacon Management/APS for two years, student scores were not only lower than they had been the year before the company took over, but they were also lower than the scores of students in other Wilkinsburg elementary schools, where scores improved considerably.[22]

These experiences are not isolated. Many public schools have begun to abandon the for-profit school management concept. One recent example occurred in San Francisco. An elementary school in San Francisco's Noe Valley had been in trouble for years, with low student achievement and high truancy rates. The answer, the board thought, was to turn over the management of the school to the Edison Project. In a highly raucous and lengthy meeting of the board and citizens on June 24, 1998, the board voted five to two to hand over the day-to-day management of the Noe Valley school to the corporate for-profit management company, the Edison Project. Since then, according to supporters of the idea, evidence has shown that student achievement has improved, parents are more contented, faculty is satisfied, and the facilities are clean and functioning. But one thing did not change: the heated opposition on the part of some school board members and community members to allowing a corporation to deliver instruction and design the interface between teachers and learners. With the election of a new school board in November 2000, the school, renamed The Edison Charter Academy, is once again in the middle of public controversy.

The for-profit company expects to make profits within two more years, but that profit, say opponents to privatization, will only come through a reliance on fewer and less-qualified personnel, as well as cost cutting. They argue that the profits made by the Edison Project divert crucial monies and resources away from public schools. San Francisco school board president Jill Wynns stands in opposition to the for-profit management of schools. She contends that Edison has damaged the community's sense of cohesiveness about public education and that this has fractured the San Francisco community.[23] Newly elected school board member Eric Mar believes the board has a moral and ethical obligation to cancel the Edison contract. For Mar, it's a bigger issue than just one particular school and some parents feeling some satisfaction. It is a public policy issue of using public resources for for-profit institutions.[24]

Does running schools for profit really enhance quality education for all students and provide unique educational environments and curriculum for teachers? Edison student scores have risen in recent years in San Francisco, but critics claim that this rise is due to "creaming and skimming," which we discussed in previous chapters. For example, there are fewer Latinos and blacks in attendance at the Academy since Edison took over and San Francisco critics maintain that this shift in demographics has produced the improved test scores among students—not some extraordinary and innovative curriculum or "management style."

Since Edison took over the school, the Edison Academy has had numerous problems with staff and teachers. In December 1998, United Educators of San Francisco filed a grievance against the district for requiring teachers at the Edison Academy to work, at the same pay scale, a school year that is 7 percent longer than those of other schools in the district. Unhappiness among teachers was so high that all but a few educators decided to return to the Edison school in the fall of 2000. The grievance forced Edison to increase teacher pay by ten percent and shorten the calendar year; however, by that time dissatisfaction was serious enough that teachers found other jobs.

Parents, too, are asking tough questions. Berta Hernandez, mother of a boy who had entered first grade at the Edison school in

1999, complained that she was "harassed and mistreated" because she questioned the Edison track record. "When per pupil spending is down, it's easy to sell out to corporate do-gooders," she told the San Francisco school board. Lindsay Hershenhorn, a first grade teacher, accused the school principal and school superintendent of pressuring the community to accept the deal while suppressing dissent. She pointed out that the hasty, last-minute effort to collect signatures for the school charter had not been preceded by meetings of the community, the parents, or the staff. When concerns for profit are put ahead of the needs of children, the result in not trustworthy decision making.[25]

In 2001, the San Francisco Board of Education received complaints that raised serious concerns regarding Edison's operation of the Academy, including high teacher turnover, elimination of the Spanish bilingual program, incomplete financial reporting, discontinuation of a free after-school program, failure to serve special education students, failure to provide counseling for African American students, failure to achieve promised and measurable student outcomes, and complaints regarding financial stability and effectiveness of the Edison project.[26] Edison denied that it had violated the charter agreement between the school board and the Academy and initiated a lawsuit that became known as *Edison Charter Schools v. the Board of Education.* The company alleged a violation of the Ralph M. Brown Act, which prevents secret and private meetings by a public entity.[27]

Meanwhile, Edison attempted to soften its for-profit image in favor of a "public service" orientation. Edison offers classes in language, art, music, and physical education, and their greatest contribution to the Noe Valley School was a gift of a home computer to all students in grades three to five. A one-time donation by a private foundation of $1.8 million dollars re-equipped the school and sanitized the environment. But the members of the new San Francisco school board were unimpressed. Board members, teacher unions, and Coleman Advocates for Children and Youth maintained it was simply unfair to give a few hundred students such educational advantages while public schools suffer exorbitant losses of finances and school programs. All students, they argue, must be given educational opportunities, not just a few elite schools and students. And although proponents and supporters of the Edison Academy say that this is precisely what school reform should look like, critics of for-profit management of schools say the Edison plan reinforces standardization of teaching and learning and is based on pedagogical principles that are regimented and prearranged—basically cookie cutter schools with a homogeneous and sanitized curriculum that must be followed by all teachers and students.

The Edison Academy was funded through a mixture of state and federal resources in the same way other schools are funded. The San Francisco school district gives Edison a base-per-pupil amount of $4,200 per year, and the Edison Project also gets federal desegregation funding, expected to be $225,000 in 2001. This is the same sum received by other San Francisco schools.

Nevertheless, with the November election of new school board members, the Edison contract was not renewed. Newly elected board member Mark Sanchez, a former teacher at Edison, says that his goal is to not have Edison be corporate run because it eventually puts a corporation in the position to make money off of public dollars.[28]

At a June 28, 2001, board meeting, Resolution No. 16–25Spl, entitled Board of Education's Directive Regarding Renewal and Revocation of the Edison Charter Academy's Charter and Management Agreement, was signed into law by San Francisco School Board members. The resolution denied the renewal of the Academy Charter and entered into a settlement agreement that allowed the company to submit a renewal petition to the California State Board of Education.[29]

CONTRACTING OUT PUBLIC SCHOOL SERVICES TO FOR-PROFIT COMPANIES

Teacher unions are wary of another privatization trend: the contracting out of vital school services to private firms. With a host of entrepreneurs literally waiting to seize the opportunities afforded by the educational marketplace, the practice of contracting out specific services such as food service, insurance, curriculum development, and maintenance is mounting. The for-profit companies that wish to enter into the educational marketplace are focusing primarily on charter schools for inroads into these contracting opportunities. Unions are especially concerned that public schools are beginning to contract out more and more regular services to for-profit, private firms. Some opponents argue that privatization is an instrument of class politics. One study found that the dangers of privatization in education are "creaming" the best students, corporations involving themselves in poor school management, union busting, conflicts of interest, discrimination against kids who need special education, and often-outright racism. All of these activities, the study claims, are presently on display in the for-profit school system.[30]

Because the cost-cutting and reduced services that accompany the privatizing of education effectively undermine public employee unions, they have also have the effect of reordering the class structure.

(This process has been carefully documented in Chile, where the entire public education system was privatized during the 1970s. Vast amounts of wealth were shifted upward during that society-wide process of privatization, which reordered not only education, but also industry and the nation's social security system. See chapter five.)

Numerous charter schools avoid using unionized public employees by contracting out such services as district maintenance, cafeteria services, and landscaping. Many charters opt to use private firms because these firms provide workers with no union protection and no salary packages or pensions; therefore the wages and benefits are less costly. Amy Wells studied this phenomenon and discovered long lines of entrepreneurs eager to profit from school reform. Among these new cottage industries she lists charter school management consulting agencies (which usually offer a broad array of services), payroll and insurance companies, food services, maintenance, curriculum specialists, and networking organizations. Wells found that the contracting-out process usually develops gradually, beginning with just one or two outside firms, and that charter schools were not the only ones to resort to this process. Traditional public schools often contract out transportation, food services, special education, building maintenance, and custodial services.[31]

In California, the courts considered the issue. A charter school contracted with a private landscape company for maintenance and was then sued by the classified staff's union, which argued that the school is obligated to use district employees. The court decided in favor of the charter school, granting it the right to hire the cheaper private company for landscape and garden maintenance. [32] However, unions raise an important objection. Since maintenance is often provided by minority workers who, because of their union affiliations, enjoy benefits, adequate compensation, and safe working conditions, the practice of contracting out these services to for-profit private firms endangers these workers' ability to provide for their families with decent livable wages, let alone educate their children privately.

In an attempt to confront "niche" contracting, which is becoming increasingly pervasive, the National Education Association (NEA) is developing strategies and criteria that will judge private sector involvement in contracting out public school services. Nevertheless, it is clear that unions have begun to capitulate to some privatization demands and now promote what they term a "public/private arrangement."[33]

The relationship between free enterprise and public education is certainly nothing new. For over 100 years, public education was designed to produce a factory-ready, disciplined workforce. However, since then, public education has become a battlefield between corporate interests and those school reformers who see privatization as a nonequalizing power in society. Many citizens would argue that the relationship between the needs of the post-modern workforce and the exigencies of education in the new "knowledge-based" economy means some kids will unavoidably be left out—and they are almost certain to be low-income children of color in poor school districts. Some teachers and parents fear that just as HMOs have made the financial bottom line the standard for health care delivery, Educational Maintenance Organizations (EMOs) will be more accountable to corporate investors than they will be to students. In fact, the for-profit companies are not really interested in running the entire school system.

To be sure, taxpayers already pay for many services at private and public schools, which relieves those schools of significant financial obligations such as transportation, textbooks, hot lunches, counseling and speech therapy, as well as those costs linked with educating disabled and special needs children. By the 1989–1990 school year, more than half (51 percent) of all school districts in the United States had entered into public-private partnerships, involving about 2.6 million volunteers, with an estimated value of $225 million—an increase of 125 percent since 1986. About 30 million, or 65 percent of all students in 1989–1990 school year, attended schools in districts that had affiliations with business interests. And according to the U.S. Department of Education, about 50 percent of these partnerships involved the private donation of goods and services.[34] Approximately one fourth of public school spending in the United States goes directly to for-profit firms to buy goods such as books, computers, food services, building maintenance, and the like. In an analysis by the National Education Association, research found that public schools spent $80 billion in 2000 on "niche" purchases of goods and services. As businesses seek to enlarge their presence in public education as a provider of these services, they may move increasingly into instruction, as we have seen with the growth of sponsored educational materials (SEMs). Sylvan Learning Systems, for example, provides Title I services under contract to school districts, and Kaplan Educational Centers is poised to follow the Sylvan example.[35]

According to figures published by the NEA, U.S. educational spending for goods in the private sector during the 1997–1998 school year was allotted as follows:

regular classroom instruction	$10.7 billion
student services (e.g., guidance and speech pathology)	$0.9 billion

instructional services and in-service media centers	$1.9 billion
central administration	$2.4 billion
school administration	$0.7 billion
maintenance and operations	$13.6 billion
transportation	$5.8 billion
food services	$6.1 billion
other services and operations	$2.3 billion
capital expenditures and interest expense	$35.1 billion[36]

In some cases the private firms receiving these contracts are unionized so wage levels remain the same. In New York City, for example, school bus drivers under the new private contract were represented by the same union and the district realized no cost savings through privatization. However, even though privatization does not always result in lower costs through lower wages, this is not the result that privatization advocates hope for. The goal of the privatization policy—providing the same services more cheaply—makes it reasonable to assume that lower wages will usually result. This trend is troubling to teacher unions and their members, who have relied on collective bargaining for decent, livable wages and secure retirement benefits.

Advocates for privatizing education by contracting out needed services—an arrangement that has been termed "private-public partnerships"—contend that continually rising costs, coupled with restrictions on revenues, leave many school districts with few options other than cutting back on expenditures for classes, teachers, teachers' salaries, and infrastructure; or raising money through additional taxes. Neither alternative is desirable or simple to execute. A partnership between the public schools and the private sector, they argue, may lessen the pressures on school districts, enabling them to continue to provide fundamental services and infrastructure.

In thinking about contracting out of public school services, citizens should ask:

- Should business be involved in the provision of services to schools, and if so how?
- Which services should schools contract out?
- Is anyone harmed by this course of action—students, employees, the wider community?
- Can private contracts be structured to protect students, employees, and public interests?
- What guidelines should we as citizens develop, if any, for the contracting out of vital school services?

➠ Does privatization slowly erode public schools by capitalizing on lack of public resources? If so, is the answer privatization or more expenditures of public funds?

SUMMARY

Members of both the American Federation of Teachers (AFT) and the National Education Association (NEA) feel increasingly threatened by privatization and the practice of contracting out of school services. Are unions, teachers, and the public right to be concerned? Many privatization proponents have argued that market forces will serve to require teachers, who become complacent in their professions, to figure out how they can operate more effectively. In this scenario, teacher unions and public schools are self-interested protagonists responsible for driving up educational costs while accepting lower student achievement. The market, argue privatization proponents, will assure that quality is enhanced and achievement guaranteed.

Opponents of privatization passionately disagree. Progressive school reformers argue that *all* schools should be elevated to first class status—not simply a few "good" schools. But with privatization and for-profit management of schools, the characteristics of a good education—innovative teachers, small classes, access to computers—would be found only in a few public schools. To solve the funding dilemma, they advocate a tax structure that would require corporations to pay their fair share of the costs of public education.

Providing educational services for all schoolchildren would not be profitable, the privatization advocates argue, and few of these private education companies have paid off for investors. Yet they have introduced a profit-oriented perspective into our education system. For more than a decade, they have been organizing around school reform, tapping into real concerns about failing schools and lack of options. But before we grasp for a quick marketplace fix for our public education system, we must ask ourselves, Is this really the answer to long-term educational reform?

Regardless of how we answer that question, there can be little doubt that corporations have taken advantage of our frustrations with lack of resources and moved into the educational arena. Progressive educators opposed to privatization argue that we can reverse that process and regain control of education by offering another vision—one that admits to the problems associated with public education and public society in general, one in which corporations pay taxes instead of receiving tax write-offs and free advertising in schools. To progressive educators, educational choice and a good education must remain the right of all families, not just a few. Disparities in school resources simply open the door for corporations to fill the gap.

Can privatization through for-profit management of schools and contracting-out of school services accomplish the mission of authentic educational reform? This is one of the central questions that we as a nation must answer as we attempt to stimulate reasonable reforms in education for all our nation's children.

*Serious financial and legal difficulties plague Edison, making its future uncertain. In 2002 Edison lost its longtime contract for a large charter school in Boston and lost a contract in Dallas; Edison's relationship with its biggest client, the Las Vegas school district, soured in 2002. Edison was forced to settle an inquiry by the Securities and Exchange Commission for falsely reporting revenues and failing to maintain adequate financial controls. The company agreed to hire an internal audit manager and to revise its reporting methods. Edison's stock value plummeted and in August 2002 NASDAQ threatened to delist Edison. By November 2002 Edison stock was trading at sixty-seven cents a share.

NOTES

1. Symonds, W., and A. Therese. (February 2, 2000). "For Profit Schools." Business Week. 3667:64.

2. The National Education Association. "Charter Schools Run by For-profit Companies." http://www.nea.org.

3. Jennings, W. (1998). "Educational Entrepreneurs Show Reform Is Moving on Many Fronts." Speech given at the Association of Educators in Private Practice (AEPP) eighth annual Edventures conference held in Northwestern University in Evanston, Illinois, July 30-August 1, 1998.

4. National Education Association. "For-profit Management of Public Schools." http://www.nea.org.

5. Ibid.

7. Molnar, A., J. Morales, and A. V. Wyst. (2000). "Profiles of For-profit Education Management Companies. Center for Education Research, Analysis, and Innovation-University of Wisconsin–Milwaukee. http://www.uwm.edu.

8. Ibid.

11. Goodnough, A. (February 13, 2001). "Both Sides Courting Sharpton on School Privatization Plan." p. 1. *The New York Times* on the Web. http://www.nytimes.com.

12. Light, J. (2000). "A Local Battle Highlights the National Debate Over EMOs." Corporate Watch. http://www.corpwatch.org.

13. Ibid.

14. Advantage Schools. http://www.advantageschools.com.

15. Slowey, D. (February 22, 2000). "Credit Suisse First Boston Equity Partners, L.P., Leads $28 million Investment in Advantage Schools. *Boston Globe.*

16. Ibid.

17. Symonds, W., Therese, A. (February 2, 2000). "For Profit Schools." *Business Week Magazine.* 3667: 64.

18. Ibid.

19. Ibid.

20. Corporate Watch. (1998). "Charter Schools Run by For-profit Companies." http://www.corpwatch.org.

21. Ibid.

22. Ibid.

23. Guthrie, J. (February 13, 2001). "San Francisco Poised to Cancel Edison Charter." *The San Francisco Chronicle,* p. A13.

24. Ibid.

25. Light, J. (2000). "A Local Battle Highlights the National Debate over EMOs." http://www.corpwatch.org.

26. San Francisco Unified School District Board of Education. (June 28, 2001). Superintendent's Proposal. Resolution No. 16-25Spl. Directive Regarding Renewal and Revocation of the Edison Charter Academy's Charter and Management Agreement. San Francisco, California.

27. *Edison Charter Schools v. the Board of Education.* Superior Court of the State of California, City and County of San Francisco. Case No. 319053.

28. Ibid.

29. San Francisco Unified School District Board of Education (June 28, 2001). Superintendent's Proposal.

30. Vine, P. (September 8–15, 1997). "To Market, to Market. The School Business Sells Kids Short." *The Nation* 265:11–17.

31. Wells, A., and Scott, J. (April, 1999). *Evaluation of Privatization and Charter Schools.* p. 15. UCLA Charter School Study Prepared for the April 1999 Conference on the National Center for the Study of Privatization in Education. Teachers College, Columbia University.

32. Ibid. 14.

33. National Education Association (2000). *Education, Investors, and Entrepreneurs: A Framework for Understanding Contracting-out Public Schools and Public School Services.* Washington, D.C.: NEA.

34. David, A. (July 1992). "Public Private Partnerships: The Private Sector and Innovation in Education." The Reason Public Policy Institute. http://rppi.org.

35. National Education Association (2000). "Education, Investors and Entrepreneurs."

36. Ibid. Projections based on the U.S. Department of Education National Center for Education Statistics. School year 1993–1994 detailed expenditure data.

Chapter Nine
◆ Epilogue

In this book, I have taken on the responsibility of helping you, the reader, understand the current move toward the privatization of education as part of a larger neoliberal agenda. I believe, as I have attempted to demonstrate, that privatization represents a complete overhaul of societal services, social relationships, identification of self, and the notion of public community. Privatization, as all social actors agree, will not only affect public-private arrangements but will change the underlying political values, understandings, and capacities for collective action and community building within society. Turning public tenants into private homeowners, public employees into private employees, educators into managers, students into products, and Social Security beneficiaries into investors in private retirement accounts will also change citizens' frames of social, individual, and political thought. In other words, privatization does not just create new material conditions for the satisfaction of human needs and wants, it changes everything: human consciousness, ideological formations, human relationships, intellectual controversy, public discourse, democracy, and the material conditions under which we live our lives. In fact, the consequences of neoliberal policies foster a consciousness that is atomized and alienated, replacing public empathy with privatized self-interest.

Within education, efforts to privatize schooling are becoming more numerous and increasingly diverse. As I have attempted to demonstrate, it is unlikely that contracting out public services, awarding private vouchers, developing corporate curricula, or allowing for-profit companies to manage public schools will reduce pressure on government spending. In fact, as experts on both sides of the debate have pointed out, private contractors and corporations are as likely as public employees to lobby for larger budgets, special entitlements, social legitimacy, and an ever-increasing market share.

I have also attempted to demonstrate that support for privatization activities in schools is not limited to corporate curricula, private vouchers, SEMs, direct advertising, or corporate contests. IBM and Apple Computer, for example, have set their sites on schools-for-profit just as more and more multinational companies are beginning to consider the idea.[1] If we add to this the Burger King Academies—owned and operated by Burger King's British transnational corporate owner—which are fully accredited, quasi-private high schools in fourteen U.S. cities, it becomes clear that we are observing the radical transformation of public spheres into publicly financed private realms. And this is just the tip of the iceberg. "Partnerships" between the private sector and public sector are mushrooming. In New York City, for example, the board of education recently agreed to allow a private company to place ads on school buses. The board hopes to raise $5.9 million per year in this way—a noticeable contribution to the system's $8 billion annual budget. In Seattle, which faced a projected deficit of $35 million over three years, the school board proposed a similar solution to the districts' money woes: selling advertising. They project $1 million annually in earnings. In this case, however, the community refused to support the concept of selling access to their students. Protests erupted, and after five months the board abandoned the plan.[2]

The proliferation of Web sites and think tanks linked to organizations promoting public funding or private schools and privatization of public schools is no isolated phenomenon, according to Andrew Stark, who teaches management at the University of Toronto. It is part of a larger neoliberal trend reflected in two decades of political agitating to privatize functions that have traditionally been public. Stark points to an array of examples, ranging from private communities demanding tax transfers from the public treasury for the dues they pay to maintain their own streets and parks, to merchants in Los Angeles and Philadelphia raising millions of dollars to build police stations in their neighborhood, to the privatization of public hospitals everywhere from Boston to Tulsa.[3]

However, the issue is complex, as Stark has noted. In particular, when schools are asked to rely on private funding sources, the disparity between schools is compounded. He describes the fund-raising efforts of two schools located just a few miles from each other: Ser Ninos Elementary School, located in a poor neighborhood, and Rice School, located in one of the cities wealthiest communities. Rice held an auction. One parent paid $20,000 for a reserved parking space; others bid large amounts of money for extra attention, including the right to spend a day with the principal and to go camping with the school's teachers. At Ser Ninos, the school held a garage sale to raise money and earned $44.[4]

As the auction at Rice, demonstrates, many parents and schools have moved beyond cookie and candy sales in an attempt to get a private school education for their children on what one principal calls "the public nickel."[5] This practice raises very different issues from those we have discussed in connection with private vouchers. With choice and private vouchers, "parents use public funds to purchase services from the private schools their children attend."[6] In other words, they take state monies and give them to for-profit corporations to manage schools, develop curriculum, and provide myriad privatized educational services. But what transpired at Rice School is a paradigmatic shift: wealthy parents are using private resources to purchase services for the public schools their children attend. As a result, these public schools are transformed into elite enclaves for students fortunate enough to have parents with the money to purchase indispensable educational resources. Yet in a larger sense, the concepts are two sides of the same coin: they both symbolize the blurring of the boundary between private and public.

Perhaps one of the most troublesome oversights in recent educational debates is the definition of student achievement and how it is related to social class, race, and gender. With the growing economic and cultural chasms between rich and poor and between white and "other;" with white flight from cities and the persistence of racism, housing segregation is perhaps more extreme than during the pre-civil rights movement. Pointing out that the professional structure is class-based, Aronowitz invites us to consider why blacks and Latinos are at the bottom of the economic and cultural ladder. He also asks us to ponder if this has not led to a widening of the educational chasm between whites and blacks.[7] The issue of race is still an underlying reality in American life, as are issues of social class and gender discrimination.

These concerns are important in many ways. In many large cities, middle-class flight—black as well as white—has left cities faltering, both economically and organizationally. Structural changes in the economy have created a climate of de-industrialization that adds a critical class character to the conversation about educational equity and student attainment. As companies flee for distant shores where labor is cheaper and more compliant, they take with them many high-paying union jobs. As a result, many rural and urban communities in the United States find themselves left without decent education, recreation, housing, and health facilities—not to mention basic environmental protections such as clean air and water. Cities are now finding that they lack the tax base to provide crucial social services, and this grim reality must be taken into consideration when formulating educational policies.

The issue of student achievement and the states' obligation to provide an "adequate education" has found new and controversial expressions in the judicial arena. In the 1970s, in the *Serrano v. Priest* decision in California and in similar cases in Michigan, New Jersey, Texas, and

a half dozen other states, the courts have ruled that when a state constitution promises free public schooling to all children, the state has the responsibility to assure that the funding for these schools exists and is relatively equal for each child—regardless of the local-property tax base
and other economic realities within which children live. But just what is
an "adequate education"? Both courts and scholars have grappled with
this question for years without producing many satisfying answers.

However, in the past few years, courts in Kentucky, Massachusetts, New York, North Carolina, Ohio, and Wyoming have embraced a
far more radical consideration of this educational concept. These state
courts have dealt with the issue of "educational adequacy" by arguing
that the state is responsible for providing a twenty-first-century education, even if this means allocating more funds for remediation. As the
Washington State Supreme Court recently ruled, "educational adequacy" means schooling that will equip students for their roles as citizens and enable them to succeed both economically and personally.[8]
But precisely what does this mean? The court's attempt to define legal
guidelines for educational adequacy merges with the argument that the
idea of student achievement, an equally illusory and ambiguous concept, has never really been defined for public policy purposes. Decades
of discussions over educational purpose from diverse academic perspectives have left us with a notion of student achievement more and
more wedded to standardized tests. Where once we debated the issue of
educational purpose and accountability, we now assume that student
achievement means passing state-mandated tests.

Yet in an important legal decision in New York in January of 2001,
Justice Leland DeGrasse of the state supreme court ruled that the state's
system of school financing deprived children in New York City, especially Latino and black students, of the sound basic education guaranteed by the state constitution. In his written opinion, DeGrasse discussed at length the fact that 40 percent of New York City's children
come from welfare homes. He noted that 70 percent are poor enough to
qualify for low- or reduced-priced lunches. He spoke about dilapidated,
overcrowded, and often-unsafe school buildings. He pointed out the
lack of highly professionally trained teachers, and he addressed the lack
of educational resources including textbooks, laboratories, science facilities, computers, and the pedagogical equipment needed to learn.
DeGrasse's opinion was unambiguous in two aspects.

First, instead of basing his decision on the state's funding formu-
las, he relied in his ruling on the constitutional right of every child to a
decent and equitable education. Second, he ruled that this education
cannot be elementary aimed at achieving minimal levels of literacy but

must be an education for productive citizenship. Education for productive citizenship, he wrote, is not just a matter of understanding how to cast a vote or participate on a jury, but of learning to do so proficiently and capably. He also addressed the issue that education must shift its emphasis even in the area of productive needs, arguing that it must address the changing nature of the labor force in America and the accelerating transformations in technology that are impacting social life. He aimed his opinion directly at what he termed the "digital gap" and set the standard for "educational adequacy" as democratic citizenship education, much as W. E. B. DuBois and John Dewey so vehemently argued in the last century.

What DeGrasse and other judges are doing is legally defining, with the aid of expert witnesses, what it means to be educated in today's rapidly changing global world and then rendering verdicts and rulings that will allow the best possible system to arise, a system that will ensure educational adequacy for all students. These judges understand that the notion of educational adequacy is interwoven with the multidefinitional standards regarding student achievement and cannot be separated. Many educators now claim that this "adequacy" approach allows the courts to move away from complex tax reform schemes and simply rule what guidelines will be used to define educational adequacy and then implement judicial decisions that mandate the funding for state and local communities to assure its availability.

The Campaign for Fiscal Equity, a New York nonprofit that seeks finance reform in New York school systems, believes that by concentrating on issues of educational adequacy when defining both students' opportunities and their achievement, citizens are forced to include the wider issues of race and economic class in their deliberations. Educational adequacy as a judicial and academic debate gives progressive educators the opportunity to raise the expectations for all students by arguing that opportunities to become educated must be provided in public schools. Instead of talking about how to "slice the educational pie" by moving monies from rich districts to poor ones, the idea of educational adequacy fosters a debate among citizens that will increase the amount of pie for all and move the definition of student achievement toward societal and human ends.[9]

Although the idea faces intense resistance from many politicians and public policy interests committed to standardized tests as a baseline for student achievement, most state constitutions are clear that in the end, districts are merely augmentations of the government. If public schools fail, then the state has failed. And with the intrusion of high-stakes state mandated testing, mushrooming accountability requirements, and elaborate and complex testing systems, most states have admitted to their own culpability and accountability in providing educational adequacy to all students.

What direction will this discussion ultimately take? It is impossible to say. But it is clear that the criteria for what constitutes the "sound education" guaranteed by the states are being discussed more widely within legal and academic forums. But until the debate becomes public and all stakeholders are at the table, it is difficult to see how a private-public policy can solve a problem we have not yet defined.

THE INTERNATIONALISM OF PRIVATIZATION: NEOLIBERAL POLITICS AND EDUCATION

Defunding public education is not simply an American phenomenon but a worldwide trend. In many countries, it is part and parcel of structural adjustment policies, imposed by such organizations as the International Monetary Fund (IMF) and World Bank, which involve broad privatization efforts to eliminate or reduce the social safety net. According to Erika Shaker, of the CCPA Project in Canada, an organization that monitors neoliberal policies throughout the Canadian provinces, the world is witnessing a large-scale, fundamental reorganization of the public education system on the basis of a crisis manufactured in the private sector: the claim by corporate interests that the schools are not turning out suitably "educated" students. The National Alliance of Business, for example, claims that schools have neglected their primary responsibility, which they see as teaching basic skills. Thus, from their point of view, the public school system is a failure.[10]

Take for example, the country of Mexico. With the signing of the North American Free Trade Agreement (NAFTA) in 1992–1994, a new national economic and educational model was finalized for Mexico. But according to some social economists, this neoliberal development model is increasing poverty in both rural and urban areas. According to the most recent census in 2000, fully 75 percent of Mexicans currently live in poverty, and one third of these live in extreme poverty. This is compared with 49 percent living in poverty in 1981, before the neoliberal restructuring policies were imposed.[11]

This new economic model is presided over by a Mexican government that has discarded its responsibility to society in order to become a catalyst for private capital investment. The first step in the privatization process was the privatization of publicly owned companies and the national banking system. From there privatization spread to other sectors: health, subsidized housing, and public education. For the Mexican people, the cost of privatization has been high.

Beginning on the first day of 1994, when NAFTA went into effect, the indigenous people expressed their objections forcefully. The peoples of Chiapas led an armed resistance in opposition to the notion of modernization by privatization, which they believed would benefit only a few people. Their rebellion focused attention on the depth of the crisis brought about by the Mexican government's neoliberal development model.

In Mexico, the obligation of the state to provide education free of charge is written into the constitution. However, that changed in 1993. In preparation for implementing NAFTA, the Salinas de Gortari government asked the Mexican Congress to modify Article 3 of the Mexican Constitution so that the state would be required to provide only basic (primary and secondary) education. As a result, today, only primary and secondary education remains free of charge in Mexico. In response to more than a quarter of a million young people who were demanding entrance into post-secondary education, the education minister recently declared that the government did not have a legal obligation to provide education beyond a rudimentary level, only the "moral obligation."[12]

Furthermore, the global trend in educational privatization as a neoliberal policy is not simply confined internationally to the Western hemisphere. The globalization agenda for education has seldom been laid out so clearly as in a paper published in May 1997 by the Ministry of Labor of the Republic of Korea. This ministry served as the Secretariat for the 2nd Human Resources Ministerial Meeting of the Asia-Pacific Economic Cooperation, APEC, held in September 1997 in Seoul. APEC maintains that globalization is inevitable and that education must meet the terms of its economic requirements. From their point of view, education is a matter of preparing workers for business; thus it follows that business should determine the content of education, which should be the development of a work ethic and its accompanying attitudes and skills. They conclude that the world is oversupplied with educated citizens and undersupplied with trained citizens; this training, they maintain, will eliminate unemployment.[13]

SUMMARY

This book has tried to balance the arguments for and against the privatization of schools by presenting multiple points of view on the issue. The discussions in this book have been about the norms and standards appropriate under the new neoliberal circumstances that face all nations worldwide but especially the United States. Globalization and neoliberalism have a material basis in both technological change and human relationships and manifest themselves in increased trade, investments, and financial flows. However, they also enhance corporate power and control and produce an accompanying ideological shift to neoliberal, laissez-faire public and private policies. This shift is nominally in favor of "free markets" but needs to be understood in terms of a power shift in favor of private interests and corporate dominance. The discussions in this book have not been about what people deserve from their government; instead they have concentrated on the debate about the transfer of power from the public sector to the private sector, a shift that has been orchestrated by a host of private interests. The same corporate and business interests and political policies that have starved the public sector of needed funds have found a privatized means for paying for the services they want. At the same time, they have avoided paying for public schools, emergency room care, shelters for the homeless, and subsidized housing for working people. This situation is a far cry from the economic ideals offered by Adam Smith and is characterized by very different pubic-private relationships.

I hope that this book has helped you understand the issues behind neoliberal privatization attempts aimed at public schools and their implications for our communities and our nation's young people. How we handle the new wave of globalization and neoliberal policies will impact greatly on both our democracy and the level of services we provide our nation's people. The directions we take regarding privatization, both internationally and nationally, will determine the kind of educational reforms that will result and even the type of democracy we can hope to develop and sustain.

If this book has left you with many questions, that is good. For it is through critical questioning and rigorous debate that we as citizens will find the most positive public policies to support the development of educational institutions and to create opportunities for teachers, students, and society at large.

NOTES

1. Kozol, J. (1991). *Savage Inequalities.* New York: Harper Collins, p. 17.

2. Commercialfree.org "What Is Commercialism in Schools?" http://www.commercialfree.org.

3. Stark, A. (Winter 2001). "What's Wrong with Private Funding for Public Schools?" http://www.dissentmagazine.org.

4. Ibid.

5. Ibid.

6. Ibid.

7. Arnowitz, S. (March 12, 2001). "Race: The Continental Divide." *The Nation* 272: 10, 26.

8. Schrag, P. (March 12, 2001). "Defining Adequacy up." *The Nation* 272: 10, 18.

9. Ibid. 19.

10. Shaker, E. (1998). "The CCPA Education Project: Learning about the Commercialization of Education." http://www.corpwatch.org.

11. Sanders, J. (February 26, 2001). "Two Mexico's and Fox's Quandary." *The Nation* 272: 8, 2.

12. "Mexico: Neo-liberal Adjustment of the Educational Sector" (February 28–March 2, 1997). A Report for the Third Trinational Conference in Defense of Public Education. Mexican Section of the Trilateral Coalition in Defense of Public Education. Held in Vancouver, Canada.

13. Kuehn, L. (1999). "Schools for Globalized Business." The APEC Human Resources Ministerial Meeting.

Chapter Ten
✌ Selected Print and Nonprint Resources

The works listed in this chapter are divided into two categories. The first section lists books, articles, speeches, and studies that deal with the topic of educational reform specifically in the arena of the privatization of public schools. These include law journals, labor reports, government publications, and professional and academic articles. The second section contains nonprinted resources such as Web sites that pertain directly to privatization of schools.

PRINT RESOURCES

Adelsheimer, Erica, and Kate Rix. (1999) **"What We Know about Vouchers: The Facts behind the Rhetoric."** WestEd.

This report describes various publicly funded voucher programs and examines research on vouchers, the legal status of publicly funded voucher programs, and other ways to provide school choice. It offers recommendations to policymakers, educators, and parents.

American Academy of Pediatrics (AAP). (February 1995). **"Children, Adolescents and Advertising" (RE9504).** Pp. 295–297. Volume 95. No. 2.

In this study, the AAP looks at the statistically significant increase in advertising aimed at children.

American Federation of Teachers. (1992). **"National Education Standards and Assessment."** American Federation of Teachers Convention Resolution. Washington, D.C.

This report examines educational standards and how they should be applied to all public schools, including charters.

American Federation of Teachers. (1992). **"U.S. Education: The Task before Us."** American Federation of Teachers convention Resolution, Washington, D.C.

This resolution identifies necessary school reforms and the formidable problems and issues that face school reform.

Ascher, C., N. Fruchter, and R. Berne. (1996). *Hard Lessons: Public Schools and Privatization.* New York: Twentieth Century Fund Press.

This book examines the issues of privatization and public schools and explains why the movement for privatization is taking place.

Carnegie Forum on Education and the Economy. (1986). *A Nation Prepared: Teachers for the 21st Century.* Hyattsville, MD: Carnegie Forum on Education and the Economy.

Proposes the teaching and educational reforms necessary to prepare teachers for the challenges of teaching in the twenty-first century.

Chubb, J. and Moe, T. (1990) *Politics, Markets, and America's Schools.* Washington, D.C.: The Brookings Institution.

A landmark book and one thought to have sparked the voucher movement in education. In this book Chubb and Moe argue against public schools and explain why they believe public schools cannot and do not work.

Cookson, Peter W., Jr., and Sonali M. Shroff. **"Recent Experience with Urban School Choice Plans."** *ERIC Digest* (October 1997). ED413388.

This article examines the successes and failures of school choice in urban settings, focusing on student achievement in New York, Ohio, and Milwaukee.

Cookson, Peter W., Jr., and Sonali M. Shroff. **"School Choice and Urban School Reform."** (December 1997) ERIC Clearinghouse on Public Education.

This report gives an overview of choice programs examining a citywide program (New York) and a statewide program (Minnesota) and voucher programs including the Milwaukee plan.

Corwin, R., and J. Flaherty, eds. (November, 1995). **"Freedom and Innovation in California Charter Schools."** Los Alamitos, CA: Southwest Regional Laboratory.

This report emphasizes the type of freedom and innovation the authors believe charter schools offer. The authors also offer recommendations to strengthen charter schools by providing more freedom from governmental regulation.

Eberts, R., and Stone, A. (1984). *Unions and Public Schools.* Lexington, MA: Lexington Books.

What is the role of unions in public schools? Should they have a role? Does it need to be redefined? This book attempts to address these issues.

Greene, Jay P., and Paul E. Peterson. (August 29, 1996). **"Methodological Issues in Evaluation Research: The Milwaukee School Choice Plan."** In *Program on Education Policy and Governance: Occasional Paper,* Department of Government and Kennedy School of Government, Harvard University. (Available through http://hdc-www.harvard.edu).

This report is highly supportive of the Milwaukee voucher efforts.

Greene, Jay P. et al. (August 14, 1996) **"The Effectiveness of School Choice in Milwaukee: A Secondary Analysis of Data from the Program's Evaluation."** In *Program on Education Policy and Governance: Occasional Paper,* Department of Government and Kennedy School of Government, Harvard University. http://hdc-www.harvard.edu.

This study is favorable toward the results of private choice in the MPCP.

Hadderman, Margaret. **"Educational Vouchers."** *ERIC Digest* (May 2000). ED442194.

This article provides a discussion of vouchers and their constitutionality. It also looks at whether vouchers are working.

Hannaway, J., and M. Carnoy. (1993). *Decentralization and School Improvement: Can We Fulfill the Promise?* San Francisco: Jossey-Bass.

Is privatization of schools the answer to what is ailing public schools? This book examines this question and more in an attempt to forge a comprehensive approach to school reform.

Hedges, L., R. Greewald, and Richard D. Laire. **"The Effect of School Resources on Student Achievement."** *Review of Educational Research* 66:3 (1996): 391–396.

The report looks at the voucher controversy and the effect on student achievement.

Hodkinson, Phil, and Andrew C. Sparkes. **"Markets and Vouchers: The Inadequacy of Individualist Policies for Vocational Education and Training in England and Wales."** *Journal of Education Policy* 10:2 (March 1, 1995), 189.

This article is highly critical of privatization efforts in vocational education training in England and Wales.

Howe, Harold, II. **"The Continuing Question: Will Public Schools Make It in America?"** *The School Administrator* 53:5 (May 1, 1996) 14.

The former U.S. commissioner of education considers the question of whether the push to privatize public schools and add a voucher system represents a serious threat or promises a better world.

Kearney, C. P., and Arnold, M. L. (1994). **"Market Driven Schools and Educational Choices."** *Theory into Practice* 33:1, 112–117.

Highly critical of market driven schools, this article frames the issue in terms of choice and what this might mean for the national system of education.

McGroarty, Daniels, and Nadine Strossen. **"Are School-Voucher Programs for Parochial Schools a Good Idea?"** *Insight on the News* 12:30 (August 12, 1996) 24.

The authors argue that schools should be allowed to break free from the stranglehold of public education.

Molnar, A. (1996). *Giving Kids the Business: The Commercialization of America's Schools.* Boulder, CO: Westview.

This book is highly critical of the commercial efforts aimed at children in the United States.

Murphy, Joseph. **"Why Privatization Signals a Sea Change in Schooling."** *Educational Leadership* 54:2 (October 1, 1996) 60.

A review of the many types of privatization strategies and their applications to education, including asset sales, user fees, contracts, and vouchers.

National Commission on Excellence in Education. (1983). *A Nation at Risk: Imperative for Education Reform.* Washington, DC: U.S. Department of Education.

The well-known report produced during the Reagan years that sparked a new way of looking at schools and education and became a catalyst for educational reform.

Peterson, Bob. **"Teacher of the Year Gives Vouchers a Failing Grade."** *The Progressive* April 1997, 20.

This article is critical of the concept of vouchers and interviews teachers for their response.

Peterson, Paul E. (March 1995). **"The Milwaukee School Choice Plan: Ten Comments on the Witte Reply."** *Center for American Political Studies Occasional Paper 95–3,* Littauer Center, Department of Government, Harvard University. http://hdc-www.harvard.edu.

Peterson, Paul E. (1995). **"A Critique of the Witte Evaluation of Milwaukee's School Choice Program."** *Center for American Political Studies Occasional Paper 95–2,* Littauer Center, Department of Government, Harvard University. http://hdc-www.harvard.edu.

Rees, Nina Shokraii. **"Public School Benefits of Private School Vouchers."** *Policy Review* Volume 93. (January–February 1999).

Rees argues that school choice programs have improved overall student academic achievement in public schools.

Russo, Charles J., and John J. Harris III. **"Buyer Beware: State Controls over Privatization."** *School Business Affairs* 62:5 (May 1, 1996) 17.

This is a critical report on vouchers and other privatization measures for schools.

Russo, Charles J., et al. **"Legal Issues in Contracting out for Public Education Services."** *Education and Urban Society* 27:2 (February 1, 1995) 127.

This article takes a critical look at the contracting out of public education services to private entities.

Schrag, P. (November 23, 1999). **"The Voucher Seduction."** *The American Prospect* 11:1.

Examines the rationales behind the voucher movement and the ambiguous research findings on student achievement in voucher schools.

Semple, M. (August 1995). **"Legal Issues in Charter Schooling."** *The School Administrator* 52:8, 24–26.

In this article, a school administrator considers the legal issues that comprise running a charter school.

Shanker, A. (February 3, 1995). **"Classrooms Held Hostage: Restoring Order in Our Schools."** Speech to the AFT Conference on Discipline and Safety. Washington, D.C. http://www.aft.org.

In this highly critical speech Shanker speaks out against the conditions within classrooms and how educational workers must begin to construct a curriculum that works for children.

Shokraii, Nina. **"Why School Choice Can Help Children in America's Inner Cities."** *Teacher Education and Practice* 13:2 (Fall/Winter 1997) 15–27.

A Heritage Institute report on the positive effects of school vouchers.

Sizer, Theodore, R. **"New Hope for High Schools: Lessons from Reform-Minded Educators."** *The American School Board Journal* 183:9 (September 1, 1996) 37.

In this article, Theodore Sizer of Coalition of Essential Schools, discusses what works in public school instruction.

Stern, Sol. **"The School Reform That Dares Not Speak Its Name."** *The City Journal* 6:1 (Winter, 1996) 28.

In some New York City educational circles, vouchers are out of the question. But vouchers may be the best hope for reviving the failing public schools. This report looks at vouchers as a salvation for what ails schools.

Stick, Michael, J. **"Educational Vouchers: A Constitutional Analysis."** *Columbia Journal of Law and Social Problems* 28:3 (Spring, 1995) 423.

This article explores an important constitutional question regarding voucher programs: Does the inclusion of parochial schools in voucher programs violate the Establishment Clause? Stick argues that the Supreme Court could strongly support both sides of this issue.

Townley, Arthur J. **"Privatization of Public Schools: Boom or Bust?"** *Thrust for Educational Leadership* 24:7 (May 1, 1995) 43.

The privatization of instruction and support services is well under way in public schools across the nation. Townley analyzes the arguments for and against contracting out school services and offers some guidelines for school leaders considering the issue.

Tyack, D., and L. Cuban. (1995). *Tinkering Towards Utopia: A Century of Public School Reform.* Cambridge: Harvard University Press.

What have educational reform efforts really accomplished? This book looks at the history of educational reform movements, including charter schools.

Vine, P. *To Market to Market: The School Business Sells Kids Short.* The *Nation Magazine.* (September 8–15, 1997).

This article makes the argument that privatization deprives students of a quality education. Highly controversial but compelling in its argumentation.

Wells, A. S., and R. L. Crain. (1997). *Stepping over the Color Line: African American Students in White Suburban Schools.* New Haven: Yale University Press.

How are African-Americans being served in charter schools? What is their experience in public schools? This book examines the St. Louis school choice plan in which black students attended suburban schools.

Williams, Lois C., and Leak, Lawrence E. **"School Privatization's First Big Test: EAI in Baltimore."** *Educational Leadership* 54:2 (October 1, 1996) 56.

The article studies the voucher program in Baltimore, Maryland.

Witty, Geoff, and T. Edwards. **"School Choice Policies in England and the United States: An Exploration of Their Origins and Significance."** *Comparative Education* 34:3 (November 1, 1998) 211.

This article looks at school choice programs internationally.

Zollers, N., and Ramanathan, A. (December 1998). **"For Profit Charter Schools and Students with Disabilities."** *Phi Delta Kappan.* 80:4, 297–304.

What about students with disabilities? How are they faring in charter schools? This article examines the admissions process for assuring equal access to charter schools.

NONPRINT RESOURCES

Adbusters Magazine
http://www.adbusters.org

AdBusters focuses on commercialism in society, especially in schools. The magazine frequently considers commercial efforts to privatize public education. This is an excellent source for examining how advertising affects children both within and outside schools.

American Federation of Teachers
http://www.aft.org

AFT's Voucher Home Page is a comprehensive source of the vouchers information collected by the AFT.

Annenberg Public Policy Center
http://appcpenn.org.

"Media In The Home 2000: The Fifth Annual Survey of Parents and Children." This report examines the rise of advertising within society at large, but especially as it pertains to TV and home life.

Consumer Reports Center for Children, Youth, and Families
http://www.zillionsedcenter.org

This Web site offers tools for teachers, youth leaders, and parents who want to help kids eight years and older evaluate products and advertising and make informed consumer choices.

Daily Report Card
http://www.youth.net

Published by the American Political Network, the Daily Report Card offers a summary of current K-12 related news stories pertaining to political and social developments in the areas of education and educational reform. Issues include the privatization of education.

Education Policy Analysis
http://www.epaa.asu.edu

Scholarly articles and national coverage of the latest news and policy issues. A publication from Arizona State University.

Education Week on the Web
http://www.edweek.org

This online newspaper is devoted to education issues including government legislation, curriculum, and reform.

EducationNews.org
http://wwwleducationnews.org

Provides a daily news service with timely articles on the most current issues in U.S. education. EducationNews.org also provides links to the major education news articles around the country.

EdWeb
http://edweb.sdsu.edu

A site hosted by the San Diego State University College of Education, which focuses on education reform and information technology. It features information about online educational resources from around the world, and trends in education policy and information infrastructure development. Discussions offer public policy debates regarding the privatization of education.

Metcalf, Kim K., and Polly A. Tait. **"Free Market Policies and Public Education: What is the Cost of Choice?"** Online article, Phi Delta Kappan. http://www.pdkintl.org.

This article examines the evidence of the effectiveness of voucher school programs in Cleveland and Milwaukee and discusses the implications of the educational choice movement for public schools.

Molnar, A. (August 1998). **"Sponsored Schools and Commercialized Classrooms."** Online article, Commercialism in Education Research Unit, Arizona State University. http://www.asu.edu.

National Education Association
http://www.nea.org

The NEA Web site is a comprehensive source of education news, articles, and research. Its Legislative Action Center tracks education-related legislation and provides up-to-the-minute information on legislation. The Web site also provides access to *NEA Today*, the association's newsletter.

Public Agenda
http://www.publicagenda.org

"On Thin Ice: How Advocates and Opponents Could Misread the Public's Views on Vouchers and Charter Schools." This Public Agenda survey on education examines national attitudes about alternatives to public schools.

ReThinking Schools Online
http://www.rethinkingschools.org

"False Choices: Vouchers, Public Schools and Our Children's Future." This highly critical 1998 report examines the privatization of schooling through vouchers, highlighting the problems with voucher programs and the lessons that can be learned from the Milwaukee voucher program.

Stay Free!
http://www.sunsite.unc.edu/stayfree

Stay Free! is a nonprofit magazine examining commercialism and American culture.

Chapter Eleven

•❖ Directory of Organizations, Associations, and Government Agencies

The following organizations—corporations, unions, nonprofit agencies, think tanks, associations, and government agencies—provide information on the privatization of education. They are divided into seven categories. The first category lists organizations involved in educational reform. The second category describes organizations that oppose the privatization of education. The third category compiles those organizations that support the privatization of schools, either through private choice or other means. The fourth category describes organizations that provide incentive programs, such as private contests to schools. Organizations that provide sponsored educational materials (SEMs) are included in the fifth category. The sixth category includes those organizations that support for-profit management of public and private schools. The seventh category lists organizations that directly market products to students as well as those corporations that sponsor private fundraisers through corporate sales and marketing.

ORGANIZATIONS INVOLVED IN EDUCATIONAL REFORM

Government Agencies

Early Childhood Institute (ECI)
National Institute on Early Childhood Development and Education
Office of Educational Research and Improvement
U.S. Department of Education
555 New Jersey Ave, NW
Washington, DC 20208
(202) 219-1935
Fax: (202) 273-4768
eci@inet.ed.gov

The ECI provides grants for educators and community members in the areas of national research, educational development centers, and field studies. It also houses information and referrals on families and early childhood development and education.

National Assessment of Educational Progress (NAEP)
National Center for Education Statistics
Assessment Division, 8th Floor
1990 K Street, NW
Washington, DC 20006
(202) 502-7400
fax: (202) 502-7440

The NAEP is sometimes called "the Nation's Report Card." It is a nationally representative organization that conducts assessment of what America's students have attained in terms of knowledge and their performance in various subject areas. Since 1969, NAEP has carried out assessments of students in reading, mathematics, science, writing, U.S. history, civics, geography, and the arts. The Commissioner of Education Statistics, who heads the National Center for Education Statistics in the U.S. Department of Education, is responsible for carrying out the NAEP project. The National Assessment Governing Board is appointed by the Secretary of Education. Their report studies students from both public and private schools and reports results for student achievement at grades 4, 8, and 12.

National Educational Research Policy and Priorities Board (NERPPB)
80 F St., NW, Suite 100
Washington, DC 20208-7564
(202) 208-0692
Fax: (202) 219-1528
nerppb@ed.gov

NERPPB works in cooperation with the Assistant Secretary of Education to determine research priorities and evaluation standards. In addition, the board attempts to determine priorities that ultimately provide guidance to Congress in its oversight of education. NERPPB guides the nation's educational research, development, and dissemination agenda.

National Endowment for the Humanities (NEH)
National Endowment for the Humanities
1100 Pennsylvania Avenue, NW

Washington, DC 20506
(202) 606-8400
http://www.neh.fed.us
education@neh.gov

NEH assists teachers, including those in private schools, who seek to strengthen and expand their understanding of history, literature, foreign languages and culture, as well as other areas within the humanities. With NEH support, teachers have the opportunity to participate in formal study sessions during the summer, as well as plan a sabbatical for a year of independent study.

National Institute on Educational Governance, Finance, Policymaking, and Management
National Institute on Educational Governance
Finance, Policymaking and Management
OERI, U.S. Department of Education
555 New Jersey Avenue, NW
Washington, DC 20208-5510
(202) 219-2032
Fax (202) 219-2159
http://www.ed.gov
gfi@ed.gov

NIEGFPM is part of the Office of Educational Research and Improvement (OERI) in the U.S. Department of Education. The Institute's mission is "to carry out a coordinated and detailed program of research and development. It seeks to improve student achievement through school restructuring and reform. It conducts research necessary to provide a firm basis from which to identify, develop and evaluate various approaches in elementary and secondary education, especially in the areas of governance, finance, and policymaking, as well as management at the state, local, tribal, school building and classroom level."

National Institute on the Education of At-Risk Students (At-Risk Institute)
U.S. Department of Education
OERI/At-Risk Room 610
555 New Jersey Avenue, NW
Washington, DC 20208-5521
Fax: (202) 219-2030
http://www.ed.gov

The At-Risk Institute is one of five institutes created by the Educational Research, Development, Dissemination and Improvement Act of 1994. These institutes are located within the Office of Educational Research and Improvement at the U.S. Department of Education. The At-Risk Institute conducts a wide range of research and development activities to improve the education of students at risk of educational failure because of poverty, race, and geographical location, and limited English-language proficiency.

National Library of Education
400 Maryland Avenue, SW
Washington, DC 20202
(800) 424-1616
Fax: (202) 401-0552
http://www.ed.gov

NLE is the federal government's primary resource center for educational information. The staff responds to inquiries regarding programs and activities in the Department of Education. The Department publishes educational materials from other federal agencies and provides services and resources available through the Educational Resources Information Center (ERIC), research institutes, and the national education dissemination system.

Office of Educational Research and Improvement (OERI)
555 New Jersey Avenue, NW
Washington, DC 20208

OERI provides national leadership for educational study and statistical gathering. OERI attempts to promote excellence and equity in American education by carrying out research and projects that are funded through grants designed to help to improve education. They collect statistics on the current standing and progress of schools and education throughout the country.

Office of Elementary and Secondary Education (OESE)
400 Maryland Ave., SW
Washington, DC 20202
(202) 401-0113
Fax: (202) 205-0310
oese@ed.gov
http://www.ed.gov

The Office of Elementary and Secondary Education is designed to promote academic excellence, assure educational opportunities and equity for all of America's children and families, and to improve the quality of teaching and learning. They provide leadership, technical assistance, and financial support to schools and districts.

United States Department of Education
U.S. Department of Education
400 Maryland Avenue, SW
Washington, DC 20202-0498
1-800-872-5327

The United States Department of Education was created in 1980 through the Department of Education Organization Act. Its mission is to ensure the quality of education for all students and to support state and local educational institutions, as well as private and public nonprofit research organizations. The United States Department of Education establishes seven priorities for public schools throughout the United States. These seven priorities are in reading, math, colleges, standards and assessment, technology, teacher development, and assuring safe schools.

Nonprofit Organizations

Annenberg Institute for School Reform
Brown University
PO Box 1985
Providence, RI 02912
401-863-7990
http://home.aisr.brown.edu

The mission of the Annenberg Institute for School Reform is to advance, share, and act on knowledge that improves the conditions and effects of schooling in America, especially in urban communities and in schools serving poor students.

The Brookings Institution
1775 Massachusetts Avenue, NW
Washington, DC 20036
202-797-6000
Fax: 202-797-6004
http://www.brookings.org

The Brookings Institution is an independent policy analyst think tank committed to informing the public about public policy initiatives. They have several books and papers written by respected scholars on the topic of school vouchers and educational reform, available in limited form on their Web site.

Center for Critical Thinking
Sonoma State University
c/o POB 220
Dillon Beach, CA 94929
707-878-9100
Fax: 707-878-9111
http://www.criticalthinking.org

The Center for Critical Thinking conducts research and disseminates information on critical thinking. Each year it sponsors the International Conference on Critical Thinking and Educational Reform. It has worked with the College Board, the National Education Association, and the U.S. Department of Education, as well as numerous colleges, universities, and school districts, to assist the implementation of critical thinking instruction.

Center for Education Reform (CER)
1001 Connecticut Avenue, NW
Suite 204
Washington, DC 20036
202-822-9000
http://www.edreform.com

The Center for Education Reform (CER) is a conservative nonprofit organization that publishes newsletters and materials about school reform. It focuses on the growth of charter schools and private voucher initiatives. Its Web site provides outlines and time lines of important legislative rulings, an "In the News" feature with current headlines regarding educational reform and school choice, and an online newsletter called *Parent Power* that addresses school choice issues.

Center for Research on Evaluation, Standards, and Student Testing (CRESST/UCLA)
301 GSE&IS
Mailbox 951522 300
Charles E. Young Drive North
Los Angeles, CA 90095-1522

310-206-1532
Fax: 310-825-3883
http://www.cse.ucla.edu

The Center for Research on Evaluation, Standards, and Student Testing carries out research on topics related to K–12 educational testing and is funded by the National Center for Research on Evaluation, Standards, and Student Testing. It also provides educational assessment tools such as books and media kits for schools interested in evaluating student progress and achievement.

Center for School Change
The Humphrey Institute
University of Minnesota
301 19th Avenue S
Minneapolis, MN 55455
612-626-1834

The Center for School Change, sponsored by the Humphrey Institute of Public Affairs at the University of Minnesota, is program that works closely with educators, parents, businesspeople, students, policy makers, and others concerned with education in the United States. Some of their initiatives are to increase student achievement and graduation levels, improve student attitudes toward learning, and strengthen community involvement in education by fostering relationships between educators, parents, students, and key community members. One of its programs, the Minnesota Charter School Resource Center, was founded with the goal of providing free, high-quality technical support and funding to people wishing to create and operate public charter schools.

Center on Reinventing Public Education
University of Washington
PO Box 363060
Seattle, WA 98195-3060
206-685-2214
correspondence@rand.org

The Center on Reinventing Public Education strives to develop and assess approaches to public education that allow individual schools, especially inner-city schools, to be focused, efficient, and accountable. The center conducts national research on charter schools, school contracting, privatization and choice, and school system decentralization with the Brookings Institution, the RAND Corporation, Vanderbilt University, and the University of Chicago. They believe abandoning public education is impractical and that public schools should be free of heavy regulation.

Charter Schools Development Center
CSU Institute for Education Reform
California State University–Sacramento
6000 J Street
Sacramento, CA 95819-6018
916-278-4611
epremack@calstate.edu

The Charter School Development Center's goal is to help public education institutions make the transition from a highly regulated, bureaucratic system to one that permits and encourages schools to be more creative. It seeks to achieve this by providing technical assistance to the charter school reform movements in California and throughout the nation.

Coalition of Essential Schools
National Office
1814 Franklin Street
Suite 700
Oakland, CA 94612
510-433-1451
http://www.essentialschools.org

The Coalition of Essential Schools is a developing and ongoing national network of over 1,000 schools and 24 regional support centers. It has moved from a centrally run organization to a decentralized network of regional centers that gives technical assistance and personalized support to schools. Although each school in the network is unique, they are unified by CES's common principles of students achieving depth of knowledge rather than breadth of coverage in core disciplines and personalized learning in which teachers are not responsible for more than 20 students in an elementary and 80 in middle and high schools.

Consumer Reports Center for Children, Youth, and Families
101 Truman Avenue
Yonkers, NY 10703
(914) 378-2000
http://www.consumersunion.org

Consumer Reports and Zillions Online are published by Consumers Union (CU), an independent, nonprofit testing and information organization. Since 1936, CU's goal has been to test products and inform the public. It gives information about products and services, personal finance, health and nutrition, and other consumer issues, including advertising in the schools. CU supports the Student Privacy Protection Act, a bill in Congress that would require parents to give informed consent before companies and marketing firms could collect information from their children in school. The act also calls for a national study on the prevalence and effect of commercial activity in schools.

Council of Chief State School Officers (CCSSO)

One Massachusetts Avenue, NW
Suite 700
Washington, DC 20001-1431
202-408-5505
http://www.ccsso.org

The Council of State School Officers is a nationwide, nonprofit organization comprising public officials who are department heads for elementary and secondary education in the states, the U.S. extra-state jurisdictions, the District of Colombia, and the Department of Defense and Education Activity. The CCSSO works on behalf of the state agencies that serve U.S. public school students throughout the United States as well as internationally by preparing legislative recommendations on current educational issues.

Council of Great City Schools

1301 Pennsylvania Avenue, NW
Suite 702
Washington, DC 20004
(202) 393-2427
Fax: (202) 393-2400
http://www.cgcs.org

The Council of Great City Schools is a consortium of fifty-seven of the nation's biggest urban public school systems. It was founded in 1956 and incorporated in 1961. The council promotes improvements in urban education through legislation, research, media relations, management, technology, and various other special projects.

Council of Urban Boards of Education

1680 Duke Street

Alexandria, VA 22314
703-838-6720
http://www.nsba.org

The council was started in 1967 to address the special needs of school board members serving the largest metropolitan cities in the United States. The council gathers information, develops recommendations, and takes legislative action to enhance and improve the quality and equality of education.

Education Commission of the States (ECS)
707 17th Street
No 2700
Denver, CO 80202-3427
303-299-3600
http://www.ecs.org

The Education Commission of the States facilitates partnerships between corporate leaders and education policy makers in hopes of developing reform in public education. The ECS has developed initiatives on teacher quality, information about educational reforms, and policy studies. The Commission also publishes reports and policy guides on a variety of educational issues, including school vouchers, that are available to order on their Web site.

Little Hoover Commission
925 L Street
Suite 805
Sacramento, CA 95814
916-445-2125
http://www.bsa.ca.gov

The Little Hoover Commission is an independent, state body that works to promote efficiency and economy in California state programs. The commission monitors California legislation, publishes reports on state programs, and researches issues such as charter schools.

Morrison Institute for Public Policy
School of Public Affairs
Arizona State University
PO Box 874405
Tempe, AZ 85287-4405
480-965-4525

http://www.asu.edu

The Morrison Institute for Public Policy is located at Arizona State University and analyzes public policy issues, informs policy makers, and counsels leaders on private choice. It provides information and scholarly perspectives on issues in school reform.

National Center on Educational Outcomes
University of Minnesota
350 Elliott Hall
75 East River Road
Minneapolis, MN 55455
612-626-1530
Fax: 612-624-0879
http://education.umn.edu

The National Center on Educational Outcomes (NCEO) was founded in 1990 to provide national leadership in educational assessment results for all students. The center also provides a thorough publications list of technical reports, updates on state activity regarding educational reform, policy documents, and self-study guides for educators and the general public.

National Coalition of Advocates for Students (NCAS)
100 Boylston Street
Suite 737
Boston, MA 02116
617-357-8507
http://www.ncasboston.org

The National Coalition of Advocates for Students is a national, nonprofit education and sponsorship organization with twenty member groups in fourteen states. NCAS works to attain equal access to quality public education for students who are most susceptible to school failure. NCAS's constituencies include low-income students; members of racial, ethnic, and/or language minority groups; recent immigrants; migrant farmworkers; and students with disabilities.

National Commission on Teaching and America's Future
2010 Massachusetts Avenue, NW
Suite 210
Washington, DC 20036
(202) 416-6181

Fax: 202-416-6189
http://www.nctaf.org

The National Commission on Teaching and America's Future is a non-profit group comprised of educators, public officials, and business leaders committed to researching and improving the quality of U.S. education. Its Web site gives links and resources to contact key players and members in the educational arena.

National Independent Private Schools Association
10134 SW 78th Court
Miami, FL 33156
305-275-8881
http://www.nipsa.org

NIPSA is for educators who are also entrepreneurs. It was founded in 1983 by a group of California school owners. NIPSA addresses the exclusive challenges and opportunities inherent in for-profit school operation. Association members are professional educators who are former public school superintendents, principals, and teachers. Others are from university faculties or from families who have been involved in school operation for many years.

New American Schools
1560 Wilson Boulevard
Suite 901
Arlington VA, 22209
703-908-9500
Fax: 703-908-0622
Info@nasdc.org

New American Schools is a consortium of teachers, administrators, parents, policy makers, community business leaders, and experts from around the country devoted to enhancing academic achievement for all students.

Professional Association for Childhood Education (PACE)
1290 Sutter Street
Suite 200
San Francisco, CA 94109
800-924-2460
Fax: 415-749-6861
http://www.pacenet.org

pace@hsmc.com

Founded in 1983 as a collaborative undertaking between the schools of education at U.C.–Berkeley and Stanford University, PACE is an independent policy research center whose primary goal is to enrich and enhance education policy debates with sound analysis. From issues of pre-schooling and child development, to K–12 school finance, to higher education outreach, PACE is devoted to defining issues and assessing the relative effectiveness of alternative policies and programs. PACE provides analysis and assistance to California policy makers, education professionals, and the general public.

Progressive Policy Institute
Education Section
600 Pennsylvania Avenue, SE
Suite 400
Washington, DC 20003
202-546-0007
http://www.ppionline.org

The mission of the Progressive Policy Institute is to define, examine, and promote progressive politics for America in the twenty-first century. Through its research, policies, and perspectives, the institute is developing a new governing philosophy and agenda for public innovation aimed at the Information Age. The institute analyzes issues regarding privatization and public education.

Regional Educational Laboratories
222 Richmond Street
Suite 300
Providence, RI 02903-4226
401-274-9548
http://www.relnetwork.org

The Regional Educational Laboratories has ten networks serving geographic regions that cover the nation. They work to assure that those involved in educational improvement reform efforts at the local, state, and regional levels have access to the finest available information from research and practice. With assistance from the U.S. Department of Education, the Regional Laboratories work as essential partners with state and local educators, community leaders, and policy makers to address difficult problems in education.

SERVE Leaders Institute
PO Box 5406
Greensboro, NC 27435
336-334-4729
Fax 336-315-7457
http://www.serve.org/leaders

The SERVE Leaders Institute is funded by a U.S. Department of Education grant. The goals of the Institute are to address the difficulties that charter school innovators and leaders face in the charter school reform movement. The Institute provides retreat activities for charter school leaders.

Southwest Educational Development Laboratory (SEDL)
211 East 7th Street
Austin, TX 78701-3281
800-476-6861
http://www.sedl.org

The Southwest Educational Development Laboratory labors to meet the information needs of public policy makers as they develop policies to improve education in their states and localities. SEDL focuses on areas of direct services and applied policy research and construction. It offers public policy suggestions and practical research information about important education topics, as well as advice for discussing educational issues. It also conducts in-depth studies on charter schools and charter school legislation.

NONPROFIT ORGANIZATIONS THAT OPPOSE EDUCATIONAL PRIVATIZATION AND COMMERCIALIZATION

Advertising Association Food Advertising Unit
Advertising Education Forum (AEF)
Boite Postale 246
1040 Brussels 4
Belgium
32-2-732-63-36
Fax: 32-2-735-39-68
http://www.aeforum.org/
info@aeforum.org

The Advertising Association is a professional organization located in the United Kingdom with its main office in Brussels, Belgium. The Food Advertising Unit examines advertising to children, how advertising is organized, what foods are advertised, and the consequences for children and ad sponsors. The organization specifically looks at privatization as it pertains to advertising food products in schools.

American Federation of Teachers (AFT)
555 New Jersey Avenue NW
Washington, DC 20001
202-393-8642
http://www.aft.org

The AFT works to protect and strengthen the U.S. system of public education and has been instrumental in the desegregation of public schools, the passage of the Elementary and Secondary Education Act, the founding of collective bargaining rights for teachers and other public employees, as well as designing programs to meet the needs of disadvantaged students. They are chief protagonists in the fight against the privatization of education.

Americans United for Separation of Church and State
518 C Street NE
Washington, DC 20002
202-466-3234
Fax: 202-466-2587
http://www.au.org

Americans United for the Separation of Church and State is one of the most esteemed organizations working to preserve this nation's heritage of freedom. With national offices in the Washington, D.C., area and a network of members and volunteers in all fifty states, Americans United fights enthusiastically on behalf of all citizens. The organization is concerned with privatization as it relates to the separation of church and state and opposes private vouchers for education.

Applied Research Center (ARC)
3781 Broadway
Oakland, CA 94611
510-653-3415
Fax: 510-653-3427
http://www.arc.org

The ARC is a public policy, educational, and research institute that focuses its efforts on issues of race and social change. The Center's ERASE project works with local groups in six U.S. cities to challenge institutional racism in public schools. It publishes research analysis on the effects of vouchers on schools, educational issues of race and class, and myriad education policy debates.

Canadian Teachers' Federation

110 Argyle Avenue
Ottawa, ON K2P 1B4
Canada
613-232-1505
Fax: 613-232-1886
http://www.ctf-fce.ca

Reduced funding for curriculum development and for the purchase of high-quality materials makes it more likely that school boards will enter into contracts that expose students to curricular materials that promote corporate interests. The Canadian Teachers' Federation believes that materials intended for classroom use should be subjected to meticulous evaluation. The Federation examines educational materials and offers suggestions for eliminating student exposure to privatized educational materials that promote corporate interests.

Center for a New American Dream

6930 Carroll Avenue
Suite 900
Takoma Park, MD 20912
301-891-3683
Fax: 301-891-3684
http://www.newdream.org

This organization helps individuals, communities, and businesses establish ongoing practices that will assure a healthy planet for future generations. Among the myriad issues they address is that of education and specifically how education serves to promote commercialization and corporate exposure to students.

Center for Commercial-Free Education

1714 Franklin Street
Nos 100-306
Oakland, CA 94612

http://www.commercialfree.org

The Center for Commercial-Free Education is a national nonprofit organization that monitors the issues of commercialism in our public schools. The Center was established in 1993 during an outpouring of resistance to Channel One, a twelve-minute TV program composed of ten minutes of news and two minutes of commercials. The organization analyzes and examines educational materials with the aim of informing the public of materials that promote commercialism in schools and is concerned about privatization of schools as it pertains to permitting these materials to be exposed to students.

Commercial Alert
1611 Connecticut Avenue NW
Suite 3A
Washington, DC 20009
202-296-2787
Fax: 202-833-2406
http://www.essential.org

Commercial Alert helps families, schools, and communities defend themselves against commercialism, advertising, and marketing. The organization publishes Web site information about commercialism and its impact on schools.

Commercialism in Education Research Unit (CERU)
Education Policy Studies Laboratory
Department of Educational Leadership and Policy Studies
College of Education
Arizona State University
Box 872411
Tempe, AZ 85287-2411
480-727-7728
http://www.asu.edu/educ/epsl/ceru.htm
alex.molnar@aus.edu

CERU is an academic research center in the Department of Curriculum and Instruction at the University of Wisconsin–Milwaukee, and is directed by Professor Alex Molnar, author of *Giving Kids the Business: The Commercialization of America's Schools*. CERU provides educators, policy makers, and the general public with information about the impact of commercial activities in schools in an effort to promote safe educational practice and sound public policy.

Corporate Watch
PO Box 29344
San Francisco, CA 94129
415-561-6568
Fax: 415-561-6493
http://www.corpwatch.org

Corporate Watch works with people who are directly affected by corporate abuses as well as with others fighting for corporate accountability, human rights, and social and environmental justice. As part of an independent media, Corporate Watch is free of corporate sponsorship. The organization is formally against privatization of education in all realms including the commercialism of educational policy.

Media Channel
1600 Broadway
Suite 700
New York, NY 10019
212-246-0202
Fax: 212-246-2677
http://www.mediachannel.org

Media Channel is a nonprofit, public interest Web site devoted to global media issues. Media Channel provides news, reports, and commentary from its international network of media-issues organizations and publications, as well as unique features from contributors and staff. Media Channel is in direct opposition to the privatization of education in all areas.

National Education Association (NEA)
1201 16th Street, NW
Washington, DC 20036
202-833-4000
http://www.nea.org

The NEA is America's oldest and largest organization dedicated to advancing the cause of public education. The NEA has over 2.3 million members who work at every level of education, from preschool to university graduate programs. The NEA has affiliates in every state as well as in over 13,000 local communities across the United States. At the international level, NEA connects educators around the world in an ongoing dialogue devoted to making public schools as successful as they can be.

Obligation, Inc.
Barbizon Building
3100 Lorna Road
Suite 311
Birmingham, AL 35216
205-822-0080
Fax: 205-822-3336
http://www.obligation.org

Obligation, Inc. informs businesses and governments of their responsibility to children. Obligation has become very involved in television issues, especially as these issues affect the privatization of schools. They adamantly oppose commercialism in schools. Obligation commits itself to empower citizens with information that will allow them to make television better for children.

ReThinking Schools:
1001 East Keefe Avenue
Milwaukee, WI 53212
414-964-9646 or 800-669-4192
Fax: 414-964-7220
http://www.rethinkingschools.org

ReThinking Schools is a nonprofit, independent publisher of educational materials. It promotes elementary and secondary education reform, emphasizing equity and social justice. The organization is in adamant opposition to privatization of schools on every level.

PRIVATE ORGANIZATIONS THAT SUPPORT SCHOOL VOUCHERS

The following is a list of corporations paying for or subsidizing school events and/or one-time activities in return for the right to partner their name with the events and activities.

American Enterprise Institute (AEI)
1150 17th Street, NW
Washington, DC 20036
202-862-5800
Fax: 202-862-7178
http://www.aei.org

The American Enterprise Institute for Public Policy Research promotes the preservation and strengthening of basic freedoms within government, private enterprise, and cultural and political institutions. AEI is one of the largest conservative think tanks in the United States. They strongly favor the privatization of education.

California Interscholastic Federation (CIF)
664 Las Gallinas Avenue
San Rafael, CA 94903
415-492-5911
Fax: 415-492-5919
info@cifstate.org
http://www.cifstate.org

CIF is a a for-profit network of schools organized to develop and manage corporate sponsorship deals.

Cato Institute
1000 Massachusetts Avenue, NW
Washington, DC 20001
202-842-0200
Fax: 202-842-3490
http://www.cato.org

The Cato Institute looks to expand the parameters of public policy debate to allow consideration of more options that they feel are consistent with the traditional American principles of limited government, individual liberty, and peace. The Institute promotes increased participation of citizens in questions of policy and the proper role of government. They are staunchly for the end of public education and the privatization of schools.

Children First America
PO Box 330
Bentonville, AR 72712-0330
479-273-6957
Fax: 479-273-9362
http://www.childrenfirstamerica.org/

Children First America is the national clearinghouse of information on private voucher programs. They provide support services that range from administrative training to program consulting. They have experienced participants, as well as specialists in certain fields of education. They support the privatization of education through private vouchers.

Children's Scholarship Fund (CSF)
7 West 57th Street
New York, NY 10019
212-752-8555
Fax: 212-750-4252
http://www.scholarshipfund.org

CSF works to provide private tuition scholarships to eligible candidates, such as low-income children, so they might attend the private schools of their choice. They are provoucher.

Christian Coalition
1801-L Sara Drive
Chesapeake, VA 23320
757-424-2630
Fax: 757-424-9068
http://www.cc.org

The Christian Coalition is a nonprofit, taxable corporation and Christian Coalition of America, its member group, is a 501(c)(4), tax-exempt organization. The Christian Coalition is a significant player in the provoucher initiative movement both in legislative and citizen initiatives.

Citizens for Educational Freedom
9333 Clayton Road
St. Louis, MO 63124
314-997-6361
Fax: 314-997-6321
http://www.Educational-Freedom.org

Citizens for Educational Freedom is a national, nonprofit corporation that was established in 1959, with headquarters in St. Louis, Missouri. It consists of citizens and groups of every race, color, creed, and political party. Its primary purpose is to promote the rights of parents to freedom of choice, and justice and quality in education for all, including the right to choose private schools through vouchers.

DD Marketing, Inc.
103 N Main Street
Suite 300
Pueblo, CO 81003
719-546-3333
Fax: 719-544-4549

http://www.ddmktg.com

DD Marketing Inc. is the most significant promoter of exclusive pouring rights agreements between school districts and soft drink bottlers.

Education Leaders Council (ELC)
1001 Connecticut Avenue
Suite 204
Washington, DC 20036
202-822-9000
Fax: 202-822-5077
http://www.educationleaders.org

The ELC's beliefs are straightforward. They focus on education and believe that the aim of education should be on students, not the school system. They also maintain that student achievement and performance should be reported in a way that is easily understood by parents and taxpayers. The ELC believes that parents and teachers should be empowered to find various approaches to education and they support the privatization of education.

Education Policy Institute (EPI)
4401-A Connecticut Avenue, NW
Box 294
Washington, DC 20008
202-244-7535
Fax: 202-244-7584
http://www.educationpolicy.org

EPI seeks to improve education through research, policy analysis, and the development of accountable alternatives to existing policies and practices. EPI's goal is to provide increased parental choice in education, develop a competitive education industry, and to encourage policies that address the problems of both public and private schools.

Empower America
1701 Pennsylvania Avenue, NW
Suite 900
Washington, DC 20006
202-452-8200
Fax: 202-833-0388
http://www.empower.org

Empower America is devoted to ensuring that government actions favor economic freedom and individual responsibility. They are a conservative organization that favors the privatization of schools.

Family Research Council
801 G Street, NW
Washington, DC 20001
202-393-2100
Fax: 202-393-2134
http://www.frc.org

Family Research Council believes that America must reinstate decision making authority over school policy and finance to parents, locally elected school boards, and taxpayers. They support the privatization of education through vouchers.

The Heritage Foundation
214 Massachusetts Avenue, NE
Washington, DC 20002-4999
202-546-4400
Fax: 202-546-8328
www.heritage.org

The Heritage Foundation is a research and educational think tank whose objective is to formulate and encourage conservative public policies based on the principles of free enterprise, limited government, individual freedom, traditional American values, and a strong national defense. It supports the privatization of education through private vouchers.

Lexington Institute
1655 North Fort Myer Drive
Suite 325
Arlington, VA 22209
703-522-5828
Fax: 703-522-5837
http://www.lexingtoninstitute.org

The Lexington Institute believes in limiting the role of the federal government to those functions explicitly stated in or implicitly spelled out in the Constitution. The Institute actively opposes the unnecessary infringement of the federal government into the commerce and culture of the nation, and they strive to find nongovernmental, market-based solutions to public policy challenges. They are staunch supporters of the privatization of education.

Milton and Rose D. Friedman Foundation for School Choice
PO Box 82078
One American Square
Suite 2440
Indianapolis, IN 46282
317-681-0745
Fax: 317-681-0945
http://www.friedmanfoundation.org

The Milton and Rose D. Friedman Foundation for School Choice was established on the ideals and theories of Nobel laureate economist Milton Friedman and economist Rose D. Friedman. The Friedman Foundation seeks to educate parents, public policy makers, and organizations about the need for a shift of power to parents whom they believe have limited choices and voices in the education of their children. They are staunchly proprivatization of education through private vouchers.

National Science Teachers Association
1840 Wilson Boulevard
Arlington, VA 22201-3000
703-243-7100
http://www.nsta.org

The National Science Teachers Association supports the privatization of schools as well as commercialism within schools. Several examples of corporate-sponsored contests can be located on the association's Web site.

Religion in Public Schools
15 East 84th Street
Suite 501
New York, NY 10028
202-543-1517
http://www.ed.gov

This organization provides joint statements drafted by thirty-five religious and public policy organizations in an effort to find common ground on the issue of religious expression in public schools. They seek to unite coalitions across the nation. The organization is staunchly in favor of the privatization of education.

SponsorKIDS
411 West Ontario Street

Suite 719
Chicago, IL 60610
(312) 573-1113
FAX: (312) 573-1115
spnsrkids@aol.com
http://www.sponsorkids.com

SponsorKIDS is a marketing agency that assists companies in developing corporate sponsorship deals with schools. They specialize in national and international events and promotions to raise funds for their sponsorKIDS charities, which are supported by corporate interests eager to market their wares to students within schools.

INCENTIVE PROGRAMS

The following is a list of corporate programs that provide money, goods, or services to a school or school district when its students, parents, or staff engage in a specified activity, such as collecting particular product labels or cash register receipts from particular stores.

Box Tops for Education
PO Box 8998
Young America, MN 55551-8998
888-799-2444
Fax: 800-353-1341
boxtops@young-america.com
http://www.boxtops4education.com

An incentive program encouraging schools to promote General Mills' breakfast cereals, Box Tops for Education is one of America's most profitable and recognized school fundraisers. Created by General Mills in 1996, this so-called grassroots initiative has produced over $50 million for 60,000 K–8 schools nationwide. The company offers three ways to participate: clipping General Mills product box tops and bringing them to school to be redeemed for cash; shopping at the Box Tops for Education Marketplace and also at one's favorite online stores with ten percent of the total purchase contributed to the school of one's choice; and charging with a Box Tops Visa card that allows one percent of all credit card purchases to be contributed to the designated school of one's choice.

Campbell's Labels for Education
4001 Clearwater Road

St. Cloud, MN 56301
800-424-5331
http://www.labelsforeducation.com

Campbell's promotes commercialism in schools by asking students to collect soup labels that are then returned to the company in exchange for educational materials such as videos, learning kits, and equipment. They promote the private commercialization of product advertising in schools through their label collection practices.

Cover Concepts Marketing Services Inc.
172 Madison Avenue
New York, NY 10016
212-508-6890
http://www.primedia.com

This organization provides designs for textbook covers that promote product logos and/or product advertising.

School Marketing Partners
32302 Camino Capistrano
Suite 207
San Juan Capistrano, CA 92675
Tooned-In@msn.com
http://www.schoolmenu.com

School Marketing Partners produces ad-bearing school lunch menus that promote products and commercial logos.

ORGANIZATIONS THAT CREATE AND SUPPORT SPONSORED EDUCATIONAL MATERIALS (SEMS)

The following is a list of corporations and organizations that sponsor corporate educational materials. The list is not extensive but provides some examples of corporate involvement in school curricula.

Boasberg/Wheeler Communications, Inc.
4700 Belleview Avenue
No. 100
Kansas City, MO 64112
816-531-2100
Fax: 816-756-1471

lwheeler@bwcom.com
http://www.bwcom.com

This marketing company promotes advertising for corporate clients interested in new markets such as schools. They offer marketing strategies to private corporations interested in entering the educational market.

Enterprise for Education
1316 Third Street
Suite 103
Santa Monica, CA 90401
888-300-9864
310-394-9864
Fax: 310-394-3539
service@entfored.com
http://www.entfored.com

Enterprise publications provide corporate-sponsored activities based on up-to-date teaching techniques and hands-on activities. They represent many of the nation's largest electric utilities and produce colorful, curriculum-based publications for students.

Lifetime Learning Systems
200 First Stanford Place
PO Box 120023
Stanford, CT 06912-0023
203-705-3600
http://www.lls-online.com

Lifetime Learning Systems bring teachers and kids interactive, educational programs and resources that are corporate sponsored. Lifetime Learning Systems has been working with corporations and associations to provide free educational materials geared toward all ages and all subject areas.

Scholastic Corporation and Scholastic Marketing Partners
555 Broadway
New York, NY 10012-3999
212-343-6100
Fax: 212-343-6928
http://www.scholastic.com

Scholastic Inc. is a global children's publishing and media company that creates products and services aimed to educate, entertain, and motivate children through corporate sponsored educational materials.

Video Placement Worldwide (VPW)
25 Second Street North
St. Petersburg, FL 33701
Fax: 800-358-5218
http://www.vpw.com

VPW offers free corporate-sponsored educational materials to teachers, librarians, media specialists, and youth leaders throughout the United States. They offer free educational films, brochures, books, and pamphlets for use in the classroom through corporate sponsorship. They currently reach 25,000 high schools, 21,000 middle/junior high schools, and 72,000 elementary schools.

ELECTRONIC MARKETING SEMS

The following is a list of organizations that sponsor electronic curriculum materials through computers or broadcast media.

American School Directory (ASD)
http://www.asd.com

ASD is a subscription-based directory sponsored by corporations such as Computers for Education, IBM, and Innisbrook Wraps. They have over 108,000 individual Web sites, and as an Internet resource they provide every K–12 school in America, public and private, a free Internet service. Their sites are loaded with pictures, art, information, calendars, and many other promotional products. They also offer a school mall and prizes for students. They are specifically an online company with no physical address.

Channel One Communications Corp.
600 Madison Avenue
New York, NY 10022
212-508-6800 or 888-CH1-NTWK
Fax: 212-508-6870
http://www.channelone.com

ChannelOne.com is part of the Channel One Network, a PRIMEDIA Inc. company. The Channel One Network claims it is a "learning community" of 12,000 middle, junior, and high schools representing over 8 million students and 400,000 educators in the United States. They offer *Channel One News,* a daily, televised, 10-minute newscast that is shown via satellite during the school year to the 12,000 schools in the Channel One Network community. *Channel One News* features stories on breaking news and in-depth issues that affect the world, the nation, and specifically teenagers.

HighWired.Org

101 Rogers Street
Suite 200
Cambridge, MA 02142
Fax: 617-577-8030
info@highwired.net
http://www.highwired.net

HighWired assists schools with integrating technology into the classroom in ways that engage and improve performance of the entire school community. Established in 1998 to provide Web-building tools to high schools, HighWired is a market leader with nearly 14,500 schools in all 50 U.S. states and 76 foreign countries. To achieve their goals of improving the way schools teach and foster student learning, HighWired collaborates with leading education and technology companies to provide homework assignments, school news and announcements, team scores, schedules and statistics, and student activity Web sites.

Lightspan Partnership Inc.

10140 Campus Point Drive
San Diego, CA 92421
contactus@lightspan.com
http://www.lightspan.com

Lightspan was established in 1993 with a goal of using technology to help improve student achievement by connecting the school and the home. The organization supports the privatization of school policies and commercialism in schools by promoting private online assessments that are commercially made available to schools. Their Web site is accessible to subscribers only.

Oxigen (formerly ScreenAdi)

12 Automatic Road
Suite 102
Brampton, Ontario L6S 5N3

Canada
905-799-2332 or (toll Free) 1-87SCREENAD
Fax: 905-799-0081
http://www.oxigen.net

Oxigen was created to serve the internal communication needs of organizations and schools. First launched in university libraries in the U.K., it uses a state-of-the-art desktop messaging system to provide a medium for advertising agencies to reach students.

FOR-PROFIT AND NONPROFIT ORGANIZATIONS THAT MANAGE SCHOOLS

Advantage Schools, Inc.
60 Canal Street
Boston, MA 02114
617-523-2220 or 888-292-2344
Fax: 617-523-2221
http://www.advantageschools.com

Advantage Schools is a for-profit company that is running more than a dozen charter schools nationwide. Owned by Mosaica Education Incorporated, Advantage Schools is a start-up company that is on the New York Stock Exchange, and that seeks to run schools for profit.

Beacon Education Management, Inc.
112 Turnpike Road
Suite 107
Westborough, MA 01581
508-836-4461 or 800-789-1258 ext 14
Fax: 508-836-2604
info@beaconedu.com
http://www.beaconedu.com

Beacon Education Management, Inc., is a K–12, educational services corporation that was founded in 1992. It provides school management services for charter or district schools. The company delivers educational services for nearly 10,000 children at 29 full-service schools and 2 limited service schools in 5 states and the District of Columbia.

Charter Schools USA (CSUSA)
2500 N Federal Highway

5th Floor
Fort Lauderdale, FL 33305
954-202-3500 or 954-791-9910
Fax: 954-202-3512
CharterSchoolsUSA@yahoo.com
http://www.charterschoolsusa.com

CSUSA is one of the country's fastest growing for-profit development and management companies of K–12 charter schools. CSUSA provides outsourcing for corporations, government entities, developers, and nonprofits and assists with all parts of charter school design, planning, development, financing, construction, marketing, financing, human resources, curricula, and school operations. CSUSA operates the nation's first municipally organized charter high school, the first charter school-in-the-workplace, and one of the country's largest charter schools.

Edison Schools (formerly Edison Project)
521 Fifth Avenue
15th Floor
New York, NY 10175
212-419-1600
E-mail: vworthingt@newyork.edisonproject.com
http://www.edisonproject.com

Edison Schools, a private corporation founded in 1992 as The Edison Project, is a private manager of public schools. Edison has implemented its school program in 136 public schools, including many charter schools, which it operates under private for-profit management contracts with local school districts and charter boards. More than 75,000 students are enrolled in Edison partnership schools.

Excel Education Centers, Inc.
1040 Whipple Street
Suite 401
Prescott, AZ 86305
520-778-5764 or 800-417-9036
http://www.excel.apscc.k12.az.us

Excel Education Centers, Inc. is a for-profit state funded corporate charter school that was established in 1995. The for-profit company seeks to partner with other state agencies in their for-profit goals of managing charter schools.

Helicon Associates
PO Box 1014
Flat Rock, MI 48134
734-379-6810
Fax: 734-379-6745
http://www.summit-academy.com

Now known as the Summit Academy, this for-profit company manages and operates many for-profit schools. The company offers online lesson plans to teachers as well as other corporate sponsored educational resources.

National Heritage Academy
989 Spaulding Avenue, SE
Grand Rapids, MI 49546
616-222-1700 or 800-699-9235
info@heritageacademies.com
http://www.heritageacademies.com

The National Heritage Academy is a for-profit management company that has set a goal to build over two hundred for-profit managed charter schools nationwide. They stress a strong back-to-basics curriculum.

Public Strategies Group, Inc.
275 E 4th Street
Suite 710
St. Paul, MN 55101
651-227-9774
Fax: 651-292-1482
reinvent@PSGrp.com
http://www.psgrp.com

The Public Strategies Group's vision is to manage schools for profit. They provide what they call "government schools" with strategies to realize their mission. The group is looking to expand its for-profit management goals by offering "exceptional service at a reasonable price."

SABIS School Network
6385 Beach Road
Eden Prairie, MN 55344
612-829-9352
http://www.sabis.net

SABIS is a for-profit educational management organization that manages schools worldwide, serving approximately 20,000 students. Their schools are noted for their implementation of the SABIS Educational System, which emphasizes the core subjects of English, math, science, and world languages to students from 3 to 18 years of age. They are located in the United States, Africa, Asia, and the Middle East and boast a 100 percent graduation rate.

Sylvan Learning Center
1000 Lancaster St.
Baltimore, MD 21202
410-843-8000
Fax: 410-880-8717
http://www.educate.com

Sylvan Learning Center is a private, for-profit company that provides personalized student instruction to students of all ages and skill levels. They operate 900 Sylvan Learning Centers in North America and Asia.

The Tesseract Group, Inc.
3800 W 80th Street
Suite 1400
Minneapolis, MN 55431
612-837-8700

The Tesseract Group is an educational service company that runs schools for profit and is currently listed on the NASDAQ.

ORGANIZATIONS INVOLVED IN DIRECT MARKETING AIMED AT YOUTH

The following is a list of companies that develop advertising targeted at children, collect market data on young consumers, or train others in marketing to children as well as raise funds for schools through their marketing endeavors.

Brunico Communications, Inc.
KidScreen
366 Adelaide Street W., Suite 500,
Toronto, Ontario
M5V 1R9
Canada
416-408-2300

Fax: 416-408-0870
http://www.kidscreen.com

Brunico Communications, Inc. sponsors *KidScreen,* an international trade magazine that features entertainment-based information.

Edu Venture
20 Park Plaza
Suite 833
Boston, MA 02116
617-426-5622
Fax: 617-426-5431
mail@eduventures.com
http://www.eduventures.com

Eduventures, Inc. is an independent research firm that helps organizations seek profits in the new education economy. They offer research, advisory services, and executive strategy conferences that provide their corporate clients with knowledge of key industry metrics, emerging trends, and breaking news. They aid and abet the advertising and marketing to students throughout the nation.

Innisbrook Wraps
PO Box 19507
Greensboro, NC 27419
1-877-525-5608
Fax: 1-800-742-2098
http://www.innisbrook.com

Innisbrook Wraps is the nation's number one fundraising company. They have been raising money for schools for over 21 years. Headquartered in Greensboro, North Carolina, Innisbrook Wraps is a national company that markets their products to the average consumer and also to students directly online. Innisbrook Wraps has increasingly developed its business through a pledge to provide quality in all aspects of fundraising, including product, service, and incentives.

International Quality and Productivity Center
150 Clove Road
PO Box 401
Little Falls, NJ 07424-0401
800-882-8684
Fax: 973-256-0205

info@iqpc.com
http://www.iqpc.com

International Quality and Productivity Center offers company products and services to school audiences, especially targeting students. They tailor a sponsorship or exhibition package to suit business needs and complement business marketing plans. They offer a variety of ways in which companies can participate as a sponsor or exhibitor to schools including Lead Sponsorships, Co-Sponsorships, Reception Sponsorships, Luncheon Sponsorships, Breakfast Sponsorships, Refreshment Break Sponsorships, Pen & Pad Sponsorships, and Welcome Pack Sponsorships.

Kids Marketing
PO Box 66128
1355 Kingston Road
Pickering, Ontario L1V 6P7
Canada
905-839-0020
hello@kidsmarketing.com
http://www.kidsmarketing.com

Kids Marketing provides designs and development services with the goal of helping corporate clients reach and connect with kids through direct marketing. Of their list membership 27 percent are marketing and advertising professionals who are seeking to reach kids, 21 percent are in managerial positions, 16 percent are market researchers, 15 percent are media developers, 8 percent are students, and 13 percent are in various professions and working to help reach kids in some way.

Market Day
555 West Pierce Road
Suite 200
Itasca, IL 60143-2647
800-253-8169
http://www.marketday.com

Market Day is one of the original school marketing companies that serves thousands of schools across the country through fundraising drives based on sales of its products. A for-profit venture, Marketing Day sells products and then gives proceeds to schools.

Otis-Spunkmeyer, Inc.
14490 Catalina Street

San Leandro, CA 94577
888-ASK-OTIS
http://www.spunkmeyer.com

Otis-Spunkmeyer has been helping schools and organizations raise money since 1972. They market fresh-baked goods and cookies to help schools raise monies through direct marketing.

Plantation Peanuts
PO Box 128
Wakefield, VA 23888
800-233-8788
info@plantationpeanuts.com
http://www.plantationpeanuts.com

Plantation Peanuts uses part of their profits from marketing to support schools.

Rah-Rah Apparel
PO Box 694
Sparks, NV 89432
Fax: 702-359-3292
jetty@RAH-RAH.com

Rah-Rah Apparel markets clothing, and they use a portion of their profits and proceeds to fund schools and school events.

React Network
711 Third Avenue
New York, NY 10017
http://www.react.com

React Network prides itself on marketing directly to kids. They provide services to kids that include dating advice, sponsored contests, free products, movie and music reviews, and news services.

Superior Fundraising, Inc.
4584 Austin Boulevard
Island Park, NY 11558
800-526-1740
Fax: 516-889-0120
info@superiorfundraising.com
http://www.superiorfundraising.com

Superior Fundraising sells magazines, cards, and other products and donates a portion of their profits to schools and school services.

World's Finest Chocolate Inc.
4801 South Lawndale
Chicago, IL 60632-3062
800-932-3863
http://www.wfchocolate.com

World's Finest Chocolate sponsors fundraising drives for schools through the sale of their products. They donate a portion of their proceeds to educational services and schools.

●◆ Index

✏ About the Author

Danny Weil has written extensively on educational issues from curriculum to public policy. He holds a Ph.D. in education and has taught all grades from kindergarten to high school. He is the director of the Critical Thinking Institute, which provides services and consultation in the area of critical thinking and organizational management to private and public institutions throughout the world, and he has been a consultant to over fifty school districts within the United States. He is an attorney who has practiced public interest law for close to thirty years. He is the author of *Charter Schools: A Reference Handbook* and is editor of the eXtreme Teaching Series. He is an adjunct professor of philosophy at Hancock Junior College in Santa Maria, California.